sport

*A philosophic inquiry
by Paul Weiss*

southern illinois university press

carbondale and edwardsville

feffer & simons, inc.

london and amsterdam

for Marcia, Lisa, and Michael

"under whose benign

auspices . . ."

preface

I am not an athlete. For a number of years, however, I have thought about sports, watched some of them, and have taken part in a few in a minor way. Recently, I have had the opportunity to discuss questions in this area with a number of coaches, athletes, and devoted spectators. I have also read articles and books in related fields, have attended training sessions, and have chatted with players in locker rooms. There has been a remarkable willingness on the part of coaches and players to help me understand what was happening. Some of my early judgments have consequently been discarded and others replaced, sometimes by those having an almost opposite emphasis.

On physiological and related issues there are, fortunately, a number of excellent studies. Apart from these, I have not found much knowledge or insight in the literature. A considerable portion of it is anecdotal in nature, content to recall high moments in various games, or to convey the somewhat elusive personality of athletes and coaches. What little history there is, is mainly occupied with noting the times and places at which records were made. Yet records, when detached from the adventure of achieving them, are only empty numbers. The best writings are technical. They offer hints and advice for improving skills or for avoiding dangers and obstacles in the way of excellent performances. But they leave a place for only an occasional idea, and this is usually borrowed and rather frayed.

I soon found myself in an endless desert through much of which, I am sorry to say, I had to make my way without compass or guide. I had to proceed alone, and try to think through the entire enterprise afresh. Some protection and guidance was, fortunately, provided by previous reflections on the nature of man, the aims of education, and the thrust of a number of activities and disciplines which seemed to have some relevance to sport.

After considerable struggle and a number of false starts I completed a draft of a book and sent it to a number of interested coaches, directors, athletes, and philosophers. Their comments and corrections made me see how badly I had managed in my first attempt. I thereupon rewrote the entire work from beginning to end. The advance made over the previous account owes much to what I have learned from Ethan Allen, Richard Bernstein, John Blum, John W. Loy, Joseph Pullo, Eric Segal, Betty Spears, H. Vogelsinger, J. E. Williamson, and Earle Zeigler. I have also benefited from the unstinting generosity so characteristic of Robert and DeLaney Kiphuth and their staff. I have been granted the privilege of using the facilities of *Sports Illustrated*, where I was thoughtfully guided and helped by John Tibby. A grant by the Carnegie Corporation has made it possible for me to collect a good deal of data, to get this book ready for the press, and to allow me to continue my investigations both here and abroad. But I am most in debt to Arleen and Carleton Dallery, Robert Ehman, J. E. Genasci, E. Jokl, S. Kezerian, I. C. Lieb, W. E. Steinkraus, Richard Sewall, Vernon Sternberg, and Jonathan Weiss for their meticulous and sometimes line by line examination of the original text. I wish I knew how to do more justice to their wide knowledge and illuminating observations.

The present study makes but a beginning in a new enterprise, the examination of sport in terms of principles which are to be at once revelatory of the nature of sport and pertinent to other fields—indeed, to the whole of things and knowledge. The result is a work in philosophy, and not in sport. It is a work in philosophy just as a philosophy of history or a philosophy of art is a work in philosophy and not in history or in art. This need not mean that it must be without value to those who are primarily concerned with sport and not with philosophy. It is, in fact, one of my hopes that this study will prove worthwhile to anyone who interests himself in sport as a spectator or as a participant. At its best it will make evident how one might profitably approach any activity that is widely practiced and observed, but insufficiently understood.

P. W.

New Haven, Connecticut
March, 1968

contents

sport: *A philosophic inquiry*

1. concern for excellence

EXCELLENCE excites and awes. It pleases and it challenges. We are often delighted by splendid specimens
whether they be flowers, beasts, or men. A superb performance interests us even more because it reveals to us
the magnitude of what then can be done. Illustrating
perfection, it gives us a measure for whatever else we
do.

Unlike other beings we men have the ability to appre-
ciate the excellent. We desire to achieve it. We want to
share in it. Even though it may point up the fact that we
are defective, less than we might have been, we like to look
upon it. It is what ought to be.

There are many ways in which men are excellent.
Some have great character. Their public acts serve as
carriers for admirable, privately sustained virtues. Noble
beings, they give private goods a public role. Other men
achieve a stature far greater than the rest by making an art
of living, and impressing this on the course of history.
They are monumental beings, the great leaders and statesmen. Others are genuinely pious and infuse their relation
to their fellows with sacred values. Teachers of mankind,
they often outlast and outstrip those who rule nations and
control armies. And others are truly wise, sages who embody what they know. Permeating their bodies with sound
and wide-ranging knowledge, they ennoble those bodies
and what those bodies do.

These excellent men are exceptions. Large enough for
all of us to see, they are too large for most of us to imitate
except at some remove. It is easier for most men to reach,
not an excellence which requires them to first attain some

perfection privately and then to impose it on a public body
or world, but an excellence which results from a mastery
of the body or of the things in the world. It is even easier,
usually, to respect the rights of others, guided in part by
what ethically ought to be. It is perhaps even easier,
though no more common, to be a hero, having some impact
on history. Almost any man, too, can assume leadership in
some area for a time, limiting himself in the light of
whatever eternal values he is able to discern. But young
men find it easier to master their bodies than to be truly
noble, monumental, pious, or wise. We have here one
reason why they readily occupy themselves with sport.

Sport does not interest only the young; it interests
almost everyone. The fact compels a pause. Why are so
many so deeply involved, so caught up emotionally in athletic events? Are they in the grip of some basic drive? Do
they only express some accidentally acquired cultural habit
of admiration for successful violence? Are they really interested in perfection? Does it perhaps give them a special
kind of pleasure?

These hard questions have philosophic import, dealing
as they do—as we shall see—with what is close to the core
of man, what he seeks, and what he does. Yet philosophers,
as a rule have not looked carefully into the topic. They
have neglected sport. Sport, of course, is not the only
wide-spread activity that they have slighted. Sex, work,
play, and worldly success never won the steady attention of
eminent philosophers. They have given considerable
thought to the nature and desirability of achieving pleasure; they have occupied themselves with the idea of excellence and with the desire for it; they have been appreciative
of the fact that in many basic ways men everywhere are
men, with similar natures and appetites. But this has not
led them to devote their time and energy to studying some
of the most universal occupations of men.

Why is it that certain widely dispersed and evidently
attractive pursuits have not been extensively studied by the
great, or even by the near-great philosophers who dot the
history of thought? It is conceivable that these men believed that the activities expressed only some limited interest, some specialized concern for a particular good, and

were therefore the proper topics of other enterprises. We will never know for certain whether or not this or some other is the reason for the neglect, for none of the philosophers has discussed the issue.

Let us go back toward the beginning of thought, as we know it in the Western world. We will find in the Greeks some good historically grounded explanations for the neglect of sport by philosophic minds, then and later. Despite their evident enjoyment of athletics, and their delight in speculating on the meaning of a hundred different human concerns, the Greek thinkers never dealt extensively with the nature, import, and reason for sport. Since Plato and his fellows formulated most of the issues that have occupied philosophers over the centuries, the Greek failure to provide a philosophical study became a norm for the rest. Whitehead goes too far when he says that "the safest general characterization of the European philosphic tradition is that it consists of a series of footnotes to Plato," but he does thereby make conspicuous the normative role that the Greeks assumed in Western thought. Whitehead's observation also points up the desirability of asking whether it is not time to write a new text; one overrun with footnotes should be discarded for another fresh account, granted, for the sake of accuracy, that it is Aristotle and not Plato who set the standards to which most Western philosophers subscribe.

Aristotle wrote brilliantly and extensively on logic, physics, biology, psychology, economics, politics, ethics, art, metaphysics, and rhetoric, but he says hardly a word about either history or religion, and nothing at all about sport. Since he was taken to be "the master of those who know" his position became paradigmatic for most of the thinkers who followed, even when they explicitly repudiated his particular claims. They tended, with him, to dismiss labor as an affair of low-class men, and to identify worldly success with political and princely power. The fact that these subjects are studied today by economists, psychologists, and sociologists has not yet sufficed to free them from many a philosopher's suspicion that they are low-grade subjects, not worthy of being pursued by men of large vision.

Aristotle extracted a grammar from learned discourse, a logic from skilled argument, and a political theory from the practices of statesmen. But he kept away from common discourse, common argument, and common practices. He and other masters of thought did not look for the structure and rationale of what occupies most men. They tacitly supposed that the popular could not be as philosophically important as the rare, solely because it was popular. What appealed to the many, it was thought, could not contain any significant truths. Following out that idea, one is tempted to conclude with Aristotle that God thinks only of what is noble and pure, and that we ought to try to follow his example. As Aristotle put it: "It must be of itself that the divine thought thinks since it is the most excellent of things." But we men are all imperfect, living in an impure world; we at least cannot and ought not avoid a study of the finite and the corrupt. It need no more corrupt us than a study of insanity will make us mad.

From its beginning until today, philosophy has been centrally occupied with the genteel and the respectable. We come upon this fact in surprising places. In a technical discussion by Plato, for example, we find Parmenides asking Socrates, "Are you also puzzled whether . . . hair or mud or dirt or any other trivial and undignified objects . . . have a separate Form?" and Socrates answering, ". . . it would surely be too absurd to suppose that they have a Form." Socrates and his friends would have thought it equally absurd to suppose that sex, work, or sport had Forms of their own.

As befits the well-placed in a slave society, Aristotle and other Greek thinkers dealt mainly with what concerned the well-born. Later on, when the philosophers of history and religion (I refer here, of course, to the philosophers of religion of the West, for in the East they have been occupied with the issues for thousands of years) made their appearance, they too dealt primarily only with those topics that had been raised by leaders in act and thought.

The history of philosophy is a series of attempts to square the circle within which the privileged confine themselves. Among other things it neglects the history that is sweated through by ordinary men, and the life that they daily lead. It attends to dance and song only after they have made their way into the accredited theaters and concert halls. Some attention, to be sure, is paid to fate, luck, and freedom, which are certainly common concerns. But on the whole hardly anything is said about what grips mankind, what excites and overwhelms, what lures and confounds it—and therefore about what is important to the unwashed and uneducated.

Even if it be supposed that only what the upper classes do is worth reflecting on, a philosophic treatise on sports could have been written—and by the Greeks. In their athletic contests only free men were allowed to compete. There was presumably nothing low, therefore, to be contemplated in those contests, and presumably nothing untoward that would appear in the resulting reflection. The Greek thinkers did not write philosophic treatises on sport, perhaps, because they thought that the kind of power and control that athletes exhibit was within the capacity of any and all men, and for that reason was intrinsically low-grade. Some of them did say that the athletes, though free, were inferior men. A strong, but not untypical expression of the contempt that aristocrats had for athletes is reported by Isocrates.

Although in natural gifts and in strength of body he [Alcibiades] was inferior to none, he disdained the gymnastic contests, for he knew that some of the athletes were of low birth, inhabitants of petty states and of mean education, but turned to the breeding of race horses, which is possible only for the most blest by Fortune and not to be pursued by one of low estate.[1]

Veblen, characteristically, gives a more biting explanation for the aristocratic rejection of whatever the lower classes can do: "The canons of reputable living exclude from the scheme of life of the leisure class all activity that can not be classed as conspicuous leisure." [2] The sports of the rich,

1   *Isocrates*, Vol. III, trans. by LaRue Van Hook, Loeb Classical Library (Cambridge, 1961), in "Concerning the Team of Horses," pp. 194–95.
2   Thorstein B. Veblen, *The Theory of the Leisure Class* (New York, 1931), p. 258.

on this view, are necessarily different from those of the poor, but sufficiently close in spirit as to make well-off, reflective men shy away from thinking about them.

The typical philosopher disdains the common. He is justified when "common" means that which is beneath the interest of a civilized man. But "common" also means "what is widespread." No one has a right to move smoothly from the latter meaning to the former. But this is done when the common is dismissed as the vulgar—which itself was once a common term for "common."

For too many the common means little more than the brutish and the uncultivated. Let this be granted; it does not imply that a study of what is common must itself be demeaning. A clean science studies air pollution; it is a sober science that examines the history and causes of savage superstitions.

If philosophers did take the commonality of sport to be a sign of its insignificance, and then supposed that its character tainted the study of it, they committed a double blunder. The common can be good and desirable. And whether it be so or not, it can be dealt with carefully and thoughtfully, and from a perspective not necessarily known or shared in by its participants.

Whatever the reason for the neglect, the opportunity to deal with sport philosophically was let slip away by the Greeks and their followers. From their time to our own, sports have not been taken seriously enough as a source or instance of large truths or first principles.

Both when participated in and when watched, sport quickly works on the emotions; it wins men's allegiance readily and often to a degree nothing else is able to do. Mankind's enthusiasm and devotion to it is remarkable, and deserves to be remarked upon. P. S. Fredrickson observes: "There is no society known to man which does not have games of the sort in which individuals set up purely artificial obstacles and get satisfaction from overcoming them." [3]

3   P. S. Frederickson, "Sports and the Cultures of Man," *Science and Medicine of Exercise and Sports*, ed. Warren Russel Johnson (New York, 1960), p. 634.

Art, science, and philosophy make larger contributions to civilization than sport does. They demand the use of an imagination and a mind within the power of only a small number—and those only when they willingly work in solitude, outside the borders of accepted beliefs, and with a power, range, daring, and persistence backed by maturity that only a fortunate few can attain.

Agriculture, manufacture, and business play a much larger role in our economy than is possible to sport, though, of course, sport is not without economic importance. The economically more important enterprises, however, do not often arouse the full attention of most men. Rarely do they enter into men's daily disputes or lay claim to basic loyalties in the way or to the degree that sport does. It is sport that catches the interest and elicits the devotion of both the young and the old, the wise and the foolish, the educated and the uneducated.

What is not immediately evident is why men in all walks and at all ages interest themselves in sport. We cannot take it to be a sure or a great source of pleasure, at least for the participants. It is too demanding, too onerous, and sometimes too dangerous to make its pursuit desirable for one who makes this his primary aim. Spectators may find sport to be a source of delight and exhilaration; the casual player may concern himself with sport in order to relax or to increase his sense of well-being. But even here we find other and rather contrastive factors. Spectators and casual players are sometimes tensed and disappointed, angered and debilitated by what they confront.

Sport could be taken to answer to some driving common human need. But then we will have to face the question why comparatively few men vigorously devote themselves to sport. Why are most of them content to watch games, or to use them as occasions for release or for comradship, and are unwilling to enter into them with utmost dedication? If sport is the product of a primal drive one would expect all men to exhibit that drive and therefore to engage in sport.

There is some justification in holding that there is a need for sport in men, which comes to clear expression only on some occasions and which has muted forms the rest of the time. On such a view spectators would be athletes manqué, and older men would be athletes who were unable to sustain their need physically.

This approach makes it possible to give a good account of the interest men have in sport. But a price would be paid. We would slight the fact that neither spectators nor older men want to do what the active athlete does. A plausible account of the appeal of sport should explain its insistent attraction for most, at the same time that it makes clear why all do not and need not actively participate in it. The wide spread is important if it is revelatory of man or nature, or of what is beyond them both. If a study of sport is to be of philosophic interest, it should show its relation to men's basic concerns. It will then be able to make evident why sport is pursued almost everywhere.

A philosophical account of sport can have no practical value beyond that of making one aware of basic distinctions, final boundaries, unnoticed connections, and neglected possibilities, and the place that sport has in the life of man. This, though, should be sufficient to make a theoretical, speculative study of some interest, even to those whose main stress is on the practical, the technical, and the immediate.

Educators, businessmen, and newspapers give a good deal of their time to sport, and often are deeply involved in it. Some men continue to be occupied with sport long past the time when they can participate in it with distinction or even with appreciable success. Some perform exceptionally well in middle age, though these are so few in number that almost every case awakens our wonder and admiration. Most men have no athletic stature, but many of them participate in sports frequently and with great enthusiasm. It is the young men, though, who are most absorbed in sports. It is they who participate in it most passionately and most successfully.

Those who are young cannot do much to maintain or to contribute to culture; they are not experienced or developed enough to see or do things in the round. Most of them find it quite difficult to attend to the important for more

than an occasional, short period, or to be much occupied
with what is not relevant to the satisfaction of personal
desires and short-run concerns. Most young men are
largely unformed and undirected. No longer boys, they are
not yet full adults, able to function as prime factors in
society, state, or civilization. The best that most of them
can do is to be good at sport. And that is a goal well worth
their devotion.

Young men can distinguish themselves in sport to a
degree they do not, on the whole attain elsewhere. A
number of apparent exceptions come quickly to mind.
Some youthful painters, novelists, poets, dancers, actors,
and teachers are outstanding. They rightly awaken amaze-
ment and respect. Is this not due, though, to the fact that
we see them as promising to move on to still greater
heights, when they have matured? "Prodigy," our term for
so many of them, is apt. It means "to foretell." If we use
the term properly, we will not be so prone to confound a
present evidence of promise with a likely eventuality.

When we attend to the athlete it is not his eventual
success that we have in mind, but his present state and
performance, for too often he has little or no future. While
we expect our artistic prodigies to ripen with the years,
and to continue to ripen long after the athlete has passed
his prime, we realize that the athlete lives his life mainly in
the present, frequently reaching his peak before he arrives
at full manhood.

The athlete struggles to fulfill himself now; now is
when he makes himself. It is now, and not later, that he
seeks to, and can, attain the excellence which is possible to
him. He does train and he can improve, but at his best he
succeeds magnificently only when he is young. Unless
perchance he is six years old and can run a hundred yards
in ten seconds, he is no track prodigy. If he is an athlete it
is because he now is well trained, though young.

A young man's emotions are more his master than his
creatures. Quickly and unexpectedly they slip from his
control, fluctuating wildly and without reference to the
objective circumstances. Unprepared for and insistent,
they fog his mind and confuse his actions. Rarely do young

men envisage the major relevant possibilities, rarely do they see the bearing that remote factors have on what they would like to know. They need experience to teach them how to weigh probabilities, how to assess relevance, how to balance one bias with another.

Sometimes it is said that mathematicians and physicists make their mark when young or not at all. There are young poets whose thoughts have an incomparable fluidity and subtlety. But none shows much grasp of truths outside his special province. Like other young men each has a mind of only limited range.

A normal young man has much vitality, more than he knows how to utilize well. His energies spill over into a plurality of unfinished projects. Too often he follows sudden enthusiastic starts with sudden dismaying stops. Rarely can one credit him with more than a few skills, a little vision, episodic intelligence, and occasional good judgment. If he is fortunate, over the course of time he will become more and more skillful, his vision will widen, his intelligence will be steadied, and his judgment will become better informed and better directed. If singularly fortunate, he will spend his life using his energies to inquire, probe, discover, and create. But he can now, while young, gain satisfaction more readily by attending to those tasks that require the use of a well-prepared and well-toned body. In almost every other type of life it will normally take him decades before a similar satisfaction can be achieved.

It makes good sense for a young man to want to be a fine athlete; it is not unreasonable for him to suppose that through his body he can attain a perfection otherwise not possible to him. He has little hope of succeeding, however, if he is unwilling to pull his attention away from other tasks. He must hobble any desire that he might have to live an intellectual life to the full. An interest in a splendid body does not of course preclude thought. He who improves his body and uses it well must use his mind; he needs sound knowledge of fundamentals, good judgment of what a situation involves, and an understanding of what he, his teammates, and his opponents can and most likely will do. But this is not yet to say that he is one who devotes himself to a life of study or reflection.

An athlete strives to have a fine body and to use it well. Because different sports require the use of different organs, muscles, aptitudes, and training, he will arrive at his goal along one of many possible routes. How many routes are there? The answer depends on how sports are classified. Unfortunately, the subject still awaits its Linnaeus to provide it with its basic classifications. Not until he arrives will one know which new sports should be introduced, and which might be dropped because they differ too little from others which are more enriching or better established. We need this knowledge if we are to give young men the opportunity to make full creative use of their powers under the control of limiting but enabling conditions. We will then presumably be able to offer them a set of well-defined paths over which they can move expeditiously to arrive at the goal of being well-embodied men.

Though occasionally we may see a game in which there are more players than spectators, the reverse is usually the case. Despite man's great and widespread interest in sport, there are not many full-time athletes. With the advent of television, the number of the nonparticipants in sport has increased. And there are obviously far more indifferent players than there are major athletes, and far more major athletes than there are champions.

It is not necessary to suppose that all nonparticipants or even all players are imbued with a common desire. We need not suppose that they exhibit a drive that is characteristic of the most devoted and successful participant. But it is possible for them to see themselves in the players. An athlete carries out to completion one of the types of effort everyone occasionally makes to be or to become an excellent man.

All men would like to be perfected physically and mentally. Even those who dwell upon their misfortunes, who enjoy being pained and punished, or who would prefer not to be at the front of anything, aim at a state where they feel fulfilled, somehow completed. The defects they cherish are for them but opportunities for gaining a self-confidence or a social advantage; in effect those defects are agencies for reaching a mental or physical position of superiority (a not altogether reliable sign of a signal achievement). The self-defeated, like the rest of us, also seek perfection, even though they too often are content to rest uncritically with a faint simulacrum of it.

Few men work at becoming all they can be. Fewer still try to do this by achieving a disciplined mastery of their bodies. But all can, and occasionally some do, see the athlete as an expression of what man as such can be and do, in the special guise of this individual body and in these particular circumstances. In the athlete all can catch a glimpse of what one might be were one also to operate at the limit of bodily capacity.

So far as we see the athlete to be a splendid epitomization of man we look at him and his performance objectively, de-emphasizing what he is as an individual. At the same time we feel as though we ourselves had personally achieved something. By representing us, the athlete makes all of us be vicariously completed men. We cannot but be pleased by what such a representative man achieves.

The excellence that the athlete wants to attain is an excellence greater than that attained before. He wants to do better than he had; he would like to do better than anyone ever did. What he once achieved and what he might now achieve is an excellence relative to some particular period of time and circumstance. At another time and on another occasion, a superior state or performance will perhaps be produced, thereby making clear that man's final limits had not been reached before. This is a truth that will surely hold as long as men compete with one another. There is no reason, though, to believe that every record will be broken. Should we ever arrive at some limit of speed, endurance, accuracy, etc., however, we will undoubtedly use it as an occasion for modifying the circumstances, and thus for challenging man anew.

We cannot of course talk of records today with much feeling of confidence. An amazing number of what we once thought were the absolute limits of achievement have been discovered to be but momentary stops which better health, greater dedication, more favorable circumstance, more appropriate equipment, and new training methods have enabled men to pass beyond. Records, as we now understand them, are also comparatively new—hardly more than a hundred years old. Not only are the reports of performances of athletes before that time not reliable, but the conditions under which they were achieved are so dissimilar to our own that any comparison between them would be of little value. Heinz Schöbel reminds us that there were no such hard, springy, artificially laid-out tracks at Olympia as we have in our stadiums today; [4] that discuses varied in weight and size at different times and at different games; [5] and that wrestling at the Olympic Games was exclusively a stand-up fight, in which the aim was to pry the opponent loose and throw him to the ground three times.[6]

Unfortunately, many of the records we accept today are too often not definite enough to give us an adequate understanding of just what had been accomplished. Little or no account is taken of the difference which changes in rules, equipment, and circumstances make. We use such a different pole in the pole vault today that pole vaulting is actually a different sport from what it had been only a decade ago. Changes in shoes, turf, bats, balls, and other items have made it possible to attain results in running, jumping, baseball, basketball, and football that were impossible before.

Records not only record, but provide a means for comparing achievements at different places and at different times. Offering objective, public, and neutral accounts of the boundary beyond which no one could then pass, they tell us of the excellence that was possible at a certain place and time, and under certain circumstances, the limit beyond which it was not then possible to go. When the excellence exhibited is officially attributed to a team or an individual, it not only obscures the fact that it is man who is being tested, but the fact that everyone has had teachers,

4 Heinz Schöbel, *The Ancient Olympic Games*, trans. by Joan Becker (Princeton, N. J., 1966), p. 68.
5 *Ibid.*, p. 87.   6 *Ibid.*, p. 75.

trainers, and foils, that all have been molded and directed in countless ways, and that the culture and environment have to be combined to make it possible for the athlete to develop and perform.

The athlete's answers to his challenges are measured and usually accredited to him if he takes part in a public, refereed game. There he presents himself, naked before the world, with his defenses down. He is not lax of course; on the contrary, he is readied in multiple ways, but this very fact means that he is, for the moment, unprotected with respect to anything other than what he is expected to meet in the game. All energy, all alertness, he is also relaxed, standing there exposed both as an individual and as a representative of all.

The athlete, of course, is not the only man who represents or epitomizes the rest. We all represent one another when we make any statement about a matter of fact. When we say "The snow is falling" we are not giving public expression to a private surmise or belief; we are saying something that we think is true for any and every man: "There is snow there, look who will." But such judgments demand little effort or preparation. The more we are driven to be at our best, the better do we epitomize all, and the more worthily do we represent the rest. The athlete is matched here by the thinker, the artist, and the religious man. Without loss to their individuality, they too instantiate man in a splendid form, which the rest of us accept as an idealized portrait of ourselves. But the athlete shows us, as they do not, what we ideally are as bodies.

No one can separate out just what the individual athlete contributes and what is contributed by the past, his own and others', by his contemporaries, or by nature. The world's impersonal process has him as a focal point. He has, of course, a being and a will all his own; it is his prowess and virtues that are displayed. It is he who makes the judgments; it is he who struggles and strives; it is he who must contest. In the end it is the individual who must decide whether or not he is to continue beyond the point where others can or will perform. Yet the records he makes are only the records of man, showing what man can produce through his agency. It is because he is an outstanding instance of what man might do and be that an athlete is an outstanding man.

Sooner or later the athlete falls short. Eventually he reveals some failure of nerve, self-discipline, courage, insight, generosity, caution, or imagination. These limitations we treat somewhat in the way we deal with those that characterize thinkers, artists, and religious men. We tend to blame the failures on the individual, not on man, until we come to the point where we can confidently say that no one could have done better. We could have ascribed the failures to man and credited the successes to the individual, but that would stand in the way of our wanting to identify ourselves with the athlete, as one who is what a man ought to be.

Athletes are excellence in the guise of men. To be sure, there have been and are boastful athletes, and athletes who think mainly of themselves. Yet even they sometimes must surmise that the good they do lives on as an excellence which man achieved, and that they, just so far as they are superior to the rest of men, have but shown that they are worthy of representing them. The boasts and thoughts of these athletes ride on the surface of what they in fact are.

Long before they reached the stage of being full-fledged athletes, men had to prepare for it. Athletes have to discipline themselves, reorganize themselves, punish themselves. It is not easy to see why they were willing to do this. Why should young men want to be athletes, once account is taken of what they must become and do along the way? My answer has already been indicated: young men are attracted by athletics because it offers them the most promising means for becoming excellent. That answer, though, should not merely be stated, but won. This means it should be reached across the barrier of more obtrusive and apparently more plausible views.

2. the attraction of athletics

ATHLETES usually submit themselves, often with enthusiasm, rarely with reluctance, to long periods of training. They do not seem to mind having to engage repeatedly in dull exercises and tedious practice sessions. Nor do they seem to take amiss the need to control their appetites, even those that are imperious and insistent. Willingly, athletes sacrifice opportunities to be lax, give up occasions to be irresponsible, and put aside a desire simply to enjoy themselves. At times they risk injury, and in some cases death. Fatigue is a familiar. Sooner or later every one of them comes to know that he is preparing himself for defeat, and perhaps humiliation. His days are numbered, his successes rarely momentous, and his glories short-lived; he works hard and long to prepare himself for what may end in dismal failure. Why?

Why are athletes ready to give up so much that is desirable to accept what involves a good deal of wasted motion and boredom? Why are they willing to risk making their inadequacies evident, instead of enjoying the struggle of others from afar, or instead of plunging into a game without concern for how they might fare? Why do they subject themselves to the demands of a severe disciplining? Why are they so ready to practice self-denial or to sacrifice their interest in other pursuits to prepare themselves for what may prove disastrous? Why are they so prone to accept advice, often from men not nearly so competent as they themselves are? Strong, with more than the normal amount of pride and impulsiveness, why do they docilely listen to criticism which is not infrequently phrased in brutal or scathing terms?

These questions are not often asked. But unless they are, we will not learn what it is that the athlete wants or what he should get. Each question invites a number of answers. The answer that I think should be accepted—sport attracts because it offers a superb occasion for enabling young men to be perfected—will not be plausible or clear until the inadequacy of apparently more obvious explanations is laid bare.

Instead of claiming that young men want to have fine functioning bodies and, thereby, reveal what man can be and do, one might with some justice maintain that they have neither the wit nor the control to do anything else but spend their time in sport. After all, they are not much given to reflection. Few of them are singularly judicious. Most are impulsive and easily impressed. Not difficult to sway, they are easily tempted by praise, and readily lured by the prospect of sudden glory. Their experience lacks range; their understanding does not have much depth. Nor have they a great deal of knowledge. Lacking prudence, restraint, and wisdom, they are willing to take unnecessary risks. Amateurs in the exercise of reasoned judgment, they too quickly become involved in what is not worthy of a man's time or attention.

Few young men seem to be aware of the price they pay to participate in sports. Most of them are awed by authoritative figures. Today they are also pushed and pulled by advertising, publicity, and what seem to be great prizes. All appear to be easily dislocated by glamor, that instant substitute for fame. It is not surprising, therefore, that they should give themselves to sport, whether it is good for them or not, and whether or not it would have been better for them, then and later, to have spent their time at something else.

Young men are undoubtedly chargeable with most of these faults. But it is also true that young men are not without knowledge, insight, and some understanding of the desirability of being an active member of a world outside the realm of sport. Their involvement in sport cannot be dismissed as a simple function of ignorance or incontinence. Had the view spoken of boys rather than of young men, it would have been stronger, for it then would have offered a plausible explanation of why many initially became interested in sport. Ignorant and unfocused, boys are easily bedazzled; it is not too hard to tempt them to give themselves, at least for a time, to a life that is in fact more difficult and less rewarding than they suspect.

Such an account fails to show why the boys or the young men are willing to give so much time and energy to preparing themselves for what usually are short periods of display, particularly when there is a likelihood that they will be publicly discomfited. Why do they not withdraw from athletic programs once they become a little more mature? Surely it does not take long to learn that athletics demands considerable sacrifice of time, desire, and comfort. Why do the young not turn to other things once they feel the weight of fatigue? Why are they willing to hover so long on the edge of a debilitating despair? Why do they persist once they have tasted the bile discharged by defeat?

There are great moments in almost every athletic career. In few other activities are there so many sudden pleasures and excitements. The dazzling triumphs possible in sport, and sometimes its material rewards, are hard to duplicate. But none of these prevent the athlete from being haunted by a sense that he will be proved to be incompetent, not really first-rate, even if he had shown himself to be the opposite just a short while before. Despite this apprehension he continues to participate, persistently and sometimes with fervor.

A reference to young men's inexperience, immaturity, and impulsiveness can go but a little way in accounting for their devotion to athletics, despite many brackish failures. It does not throw light on their dedication. Perhaps it can explain their occasional inertia, but it does not help us to understand why they deliberately choose to train and practice, even when they are confronted with apparently more attractive alternatives.

This reply tempts the answer that young men are quickly mired in the athletic world. It is not easy for them to break their habits, even quite foolish ones. The most rebellious of them do not find it a simple thing to defy their coaches, teammates, relatives, and friends. It is hard for them to ignore the pressure others impose, coming as it does in such large doses, sustained by an apparent appreciation and even respect. Having once experienced the joy that comes from seeing that they perform better than most, young men find it difficult to return to the anonymous world of everyday. It is not reasonable to expect them to have either the desire or courage to exchange an exciting world where glory is possible, for one that is calm and undramatic.

This answer does not carry us far. It is halted by the fact that not all who give themselves to sport are successful. Most athletes know quite early that conspicuous victories are probably outside their reach. And the rest of those who spend a good deal of time at sport know that they cannot even approach the heights where champions are. Many coaches and spectators try to discourage those who do not promise to be outstanding. If they continue to practice, they must in most cases do so in the face of not only the discouragement that a knowledge of their own limitations provides, but of the discouragement which some coaches betray and most spectators express either by abuse or—what is even worse at times—by ignoring their presence.

Young men continue to practice and to perform, not because they are captives of coaches or because they hope to be champions, but because athletic activity satisfies them in a deep and special way. Though they all cannot exhibit what man at his best can do, they all can make evident the kind of work that must be done if excellence is to be achieved.

Innocence and heedlessness are not the only or the main reasons why young men actively interest themselves in sport. They are too self-aware to be seen to be anything less than willing men who obtain something of value even in tiring practice sessions. They seem to gain something even from defeat. Indeed, at times one is tempted to say that they want to suffer, that they sometimes invite failure and even death, providing only that they can then function as adventurous men who, for the moment at least, try to do something bodily exceptionally well.

Young men, their movements remind us, have a great

deal of excess energy. It surges through them abruptly; sometimes it erupts explosively. They have more energy than they can use, and they express more of it than they can control. Exhibited quite early, that energy often spends itself in destructive activities. Even when it is expressed in harmless ways, it is often subject to unpredictable changes in pace and direction. Too often it ends in frustration, leaving them with a feeling of futility.

Young men could be said to welcome training, practice, and competition because these provide them with opportunities to master the way their energies are expressed. Confidence and effectiveness seem to be gained when young men, under stern self-control, struggle with one another and the world beyond. Encounters which end in defeat often have a salutary effect on them: conceit is reduced, and judgment is sharpened. Although worsted, their efforts often leave them freed and purged. Young men apparently benefit from strenuous work; they seem to gain from being disciplined, and from being pushed to their limits. They must, it seems, live through tensions and crises before they can be at peace with themselves. The struggles they go through quiet their violence and structure their expressions to bring them into a vital relationship with their fellows. Athletics gives them a surplus of joy no matter what they do. Their failures and frustrations merely accentuate the inextinguishable glow that is theirs when they give themselves fully to a life of sport.

This account fits all athletes somewhat, and some of them quite well. Certainly in the beginning, and often throughout their careers, all are involved in the controlled expenditure of excess energy. They are usually restless; if they do not work off their energy in well-organized ways, they remain unfocused. When they become tired, more often than not they stop and rest awhile. If they feel they have passed their peak, they shift the center of their interests and allow sport to occupy them only in spare time. But not all athletes answer to this description. Many of them continue to prepare and to act, well beyond the point where they have energy to spare. Sometimes they urge themselves beyond the limit of fatigue. They call on unknown reserves to make use of energy which could have been deployed in other areas, or which need not have been tapped at all. More important, athletes, by and large, are men who obligate themselves to strive to realize a difficult goal. References to their surplus energy does not tell us how or why they make these severe demands on themselves.

Both the view that young men interest themselves in athletics because they are foolish, and the view that they do it because they have energy to spare, share a common assumption. Both treat the athlete as an isolated individual, occupied with achieving some result for himself alone. Today, under the influence of sociology, pragmatism, language philosophy, or scientism, many thinkers would prefer to adopt instead an explanation which was more alert to contextual considerations. They would be inclined to stress the fact that athletics offer the young a fine opportunity to be with and to know their contemporaries, and thereby become social beings.

Despite bouts of moodiness and sudden retreats into incommunicativeness, the young, even more than the rest of us, have a strong desire to be with others. Though they are characterized by a singular self-centeredness, which we hope experience and education will mute if not eliminate or correct, and though they exhibit a lack of sustained interest in much that goes on about them, they can and do make quick contact with others. They seem to want to belong to groups whose achievements they can adopt as their own. By playing with one another they sustain and may even accelerate and intensify a natural disposition to become vital parts of society.

This thesis seems to have considerable strength when offered as an answer to the question of why or how children become social beings. Although they are born into families, children initially know nothing of what it means to cooperate and thereby grow up together. But quite soon they learn to play, first by themselves and then with other children. Play quickly becomes their primary occupation. They *will* play; play they must. In the absence of other children, they will even play with adults. Unknown to themselves, they make things together as a way of becoming part of a rewarding, expanding world. Through play a spirit of camaraderie is engendered in them, which hopefully will ripen into a desire to be considerate. It does seem to encourage cooperation and generosity. Play appears to be nature's means for turning little barbarians into socially acceptable beings. Along some such lines as these, a social theory of sport might stake out its claims.

The question of how to turn children into social men who are at once decent, responsible, and well-adjusted is of central importance for any society. It has a dominant place in our educational theories and practices, where it is accorded many answers, a number of which have considerable plausibility. The best include a reference to the play of children as offering a promising beginning to the never-ending process by which social men are produced. But it ought not to be overlooked that much of children's play is self-oriented, even when children play together and depend on one another's participation. A child plays by itself a good deal of the time despite the fact that others are playing in the same place, and in that sense "with" it.

Let it be granted, though, that play is an agency for maximizing participation in group activities. This is not yet to make evident why young men interest themselves in athletics. What may be true of the play of children is not necessarily true of the sport which interests those a dozen or so years older. The sport of men and the play of children, subsequent discussion will, I hope, make evident, are distinct from one another in structure. They have different aims and produce different results. But even if they were rather similar, or closely linked, the social theory would not help us much in learning why some men participate in sport. Though all children seem to want to play, not all want to turn themselves into athletes; though all men seem to enjoy watching athletic events, not all want to participate in them. The theory fails, too, to explain why some men interest themselves in individually pursued activities, such as golf, diving, surfing, shooting, ice skating, dressage, or weight lifting, unless we exaggerate the truth that even individual sports have a public and social dimension.

There are athletes who are individualistically minded. Though they compete against records set by others, or against a nature which challenges them all, though they are socially trained and normally act in terms of imagined competitors, and though they judge themselves or are in fact judged by others in public, common terms, they do not always take themselves to be part of some joint enterprise. If athletics is a means for making men social, it is a means which operates against the conscious and sometimes the express intent of some men who spend a good part of their days in athletic activities.

It is usually not too difficult to compete as part of some team. If all that was sought was an opportunity to be with others or to unite with them, this could be done straight away by working with them then and there. One would have no need to subject oneself to a long and arduous discipline. The social theory does not explain why a man should willingly undergo long and grueling training, often by himself, at a pace and under conditions set by himself alone.

Perhaps it will be answered that one trains to make possible a social existence that is more successful than one that is lived without preparation or plan. But then we should expect that those who undergo rigorous training will become more socially adequate than the rest of us, or will be revealed, in their failure, to be social incompetents or singularly unwise. Neither alternative seems to be supported by the available evidence.

Men, of course, can be more cooperative than they are. They could make more of an effort to carry out their roles in the light of the roles that others assume. Athletics could promote these ends. But the ends could be achieved more simply by making room for other men to do what they should. If something more were needed in order to make genuine social beings, athletic events might perhaps provide it. If they did, they would do so only for a few, for though many are concerned with sport only a limited number of men participate in it.

No theory of sport is satisfactory if it does not throw some light on the widespread interest men have in it. It should also account for those who never participate, those who prepare only minimally, those who prepare for long periods and with great concentration, those who concentrate only on their own careers, as well as for those who perform primarily as members of a team. The social theory cannot meet all these demands. They can be met only by a view which finds room for both individualists and team men, for spectators as well as for participants. We move toward such a view when we attend to man's desire to be self-complete, directly through his own action, and indirectly with the help of others.

A more sophisticated version of the social theory maintains that sport promotes the life of those who participate in it. It does seem to be true that by engaging vigorously and persistently in some sport a man improves his body tone and keeps his muscles from atrophying. He seems to gain in health; apparently through his participation in sport he is able to improve his overall power; he there inevitably learns how to overcome obstacles and how to meet the demands that sudden crises present.

Many defenders of sport go further and claim that the athlete builds up a barrier against disease. Some say that his longevity is promoted by his athletic activities. The evidence offered, unfortunately, is fragmentary and tendential. It does seem to be true, though, that many athletes have learned the art of successfully getting on with their fellow men, at least with those who are on their team.

Jobs are often made available to athletes. And they make many acquaintances—optimistically called "friends" —some of whom prove useful in later life. Many athletes seem to have considerable attraction for women. How much of this attraction is due to the fact that performers are conspicuous men, how much to the fact that athletes are stronger than most and some times are quite graceful, how much to the fact that they are so evidently assertive, so evidently male, and how much to a simple function of the truth that they are greatly interested in their bodies, is not yet known. But the fact that many athletes think of themselves as being attractive seems to be beyond much question.

It would be naïve to suppose that no athletes are aware

that these desirable results are promoted by a participation in sport. But it would grant them much more credit for knowledge, calculation, and practical wisdom than they give evidence of possessing to hold that they have more than a dim knowledge of these advantages. Their evaluations are, more often than not, romantically unrealistic. To see how profitable an athletic life is biologically, economically, or socially requires more judgment than most young men can manage. They will have to become more mature if they are to be able to see the real import of an athletic career.

Everyone can see, of course, that some athletes prosper to a degree that some non-athletes do not. This could be enough to make a number of young men want to devote themselves to a life of sport. It is often enough to make underprivileged young men devote themselves to an athletic career. But given the amount of time, and the punishments that the athletic life involves, as well as the loss of freedom that it too often entails, it would seem that many an athlete could have made a better choice. By engaging in business or politics some of them, at least, could have accomplished much more with less effort. Except for a few men, politics or business offers less strenuous and more promising ways of assuring worldly success than sport can. Few material rewards are in fact promised by sport for those who are not of championship calibre or who do not break records. Those who can participate in it only part of the time usually find their satisfaction only then.

Sport enthusiasts—not all of whom are administrators and coaches—nevertheless defend sport sometimes as though it were a great propellant toward a financially successful life, an ideal promoter of health, and the best of agencies for social adjustment. The few administrators who say that athletics is not an unmitigated good seem to have careers shorter than the average. The rest tell us that the student learns in sport how to overcome destructive tensions. They assure us that sport makes him both virile and modest, ambitious and gentle, quiet and strong. Loyalty to country and good will toward fellow man, it is said, are promoted by sport more than by anything else. The claims are neither foolish nor entirely unwarranted. Observation backs current learning theory to support the well-entrenched view that a proper spirit is forged through a participation in sport. But it is also true that some of the comments offered in defense of athletics imply that the right spirit means little more than an enthusiastic submission to the ideas set up by generals, politicians, and business executives.

No one seems to have discovered a better way for producing fine adults than by making young men learn how to make creative use of rules which demand self-discipline, thoughtfulness, and cooperation. Such rules govern athletic events. There may be better agencies for helping young men to mature, but no one seems to know what they are. It is possible that they have not been discovered because no one has altogether mastered the art of education. The failure may also be due in part to the fact that the success that has been achieved in getting men to adjust themselves to their bodies has made it unprofitable for them to attend to possible alternative processes of maturation. But even when attention has been paid to the intellectual side of life, we can claim little success in the task of making full men. No one really knows what is the best way to make young men be at once informed and productive. How can we stimulate them and still not make them lose control of themselves? We teach many of them, and a few grow into large-sized men, but we do not know just why or how.

If these observations are justified, they point up, not the desirability of increasing the time which young men spend in athletics, but the need to improve the rest of the educational process. The primary function of an educational institution is to enrich the minds of the young. That some colleges have helped some of the young to do nothing more than strengthen and extend their bodies merely forces to the fore the question as to whether teachers are as competent as coaches.

It is sometimes contended that athletics not only builds bodies but character. Character, it has long been known, is best forged by making men face crises in the little; by being pushed up against limits they define themselves. If they are made to do this again and again in the same areas, firm habits are established, enabling the men to act without much reflection and yet with surety and precision. Properly trained, the men gradually learn how to act quickly and yet successfully; properly aimed, their action will be productive of what enriches while it satisfies. As a result of their athletic activity the men will become more alert to the insistence and rights of others, both those with whom they play and those against whom they play. If athletic training will lead to such outcomes as these more expeditiously than other means allow, it will provide a strong justification for sport programs.

To support this view, one should show that character is not or cannot be properly molded in childhood, much before there has been an opportunity to engage in athletic activities. Yet some children seem to be habituated to act well, and in ways that are appropriate to their age, size, aptitude, and promise for growth, long before they are able to participate in sports. On the other hand, it is far from clear that children, then or later, are benefited when they are herded into little leagues where they pathetically try to imitate the practices of grown men. Neither their bodies nor their characters seem to be improved by their early immersion in activities originally designed for their elders. Minute strains, lesions, and fractures suffered when quite young grow in size with the body and its bones. Rivalry and the desire to win loom larger than they should in those too young to know what really is important. Sport does not, at least for some children, help them grow properly as bodies, and may hinder their growth in character.

But, it might be argued, this does not mean that sport does not provide a singularly effective agency for building desirable bodies and powers in young men. And if it does have a value for young men, it ought, scaled down somewhat to match their smaller magnitudes, be made into an integral part of the life of a child. Such a contention overlooks the fact that some desirable traits are best ingrained only after considerable control and a sense of responsibility have been acquired. Without the support of sound knowledge and wise practice, blind sentimentality tends to replace loyalty, conceit begins to parade as confidence, and obstinacy usurps the place of resolution and decision. To benefit from a sports program, it is desirable to come to it with judgment and good sense. Fine bodies and excellent characters are not necessarily best begun by having children compete with one another. There is something to be said for fitness programs tailored for the very young, but this is not yet to say that they ought to participate in organized sport.

On the college level, athletics should be able to contribute to a young man's understanding of himself. He could learn there what it means to be committed, and how to express a devotion not easily sustained. If he could also be helped to acquire the ability to assess opportunity with accuracy and despatch, he could gain much from a participation in sport. But this will rarely happen if an athletic program is treated primarily as a means for producing a desirable character. Like many another important objective, character is most effectively achieved when attention is directed not to it but elsewhere—in this case to sport itself taken as a finality, serving no other end.

Sport often receives support from official educational bodies because it seems to contribute to the forging of good character. It attracts young men because it allows them to extend, and thereby test themselves. It warrants philosophic attention because it offers an occasion for the achievement of excellence, and because it allows one to see what a man can be and do with his body. But these outcomes are rarely at the forefront of an athlete's consciousness. They unknowingly underlie his interest in sport for its own sake, as that which deeply satisfies, he knows not why.

Sport is normally participated in brilliantly only by young men. Not all of these are in educational institutions. No study of sport can therefore legitimately concentrate only on college athletics. It should keep in mind those who never went far in school, those who continue in sport long after college years, and those who engage in sport for a living. Nor can it justifiably overlook the sad fact that in many an educational institution, athletic programs, because geared to please the public and alumni rather than to help the young mature, serve to hurt those whom it should help.

Those administrators who have taken a strong stand against any large-scale sports activity are, paradoxically, in agreement with some powerful coaches who concentrate on a few young men, and have no interest in the remainder. The reasons behind their different actions are, of course, dissimilar. While the one is afraid that a large program will entail the exploitation of a few men to make possible good publicity, large receipts, and generous donations, the other is occupied with supporting that very exploitation.

We need side with neither, but if side we must, we surely must ally ourselves with the former. An educational institution is a laboratory for the making of men, who come to them with minds and bodies which need to be improved. They are men who ought to be prepared to be vital parts of a growing civilization. Athletic programs in colleges are justified if they contribute to this end. Unfortunately, they can and do sometimes serve as an escape from the more onerous demands of study; rarely do they demand an independent, fresh use of the mind. The programs need to be redesigned. We have all the more reason for demanding that this be done when the programs involve a distortion or opposition to basic educational purposes—which is what happens when college athletes are subsidized.

*Scholar*ships presumably are created to enable young men to become educated, which is to say: have their minds stretched, their spirits lifted, and their aims corrected by becoming acquainted with the import of disciplined inquiry. If scholarships are given as a payment for engaging in athletic contests, especially those which bring in large gate receipts or strong alumni support, the aims of education are perverted. Young men's athletic promise is then used as an excuse to deprive them of the only distinctive opportunity that a college has to offer. The issue will come before us again when we deal with the problem of professionalism, but for the moment it is sufficient to remark that though there is a real danger in a strong college sport program, the upshot, on the whole, may be desirable. Not all educational institutions subsidize young men for the purpose of having them entertain their elders on the football field or the basketball court. Nor does every athlete use sport as an escape from more difficult assignments. Some are good students, doing fine work in hard courses, and almost all of them are forced somewhere near the limits of their intellectual capacities every once in a while.

When we turn to professional sport, in particular, to professional football, soccer, basketball, and boxing, the entire question of the motivation of the players assumes a different hue. Here aggressiveness apparently has a prominent role, an aggressiveness which, at least in modern times, stops short of trying to injure or to kill an opponent. Many have been tempted, therefore, to speak of sport as providing men with a comparatively safe method for expressing a native, universal insistence on themselves at the expense of others, a way of being aggressive while avoiding aggressiveness' natural tendency to subjugate and destroy.

Many games and athletic contests have a function similar to the military, and in more or less evident form exhibit something of war's relentless insistence on victory. The admonitions of coaches and spectators, even in sports having no evident military connection, are spiced with aggressive terms: "kill," "beat," "attack," "offense," "strategy." Some Freudians take aggression to be a primary human drive alongside sex; for some of them even sex is a form of aggression. Men, they hold, are inescapably aggressive beings who are forced by prudence or the pressure of society to suppress their tendency to annihilate one another. The tendency makes itself manifest nevertheless, coming out in the form of sarcasm, jokes, and the use of pejorative terms, in the act of making money with its attendant power, and in a hundred expressions of assertiveness. It is presumably present and only slightly disguised in symbols of status, with their aura of prestige and untapped strength. But properly expressed aggression assumes a physical guise. Athletics, it is thought, provides it with a fine outlet.

Almost all of those who try out for a college or professional team, and all those who are on the final line-up have the skill and power that are needed to play a game well. But usually only those find a place on a team who coaches think will exhibit a native aggressiveness more evidently and effectively than the rest. They are urged to be mean, and sometimes to become angry, to hate, and even to despise. Hopefully they will then be more energetic, putting muscle behind their natural aggressive tendency, and yet will not allow the aggression to end in disastrous or undesirable ways. What might have had serious consequences is thereby enabled, in athletics, not only to function without great injury to anyone, but with considerable benefit to him, the aggressor. Because he has allowed his aggressiveness a sublimated but full expression for a while, so the theory allows us to conclude, he emerges from his contest at once sobered and purged.

The athlete, it seems, not only does not hide what man truly is, but stops short of doing much harm. He is, therefore, a more authentic man than others are, without ever becoming the brute which every man natively is. The theory, once some of its implications are drawn, begins to sound a little less plausible than it did before.

It is by no means evident that there is a native, primary, aggressive drive. No evidence has been provided for supposing that aggressiveness is more basic or more universal than self-maintenance, kindness, generosity, or sociability. There are men to whom passivity seems more natural or more civilized than aggression. They would rather submit than fight.

Mystics, contemplatives, pacifists, and martyrs neither express aggression nor distort it; they simply have no inclination in that direction. If there is any aggressiveness in them it is enfolded within their other concerns. One can treat everyone of these men, of course, as a truly aggressive being who has found a way of hiding what is patent in all the rest. But what warrant is there for such an interpretation but the fact that one insists that every act and every type of life be understood to exhibit aggression somehow? Even if the point were granted, we would still find difficulty in understanding why some men trouble to master skills, why they are concerned with achieving grace, and why they concentrate on being accurate to a degree no need to conquer other men seems to demand.

Many sports require considerable cooperation on the part of all. All demand dedication and sacrifice. Everyone of them offers a test of a man's capacity to judge and to control himself. Unless we insist on viewing its opposites as manifestations of itself, we cannot treat aggression as a primary drive, underlying all others. Though it may be possible to consider diving, weight lifting, marathon running, and mountain climbing as offering outlets for aggression, they, and other sports, can even more readily be treated as occasions for the release of excess energy, for attracting attention, or—what I have already suggested is the proper answer—for exhibiting and testing how excellent one can be by putting all his energies at the service of his body.

The role of aggression will receive further attention later. For the moment it suffices to note that a reference to it may provide an explanation of why some men engage in some sports. But what is needed is a way of accounting for all participants, and then as men who are not radically different in principle from all the rest. This means that we have to probe behind what drives men on, consciously or unconsciously, to get to an essential human disposition which achieves a distinctive expression in those who devote themselves to an athletic career.

Each man is imperfect, each is incomplete. Outside of each are other realities. Some of these realities are alien, some congenial, some useful, and some injurious. Whatever they be, they are distinct, independent beings, revealing a man to be one who is only part of all that is real. He is what they are not; he is not what they are. But for him to be fully real, he must lack nothing; he and they must therefore be one. This result he can achieve in two ways. He can reach out to the other realities and try to subjugate them, to make them into his possessions, and on his own terms. Because his attention is limited, his powers inadequate, and the objects obdurate and remote, he can never wholly succeed in this endeavor. If he is to encompass all there is, he must have recourse to thought, for this alone can lay hold of any and everything. But it can do this only if, in compensation, it leaves behind the substance of things to content itself with a mastery of their meaning.

A man can also proceed in the opposite way, and try to accommodate himself to what he confronts. He can yield to what he faces. Since different things make somewhat different and sometimes conflicting demands on him, however, he can adjust himself to only a few, unless with a naturalistic mystic he gives up all discrimination, and seeks only to be in harmony with whatever there is. But then he does not complete himself, for this requires him to become one with each and every thing.

No man can utterly subjugate other realities. Each is obstinate, forcing him to take some account of its nature and career. Nor can he simply submit to all other realities, for he can never altogether cease to insist on himself. The two ways can serve only to reduce and never to overcome his incompleteness. Fortunately, they are never wholly sundered from one another. Every act has something of both within it. A man can therefore understand the world on his own terms without destroying the fact that it is there for him to know. And he can fit into the world even while he is impressing something of himself on it.

A man strives to make himself be complete. This result he can achieve if he can master other realities while remaining himself. It is *self*-completion which he seeks, not an impossible, impersonal perfection, pursued along one of two separate routes. Athletics provides a congenial way in which young men can make great progress in this adventure.

Aggression enables one to violently subjugate what stands in the way of an effective union; it has a significant role to play whenever a yielding to others begins to threaten one's continuance. Too often if is confounded with that insistence on oneself which prevents one from yielding altogether to what one ought in part to master. An insist-

ence on oneself is always operative, as part of the effort to
be self-complete, but aggression comes to the fore only
occasionally and then as a rule only when one is forced to
compensate for having given in too much.

Athletics puts primary emphasis, not on the effort to
subjugate others, as a theory of aggression maintains, but
on the opposite effort to deal properly with other realities,
in order to enable one to become excellent in and through
the use of a body. It attracts the young and has an appeal
to all because it is one of the most ready means—perhaps
the most ready means—by which one can become self-
complete.

There are at least three, and perhaps four, stages the
athlete goes through in his progress toward self-completion. There is first his *acceptance of* his body, carried out
in training and practice. This is followed by his *identification* with the situation in which he is, and particularly with
the equipment to be used, thereby enabling him to enter
into a contest, and there *define* what he is by what he does.
Finally, there is his assumption of the position of a *representative* in a game, where, without losing distinctiveness,
he functions on behalf of, and so far exhibits the import of,
others. The next eight chapters attend to these different
stages.

3. the challenge of the body

WE men live bodily here and now. This is as true of the most ecstatic of us as it is of the most flat-footed and mundane. No matter what we contemplate or how passive we make ourselves be, we continue to function in a plurality of bodily ways. Whatever our mental state, throughout our lives our hearts beat, our blood courses through our arteries, our lungs expand and contract. Our bodies grow and decay unsupervised, and, in that sense, uncontrolled. Only a man intoxicated with a Cartesian, or similar, idea that he is to be identified with his mind will deny that he is a body too.

Some, with the brilliant Merleau-Ponty, think that man's body is unique, not to be compared with the bodies of other living beings. Most men, instead, follow Darwin and view the human body as a minor variant on the kind of body that primates have. Today a number are reviving La Mettrie's idea that the human body is only a machine. They, and sometimes some of the others, occasionally claim that a man is nothing more than a body. Since they have at least mind enough to think there is nothing more than a body, I have no mind to follow them. The body is, of course, a precondition for the exercise of some, and perhaps even all, mental functions. This fact is sufficient to make it desirable to cultivate the body, and to consider the body seriously in any attempt at understanding the nature of man, without requiring us to suppose a man is only a body.

Everyone lives at least part of the time as a body. Occasionally our minds are idle; sometimes we sleep; we can spend much time in just eating and drinking. Though no one is merely a body, every one of us can be lost in his body for a time. Sooner or later, however, the minds in most of us awaken and we stray to the edges of reflection.

Even a dedicated sybarite has flashes of self-consciousness. Like the rest of us, he sometimes remembers and expects. He, too, looks to what lies beyond the here and now, and even beyond the whole world of bodily experience, to take account of ideals, if only to dismiss them. And sometimes, with poets and religious men, he deliberately detaches himself from his body and tries for a while to have a nonbodily career, occupied with fancies, myths, and transmundane beings.

He who gives himself to the life of the mind acknowledges as limits only what, if anything, is found to be beyond the reach of thought. But no one can totally identify himself with his mind. Bodily demands are imperious; the body's presence intrudes on consciousness. A man may escape the thrall of his body for a while, crush his desires, or focus on what is eternal, but sooner or later his body will show that it will not be gainsaid. It has needs and makes demands which must be met.

The life of thought proceeds at a different pace and pursues a different set of ends than that which concerns the life of the body. Each exhibits in a special shape what man can possibly be and do. Neither is replaceable, though the full use of either at a given time precludes the full use of the other; a career devoted to one alone is possible to only half a man.

The body is voluminous, spread out in space. Through it we express tendencies, appetites, impulses, reactions, and responses. The mind, in contrast, is a tissue of implications, beliefs, hopes, anticipations, and doubts. It has no size, and cannot, therefore, be identified with a brain. But the two, body and mind, are not distinct substances, closed off from one another. They are linked by the emotions.

Emotions are at once bodily and mental, inchocate unifications of mind and body. A controlled expression of the emotions drains them of their confusion at the same time that it intensifies the unity which they provide for the mind and the body. That is why emotions should not be allowed to come forth unchecked and unguided. Because art and sport involve a controlled expression of emotions, making it possible for minds and bodies to be harmonized clearly and intensely, they offer excellent agencies for unifying men.

Never in full possession of their bodies, men are always more than they bodily reveal themselves to be. Their bodies can only partly reflect what they are; the fullest bodily life exhibits them as less than they can be and less than they ought to be. This remains true even when the mind is put at the service of the body. A more independent and freer exercise of the mind is desirable, for the controlled expression of the emotions is then given a greater role, thereby making possible the production of a more complete man.

These remarks summarize a vast literature, bypass discussions centuries old, and hide perhaps as much as they make evident. Our minds are mysteries. The interplay of mind with body is more a matter of supposition and speculation than of solid fact, unimpeachably evidenced. But if we stop here to make sure that all will be persuaded about that which all believe, we will lose our chosen topic. This is not the place to give full attention to the nature of the mind or the emotions, and the way they can and should relate to one another or to the body. Perhaps, though, enough has been said to make what follows not be as dogmatic as it may at first sound.

At the very beginning of life the mind's course is determined by what the body does and what it encounters. Soon the imagination, aided by language, the consciousness of error, self-awareness, and the unsatisfactoriness of what is available, begins to operate. The mind then turns, sometimes hesitantly but occasionally boldly, to topics which may have little relevance to what the body then needs, to what it does, to what it may encounter, or to the ends it should serve.

One cannot live a life solely of the mind for very long. Its exercise is brought suddenly to a halt when the unsupervised body becomes mired in difficulty. To restrain, redirect, and protect the body, the mind must be forced back into the service of that body. But now it need no longer wait on bodily prompting. By itself it has learned a good deal about ideals, abstract categories, and logical consequences. Some of that knowledge it can now use to point the way the body ought to go. A mathematical notion will help clarify how this is done.

Mathematicians speak of a "vector" as a quantity having a direction and magnitude. The term has been adapted by astronomers and biologists for more special uses. I follow their lead and treat the bodily relevant mind as a vector, reaching from the present toward a future prospect. Normally that mind terminates at a bodily pertinent prospect, an objective for the body to be realized in subsequent bodily action. The mind in this way provides the body with a controlling future.

Far down in the scale of living beings, bodies are comparatively simple, but they still thrust vectorally, albeit not consciously, toward the future. What they do is triggered in good part by occurrences that are relevant to their welfare. As we go up the scale the bodies become more and more complex, and some impulses arise without any bearing on external occurrences. And some of the occurrences that elicit responses may do so at the wrong time and in the wrong way, leading the individual into disaster and maybe death.

Were there any completely unsupervised, complex bodies their health would be most precarious and their life span very short. Fortunately, the higher organisms embody an intelligence, at service to their bodies. Without effort, though, none embodies as much intelligence as it can.

The human body, like all others, on one side is part of an external world. It too is to be understood in terms of what the world offers and insists upon. To be fully a master of its body, a being must make it act in consonance with what that body not only tends to, but what it should, do. This is an accomplishment possible only to men. Only they can envisage what is really good for the body to be and to produce. Only men can impose minds on bodies. Those minds have many grades and functions, running from attention to commitment. Man uses his mind to dictate what the body is to do.

Literally, "attention" means "a stretching out" (of the mind). Since this implies a consciousness, he who is attentive evidently has a vectoral, conscious mind. By directing itself at bodily relevant prospects, that mind makes certain places and objects into attended referents for that body. Desire, intention, and commitment, as we shall see, build on this base.

The athlete comes to accept his body as himself. This requires him to give up, for the time being, any attempt to allow his mind to dwell on objectives that are not germane to what his body is, what it needs, and what it can or ought to do. But that to which he consciously attends is not always that which his body is prepared to realize. It becomes a prepared body only after he has learned how to make it function in accord with what he has in mind. Normally, he does this by habituating his body to go through a series of acts which, he has learned, will eventuate in the realization of the prospect to which he attends. Training—of which therapy is a special instance—is the art of correcting a disequilibrium between mind and body either by altering the vector, or, more usually, by adjusting the way in which the body functions until the body follows the route that the vector provides.

To function properly as a body, it is necessary for the athlete to correct the vectoral thrust, or to alter the body so that it realizes the prospect at which the vector terminates. Correction of the vectorial thrust is one with a change in attitude and aim, themselves presupposing some change in what the mind does. Alteration of the body demands a change in the bodily organization and activity. Both changes are involved at the very beginning of the process of making an athlete. To ignore the need to undergo these changes is to remain with a disaccord of body and mind, of present and future. It is to allow the body to react to what occurs, or to allow the mind to follow its own bent, without regard for what the body is to do. Most of us exhibit the disaccord too frequently in the first of these ways. It is a characteristic defect of the intellectual; in his occupation with the life of thought, he leaves his body insufficiently supervised and directed.

The correction of the direction of the vectorial thrust is promoted by the awareness of the inadequacy of a project, an appreciation of other goals, and a temptation to change. Men usually make this correction after listening to authorities. Coaches, teachers, and models help them to change their course so that they have an object of attention which they will bodily realize.

If, instead, one seeks to change the character of an act, it is necessary as a rule to break it down into smaller acts. These may in turn be broken down until we come to unit acts, or *moves*, each of which is to be mastered in isolation from the others. Those learned moves are modifications of aboriginal, unlearned movements—pulling, pushing, grasping, and crawling. Moves combine and modify the unlearned movements, and may in turn be encompassed in complex acts.

In the beginning, training often concentrates on moves, though there are some coaches who, right from the start, try to have their charges involved in complex acts, and even in contests and games. The learning of moves is, after all, a tedious process, accepted by most only because they hope that they will thereby be in a position to carry out complex acts with signal success eventually.

A complex act is more than the moves that can be distinguished within it. Not even all the necessary moves together can substitute for the act that encompasses them. To know how to pick up, hold, and swing a bat is not yet to have learned how to bat a ball. This is a single act stretching over those moves. But if one does not know how to bat a ball well, it may be necessary to concentrate on one or more of the moves. A correction of one of them may make a big difference to the quality of the whole act.

Moves, when carried out severally, have their own beginnings and endings. Often they may have some relevance to one another. They can then make up a single temporal whole in which the earlier moves have some bearing on the later. No one picks up a bat if he does not first grip it, or swing it if he does not first grip and then pick it up. But this sequence is not to be identified with the single act within which such moves can be discriminated. In the sequence the moves are distinct and come one later than the other, but in the act they merge one into the other and are merely before and after, not earlier and later than one another.

He who can perform acts without first having to master moves has aptitude. No one, though, no matter how apt, is naturally great. To be a great athlete it is necessary to become one. But to become one it is necessary to be prepared to become one. And to be prepared to become one it is desirable to have the benefit of instruction. Training, the art of getting men's bodies to move along vectorially determined routes, provides that instruction. Its object is to bring men to the point at which their bodies follow the lure of the incipient future in which their vectorial minds terminate.

Laboratory instruction in advanced science courses or in medical school, and the teaching of art, music, and drama, offer close analogies of the way athletes are trained. Little knowledge or concern for principles is there exhibited, and as a consequence instruction of this kind gets to be quickly interlarded with unanalyzed recipes handed down from generation to generation. Let a man or team which feeds on steaks be victorious over a long stretch, and steaks will become a staple item in the diet of all who hear of it, until the inevitable day arrives when the long-established victors suffer a series of humiliating defeats. Old-fashioned remedies and devices may well sustain the most severe examination, but until they are studied we cannot know whether or not we are duplicating purely adventitious accompaniments to successful outcomes.

At this late date in the history of sport we still do not know much about what an athlete ought to eat before he engages in a grueling contest. We do not know what, if anything, should be said to him before he goes out on the field, or what exercises are most appropriate to him, as having a certain kind of body, for a successful participation in a particular type of contest or game. We do not even know much about the types of sport that are most appropriate for different ages and for the different sexes. A good part of the athletic world seems not to have learned much from those who have made the body the object of a lifetime of scientific and philosophic study.

In athletic training, as in other practical affairs, instruction normally consists in repeating the lessons learned from one's mentors. Coaches, like sergeants, chefs, and teachers of typing and other skills, and of singing, sculpture, and other arts, of chemistry, engineering, and other experimental and applied sciences, mold their charges somewhat along the lines in which they themselves have been molded. Sometimes they introduce innovations, but these are largely minor variations on what they themselves had been taught. In place of theories or problems, they offer examples, advice, drill, criticism, and encouragement.

There is much merit in this mode of instruction. Large and long-lasting cultures make use of no other. It is favored in the Orient, where one looks to a guru to communicate what had been learned at the feet of a previous or superior guru. A fine method for preserving what meditation and wisdom once won, it provides present pupils with guidance by those who had learned from masters. And when, as is often true—particularly of coaches—the instructors had practiced with distinction what they themselves had been taught, their experience helps make it possible for the students to achieve distinction too.

This method of instruction does, however, have serious limitations. It is one thing to recapture the wisdom of the past; it is another to repeat what had been previously said or done. The repetition presupposes that what is being taught is sound and is appropriate to the needs, capacity, promise, and prospects of the student. Little room is left for criticism, and practically none by those who are young. Inventiveness, daring, and fresh insight—though not unknown—because they are not encouraged, are rarely found after a time.

The defects of the guruish method do not seem to overbalance its virtues, particularly in the field of religion or traditional crafts. In domains which have not been carefully analyzed and theoretically organized it is perhaps the best possible method. That does not make its defects less deplorable. One should be protected against them. This can be done by paying more attention to the rights of the learner, the particularity of the present, the novelty of the future, the suggestions of theory, and the value of making errors in the course of a process of self-discovery.

If young men are kept only in established grooves, some of their distinctive potentialities are bound to be overlooked. One will more likely than not ignore (and will lead them to ignore) alternative and possibly better avenues along which they might become completed. Young men need personal counseling. They can benefit from advice that bears on their individual needs and differences. They should be encouraged to adventure—even to blunder —so that they can learn what their limits are. Given an opportunity to experiment, to make errors while retaining the confidence and support of their teachers, they will come to know themselves better. Denied the opportunity to make mistakes in a congenial atmosphere, they might conceivably achieve the excellence of a craftsman, working along proven lines, but they will probably not grow to full stature. To become a mature man it is desirable to discover for oneself what one can and cannot do.

Young men should try to push to the limits of their capacities, and there court failure again and again. When they stay within the limits set by others, because these had been the limits which other men accepted, they are not tempted to make full use of their abilities. If it is primarily grown men we wish to make, we must help the young to create while they grow, and to experiment as they learn.

Training, speaking strictly, should be distinguished from conditioning. The one is directed at the improvement of skills serving to realize some prospect effectively and precisely, but the other relates only to the improvement of bodily functioning. The former presupposes the latter; skills are displayed by well-conditioned bodies.

Body building exercises, though they may improve the body tone, do not finally satisfy, because they point one only toward the end of being in good condition, when what is wanted is to have a good condition which is used to do something well. But this usually means that one must undergo training. Taking advantage of the responses, reactions, impulses, and habits characteristic of all men, this both refines what is usually done and creates new patterns of activity.

A training program's central purpose is to make men well trained. By making them go through various moves and acts many times its aim is to get their bodies to function in accord with what those bodies are expected to do. Training helps them to be their bodies, to accept their bodies as themselves. It makes those bodies habituated in the performance of moves and acts while enabling them to function harmoniously and efficiently, and thereby be in a position to realize the projects at which the vectorial minds terminate.

Some men do not train. Their bodies proceed from beginning to end, often without needing to be redirected in the course of it. Eventually, it is hoped, he who trains by mastering distinct moves will reach this state too, though it is a question whether he will then ever do more than blur the checking points that his moves provided.

To hit a ball properly it is necessary to know how to grip a bat, how to hold it in readiness, and how to swing it. To achieve excellence, it is usually necessary to go through each of these moves again and again. But before it is possible for a batter to hit the ball as a player in a game of baseball, something else is needed which will enable us to say that the batter is not merely holding his bat but is prepared to hit the ball.

A batter who grips his lifted bat while waiting for a ball to reach the plate may be indistinguishable in a photograph from a batter who merely grips a lifted bat. But the two differ radically. A batter who is waiting for a ball to reach the plate is at the beginning of an act which ends in a decision to swing or not to swing, whereas he who merely grips his lifted bat is at the end of a move or a subordinate act. A mere gripping of the bat can be followed by a holding of it while the ball travels to the plate, and this in turn can be followed by a swing at the ball. He who goes through such a sequence does not play baseball; he merely continues to train, but now in public and within the frame of some game.

An act is a present, temporal occurrence, whose beginning is inseparable from its end. Its beginning separates it from a preceding act, and its end separates it from a succeeding one. The beginning and the end are themselves parts of one present whole, related to one another as before and after, and not as earlier and later. They are in an order, but not in a temporal order, though the whole act in which they are encompassed is a part of a temporal world.

There is progression in an act because of the order, but since the act is not internally temporal there is no sequence of moves in it. If there were such a sequence, the act would be broken up into smaller occurrences, each of which would itself be a present, temporal event, in turn either brooking no further subdivisions or allowing for further subdivisions, and so on and on, without end. Either there are acts which take place over an extended, indivisible present moment, not to be subdivided without losing the act altogether, or there are no extended present moments, and therefore no acts at all.

A complex act may encompass a number of smaller acts. Moves can be distinguished in both the larger and the smaller. The moves and the smaller acts can be performed apart from the larger acts. They then have a quality and boundaries that they do not have as encompassed in the larger. No one of them, and no collection of them, could be in the act without losing the quality and the boundaries that they have when performed alone.

Each encompassed act and move has a distinctive structure. No one of them can be subdivided without having its structure destroyed. But any one of them, and of course their encompassing act, can be subdivided mathematically. There is no limit to the number of parts we can mathematically distinguish by producing smaller and smaller numerical fractions of an act or move. But not every mathematical operation or product has something matching it in fact. We can mathematically divide and divide, multiply and multiply, but we will not thereby have referred to existing moves or acts.

A coach may stress moves or he may stress acts, or he may combine them in various ways. No matter how good his instruction, however, he will not make major athletes out of all who try. Only some men can make clear what it is that man can possibly attain. Still, it is not a careless thing to say that every young man who enjoys something like the normal range of health, and who possesses the usual bodily parts, can gain something from the instruction of a seasoned coach.

A good coach recognizes that each man is unique, deserving some degree of individual attention. Though he can teach the common moves to many at the same time, leaving for individual instruction only the more advanced and subtle modifications of an act, it is his task to bring each man to the position where he carries out, with accuracy and efficacy, a distinctive way of acting. It is not enough to make the young acceptably decent and sensible; one should try to make them grow daringly into a maturity that does justice to their promise. More likely than not, one will then discover abilities in them they hardly knew they had.

We all gain when the comparatively inept are converted into the efficient, the indifferent are turned into the cooperative, and skill is made to conspire with commitment and good judgment. All of us gain when young men learn how to interweave sensitivity and courage, and to back justified hopes with proper action. So far as a coach contributes to this result he is an educator, one who educes, draws out, elicits what is latent; and just so far he deserves an honored place in educational institutions.

Young men vary considerably in their gifts. The reflexes of some are faster than those of others. Some have fine bones, others are of unusual size, or have comparatively great strength. But all need and all deserve help. All must and ought to learn to be exact and exacting, particularly with respect to basic efforts at meeting crucial demands.

Young men should be helped toward a fulfillment alongside others, hopefully in such a way that they will use the major parts of their bodies maximally and in harmony. The production in them of enduring and effective habits of working well ought to be combined with a presentation of many different paths to pursue. The type of activity most suited to their different native temperaments and powers can then be more readily found. We should make it possible for them to participate in many different types of sport, calling for different abilities. The use of more organs and channels is to be encouraged, in school and out of school.

Bad advice and the wrong kind of discipline may make a man lose the advantages he initially had. This means that even more than at the beginning he will need good instruction. All can profit from learning how to become one with their bodies, and skilled in their use.

He who refuses to take advice, to be redirected, or to learn special techniques, will end by "playing at" sport instead of "playing in" it. "Playing at" occurs when one does not care which way things develop and end. But to "play in" a game is to try to help determine its course and outcome. This usually requires that one first be willing to train and practice, guided by coaches who are knowledgeable and perceptive.

Men become coaches for many reasons. By expressing what they know they come to know it better. Some sense that they can grow in the course of the attempt to show younger or less experienced men along which paths they ought to go. Teaching bolsters the coach's ego and increases his self-confidence; his ability to give advice offers a silent testimony to his superiority, as well as to the fact that he has the judgment and knowledge that all ought ideally to have. A coach also has a good deal of power and considerable prestige. He is vicariously enriched by the achievements of those whom he leads. Able to alert the young to a degree that parents at the time cannot, he seems to himself and others to possess a special ability, the mysterious and undefined character of which marks him off as an unusual being. Financial reward, publicity, the admiration of the young also play a role in the decision of many coaches to begin and to continue in the vexatious task of turning the awkward into the dexterous, the unfocused into the mature. But whatever their motives, if they coach in schools they have assumed the obligation of enabling young men to grow into excellence, and if they coach elsewhere, they have assumed the obligation of at least showing their charges how to play a game.

A coach who knows only his sport can aspire no higher than to be a foreman. If he knows only his men he can aspire only to the role of a confessor or friend. The good coach knows both his sport and his men. He is foreman, confessor, and friend in one. He is also more. Ideally, he knows what it is necessary to do and be before one can become a full man. It is, therefore, regrettable that his work is so often judged on the basis of how well his men make out in competition, usually with a traditional rival, for the work he is supposed to do is more subtle and has a greater range than can be so quickly and easily made evident. If character is one of the objectives that at least those who are associated with educational institutions ought to promote, scores cannot be a primary way of determining how well coaches do their work of guiding, instructing, and eventually making well-embodied men. And unless the coaches of professional teams are to be only managers of a troupe of entertainers they cannot be occupied with anything less than making those they coach be full men in a game.

Ideally, a coach is a model man, a unified whole in whom character permeates the body, and sensitivity is fired with imagination. He inspires his charges to possess something like his spirit, sutained by a self-assurance that is appropriate to one who is at home with his tasks, himself, his fellow man, and his sport.

Having awakened a trust in himself, mainly by his confident mastery and understanding of himself and them, the good coach often awakens in his men a desire to model themselves on him. That desire need not be destroyed, but it should be muted. If it is not, it will tend to degenerate into an effort on the part of the taught to identify themselves with their mentor, and thereby lose the opportunity to become men themselves. They should instead be prompted to work on their own behalf so as to make themselves be their bodies and be ready to exhibit themselves in public as bodily skillful men. They are not to be the man the coach is; they are to possess the virtues he has, but in an individual form, as a consequence of the way in which they meet the tests that are theirs when they participate in games.

For a young man to acquire a center in himself in relation to other self-centered men, he must be helped to face controllable crises and selected boundary situations. Ahead of time, and without undue risk of injury or discouragement, he must not only learn what kind of problems he will eventually face, but must learn how best to face them. He will then be brought to the point where he is able to understand better than before who he is, what he can do, and what he can become. This demands that he be protected against his own double tendency to over-evaluate and to under-evaluate himself. Instead of identifying himself with either his successes or his failures, as he is wont to do, he is to take these as indices of what he can and cannot accomplish. If his growth is not to be perverted or delayed, the conceit and despair that hover on the edge of every consciousness, and which constantly intrude on the spirits of the young, must be kept at bay.

In his own way, a coach must do only what every adult should do on behalf of youth, and what all should try to do for themselves. From many different beginnings, and along diverse routes the young are to be helped to become more generous and thoughtful, at once adventurous and controlled, creative and disciplined, individual and social, cooperatively acting as parts of a single mankind, living inside an indifferent cosmos. Many a coach, like many another adult and like most young men, finds this goal at once too remote and too difficult to be worth the effort to attain. Yet if coaches were to occupy themselves with lesser objectives than that of making men be as complete as men can possibly be, in and through their bodies, the coaches could expect to be little more than technicians who teach specialties that serve limited goals. The pursuit of these goals needs justification. This can be obtained only from nobler ends which the goals might effectively serve. At least tacitly, all specialized learning leans on the acceptance of ideal goods as the objective and control of what is now to be done.

One thing no one has a right to do, and that is to stand in the way of those who ought to be helped. Yet something like this sometimes occurs even where amateur sports alone are of utmost concern. That matter, too, will be treated later when we come to the problem of professionalism. For the moment it is sufficient to observe that if we do not take it to be our main task to have men become excellent we will tend to treat athletes, not as individuals who are to be prepared for a civilized life, but as apprentices or as workers who are to be paid for work done.

The minimum qualification for a coach is a knowledge of the major acts required in his sport. In some sports, such as football, with its backfield coaches, line coaches, etc., there is considerable concentration on the teaching of moves, and on those minor acts which are traversed by the acts appropriate to a game. By trial and error, by using champions as guides and models, and by applying an elementary knowledge of kinesiology, these coaches habituate their students to live in the moves and to have these moves ordered in relation to one another.

A considerable number of the men, having about the same ability, can produce desired moves in a prescribed order. They nevertheless differ in the degree that they succeed in learning what is being taught. Learning at its best leaves men satisfied and dissatisfied at the same time. Satisfied, they are more than men who must look to the future alone for their rewards; dissatisfied, they will refuse to be content with what they are now able to achieve. But some of them are too quickly satisfied, while others remain always dissatisfied.

We have here an illustration of a problem that haunts all educational theory and practice. Every educator, be he academic or coach, has to find ways in which students who are satisfactorily going through certain moves or acts are to be made dissatisfied, and thereby led to engage in new moves or acts.

No period, perhaps not even a moment of life, need be without its satisfying facet. None should be made into a mere condition or means for some good to come; a human being lives now and deserves now to live a good life. Child, young man, and adult, all have the right to be satisfied at every instant. This does not mean that they are to be perpetually pleased. Satisfaction has its abrasive moments; it can be streaked with pain and strain. What it does is mark the fact that one is willing to keep himself confined to what he now is or has. Were it not counterbalanced with a dissatisfaction, there would be no reason for anyone to act, until the satisfaction faded because of familiarity or the awakening of a new appetite. But it is when and as one is satisfied that one should be dissatisfied because faced with a desirable goal yet to be attained. Rightly dissatisfied because one is not yet at the desirable goal, one should nevertheless be satisfied by what is now achieved.

A present dissatisfaction is produced by a desirable prospect. That prospect need not be focused on or even consciously entertained. But it is operative, and should be kept in mind by those who would educate or train. They will then not only see to it that satisfaction is achieved, but that there is a strong accompanying dissatisfaction, prompting a readiness to move on.

A man might be content to follow instructions or to copy some model. He might avoid looking beyond the present, cutting himself off in spirit as well as in effort, though not in being, from what is now only possible. He might concentrate on making moves, or go through various exercises so as to improve his skills. But if he is to be an athlete he must, both in training and in performance, attend to a possibility and try to realize it.

No one is completely ripened, incapable of being improved through training. Whether young or old, all must learn not to yield to the body, not to allow its reactions and responses to determine what will be done. The body is to be accepted, but only as subject to conditions which make it function in ways and to a degree that it would not were it left to itself. He who refuses to do this is self-indulgent, almost at the opposite pole from the self-disciplined and controlled athlete. Men do not play well persistently unless they are well trained.

A man who is content to be successful in the perpetual adventure of withstanding or overcoming the world he encounters is hard to distinguish from a well-functioning animal. A man should do more. He should use his mind to quicken and guide his body. He should make his body a locus of rights and duties, and a source of acts, desirable and effective. Only if he so structures and direct this body will he have a body that is used and not merely worked upon by what is external to it. Only he who expresses his emotions through such a possessed and structured body can become well-unified and not be undone by what he feels.

Most men, a good portion of the time, are in control of their bodies. What they do part of the time, without much thought or concentration, the athlete does both persistently and purposively. It is tempting, therefore, to say that for the athlete the body has an exclusive role, in contrast with the intellectual for whom it serves only as a place in which, and perhaps as an avenue through which, he expresses what he has independently discovered. But no athlete lives entirely in his body, any more than a thinker has only thoughts that are entirely unrelated to what is going on somewhere in the physical world.

Athlete and thinker differ in the attention they give to improving their bodies and their bodies' performance. The former, but not the latter, pushes himself toward the state where he so accepts his body that he cannot, without difficulty, distinguish himself from it. Mind and body are united by both. In neither case are mind and body related as are hand and glove. Their connection is more like that of fingers to one another. They presuppose a self just as the fingers presuppose a hand.

One trains not only to have an acceptable body, but to increase a store of energy and the ability to make effective use of it. A jumper may improve his leap by lifting weights. A swimmer may be taught on dry land, and there made to go through a series of exercises which have no immediate or evident bearing on the moves and acts he must exhibit if he is to speed through water. The exercises help him to hold his insistent breath for longer and longer periods, and to withstand the searing pull of remorseless fatigue. They are not the moves or acts which swimming requires, but the acts and moves which help him to be in an improved condition.

Today, some good runners train by interspersing greater with lesser efforts. Bannister followed this interval method in preparing himself to break the four-minute mile. He ran for a short distance at full tilt, rested or jogged for a prescribed interval, and then ran for another short distance, and so on. The short distances covered in this way can be viewed as moves which are to be eventually run as phases inside a single act of covering a longer distance. When the longer distance is run, the runs over the shorter distances are not repeated. Inside the one act those runs melt into the rests and joggings. A run over a long distance is an entirely new act in which arms, legs, and lungs work in a new way from beginning to end.

He who follows the interval method trains not to run the race he will eventually run, but instead prepares himself to be in a good enough condition to run a given distance as a single act performed at maximum speed. And what is true of him is true of those who follow the two other methods in wide use today for training runners—fartlek, or free, relaxed running, and circuit, or progressive loading of muscles. The former of these has analogies in the modern training methods employed in soccer and basketball, where there is a de-emphasis on the mastery of moves and a stress on the performance of a number of acts to be carried out in actual games. To suit the needs of different men, these various methods should of course be combined in various degrees and ways, but this is not yet often done.

The well-trained athlete acts superbly, using his body effectively, in the light of what others do and will do. He makes his expectations part of himself before he enters into a game, and then continues to regulate himself by means of his play throughout the game. A batter does not merely wait for the ball to arrive at the plate; he notes where the fielders are, and looks to see how many men are on base. Aware of the characteristic strengths and weaknesses of the pitcher and the catcher, and of some of the other players as well, his act is affected by what he knows of his opponents and what he expects of them. What he does is structured in terms of what he and the others might reasonably do at that juncture. They, in turn, face him with some awareness of his tendency to hit toward the right rather than toward the left, to swing late, to have difficulty with a high pitch, or to deal awkwardly with balls which cut the outside of the plate, and so on.

Since an act in a team sport tacitly or explicitly involves the interplay of supporting or opposing individuals or groups—sometimes both—it cannot be mastered solely by one who completely ignores the others. Each individual should be aware that what takes place involves the activity of a number of men, together bringing the act about in harmony or in opposition to one another. A coach must, therefore, not only keep in mind the need to condition his men, and the need to have them act well, but also the need to have them act in the light of the fact that others also act to score and win.

Because the end to which one athlete is committed is the end for the others as well, what each does has a bearing on that at which all aim. If a player does not understand and anticipate what others might do with reference to the very end which all of them seek to realize, he will not be able to take advantage of the support that his teammates provide, or will overlook the opposition which his opponents might offer. The well-trained athlete is prepared to realize from one position what it is that all aim to bring about—a victory in a game well played.

When men perform as individuals, or train by themselves, they do not act in true solitude, for even the most solitary of pursuits involves some awareness of others. The individual fisherman or golfer makes at least a tacit reference to what someone else might do or judge. By envisaging others or by making himself subject to rules which others, were they present, would enforce, the activity becomes more than a mere exercise which can be begun, ended, or altered as he likes. To train for or to engage in a sport is to be rule-bound.

An athlete makes use of his good condition to vitalize moves and acts under restrictive rules, both in practice sessions and in actual contests and games. He prepares himself primarily to be ready to discover in the course of a genuine struggle how good he is in comparison with others. Until he meets that test, although he is fulfilled as well-trained, he is still unfulfilled as an athlete.

The good coach makes a preparation be more than an exercise and less than a game. He understands that the body offers a challenge to one who would achieve excellence through bodily acts, and that it must be structured, habituated, and controlled by the object of a vectoral mind. This makes it possible for him to see to it that his athletes are in fine condition, and that this condition enables them to perform well. No preparation can, of course, guarantee a fine performance. The circumstances may be untoward, or the athlete may be out of sorts at the time.

The art of training and coaching is the satisfying and dissatisfying of athletes at one and the same time. It is also part of the art of making men. That art comes to completion when the athlete makes himself be not merely a fine body, but a body in rule-governed, well-controlled action. Athletics is mind displayed in a body well made, set in particular situations, involved in struggles, and performing in games.

WHAT can crowd out room for itself in a spatial, dynamic world is in the present, and nowhere else. What exists, exists then. Only then can beings react, move or rest, push, yield, or stand their ground. Only then can they insist and resist. Since these and all other actions have magnitude, and since the present is where beings act, the present evidently cannot be a simple, unextended point in time.

Not an island surrounded by nothingness, the present has connections with what had been and what will be. The past is not devoid of all reality, nor is the future nothing at all. But they do not contain anything palpable, concrete, substantial, or active. Present beings arrive bearing the marks of what had been, and then face possibilities expressing the kind of beings they can be and the things they can do.

Like everyone else, the athlete acts in the present. And like everyone else, he has a past which conditions and partly explains him. Had he not had just those parents, opportunities, teachers, education, and training, what he now is he would not be. Nor would he be able to do just what he now is doing. The acts, of course, are his; they are not simple consequences of what had been.

Present acts are newly forged. But each is affected, qualified, conditioned, shaped in part by what had previously occurred, by what is attended to, desired, intended, and by what it is to which one is commited and dedicated. An understanding of each of these is a prerequisite to an understanding of the way in which an athlete can come to unite himself with his body, equipment, and the situation in which he finds himself.

Attention is double-pronged. It involves a focusing on a future prospect and an elicitation of acts, usually bodily in nature. If no acts are elicited, one can be said to be alert but not yet attentive. Though there then might be something focused on, there will be nothing which plays the role of an object of attention. Because the boxer attends to the prospect of warding off a blow, he looks down and to the right, starts to duck and to move with his left. He may not be altogether aware of what he is doing. Sometimes what he does may be undesirable; it might have been better for him to fend off the blow with his right. Whatever it is that he does, it is produced by him because he has made some possibility into an attended prospect.

A prospect focused on has no control over what is elicited; the one is not the cause of the other. What is done may, therefore, have nothing to do with bringing that prospect about. What a man does may not, consequently, be relevant to the realization of what he has before his mind. If he *desired* that prospect instead, his acts would not merely be elicited; he would favor some of those which promote the realization of the prospect. A hockey player attends to a game as possibly won and finds himself skating toward the goal; if he desires the victory as well, he tries to get the puck past the goalie.

Desire elicits acts which are relevant to the realization of a prospect focused on. It is to the advantage of the athlete, therefore, to desire and not merely attend. This he does mainly by substituting one prospect for another until a prospect is found in whose presence the relevant acts are elicited. As a rule, we take it for granted that young men will accept the prospects of honor, power, self-esteem, good opinion, and the like. We, therefore, offer these prospects to them at times when there are no competing attractions, in the hope that they will make those prospects the focused objects of their desires. And we try to redesign the young men, to habituate them, and to train them so that when they are faced with those objects of desire they will produce only those relevant acts we think they should engage in. Sometimes we are content to offer prospective objects of desire which *we* favor, and then in so attractive a guise that they will be preferred to other objectives. We face young men with what we hope is a luring prospect of expending energy with success, exhibiting power, or discovering limits, trusting that these will crowd out other prospects which might seem to promise, or which might in fact promise, more to them.

However produced, the object of a desire is only a possibility. It is in the future, not yet actual, and therefore lacks the concreteness and detail which characterize what is present. Desire adds specificity to the attended prospect; the moves and acts elicited are not only elicited, but are relevant to the prospect desired. That which we desire is, therefore, both more determinate than a possibility merely attended to and is accompanied by wanted acts. He who desires to throw a ball into a basket flexes the muscles of his arms and legs, looks at the basket, and holds the ball before him. His moves and acts are both prompted by and made desirable by the prospect he desires, and thereupon function as means by which the prospect is realized.

Does the desired object dictate what acts will be elicited? I think so. But there is no harm in taking the more cautious view, and holding that we have desire whenever we have focused objects accompanied by relevant acts, no matter how these are produced. I take the other alternative because it explains not only why the relevant acts occur but their relation to one another.

Sometimes men speak of desiring something, though they do nothing to realize what they say they desire. Above all things, they say, they desire to become great athletes, but they do not train, do not practice, or do not watch their diet. The harsh truth is that they do not in fact desire to be great athletes. They only *wish* to be so. The exercise boy who desires to be a jockey finds it desirable to try to ride horses again and again, while others are content merely to think about riding as they remain firmly on the ground.

An athlete usually has a strong desire to perfect his body and to subject it to a final test. The object of his desire seems to affect his attitude, and as a consequence he inclines toward a sequence of moves and acts which promote the realization of the desired prospect. Apart from that desire, he would engage in a number of moves or acts which had no necessary import for one another. Because the desired possibility affects a man as a single, unitary being, it leads him to act in concerted ways, with moves and acts which not only are relevant to the prospect but which have a bearing on one another.

Men can move and even act in such a way that what they do at one moment may have no relation to what they do at another; neither might have relevance to what is to be achieved. The moves and acts may just follow on one another. This they will tend to do if the men are asked to go through a series of pointless responses. It is no surprise, therefore, that when the men are put into an empty room and made to react to what are for them detached stimuli, they just do one thing after the other. But in sport, a set of interrelated relevant acts are produced, due to the fact that the players are unitary beings subject to objects of desire.

Young men neglect their studies, skip their violin lessons, pass up opportunities to eat well, and the like, because they desire to be successful or conspicuous in a contest or game. The object of their desire makes them, as single beings, do what will bring that object about. Their desire, though it elicits desirable means, does not, however, dictate that what is done will be in consonance with their character or temper. No matter how strongly a man desires to win a race, he may not be ready to run well or to run as he ought. He will run, and toward the goal, but there is no assurance that he will give himself to the running. To reach such assurance he must move beyond desire.

No one always does what he should. No one, in pursuit of his desires, always acts in accord with his central outlook. The honors, rewards, admiration, success, etc., that an athlete desires may help give order to what he does, but they do not define what *he* is then to do. To act in ways that are relevant not only to a desired prospect but to oneself, it is necessary to intend. An *intention* makes a possibility as determinate as a possibility can be. This is because, in intending, one reads into a prospect something of oneself. The intended possibility thereby acquires relevance to what one is, and as a consequence precludes some of the relevant acts which a mere desire might elicit.

An intention elicits the acts of an individual which contribute to the realization of a prospect. The individual's nature, character, and interests here play a role; they help dictate what acts will be promoted by, and will in turn promote, his intended prospect. Though he will not then determine exactly what will be done, he will do that which is both pertinent to the prospect and suited to himself as he is at that time. Because the golfer intends to hit the ball, he, as an organic unity, holds his club and body in one way rather than in another. When that intent gives way to another, he may still continue to desire to cover the course in a certain number of strokes; though his intentions, and the moves, and the elicited acts will change, his desire for that goal will continue unchanged.

A desire points one in a particular direction which can be maintained despite changes in intention. But we may change our desires arbitrarily, desire what we ought not, or change our intentions too quickly or too often while pursuing some fixed object of desire. It is better to face a prospect which constantly obligates, for this will not change too readily, and yet will make a claim on us and steady our intentions. This, *commitment* provides.

A commitment is somewhat like a desire, but with a steady objective which requires a man to continue to act in certain ways. It is an obligating of oneself by a comparatively remote prospect, while intending a goal comparatively immediate. If a man commits himself he insists on some prospect, and thereby assures that he will not give up trying to do that which will bring it about even while intending any one of a number of less remote projects. He who does not commit himself leaves himself open to a plurality of activities which may have nothing to do with one another because they are pertinent to different objects of desire or intention.

Through attention we focus on a goal; through desire we elicit acts which serve to realize a goal; through intention we elicit acts which are also relevant to the unitary nature of the individual (usually while we desire a goal more remote than that which we intend); and through commitment we are obligated to hold to a project, keeping it steady when we vary our intentions. All these are instituted in private. This does not preclude our ever knowing when a man merely wishes rather than desires, desires rather than intends, and intends rather than commits himself. If the acts elicited are not relevant to the realization of a prospect, he only wishes to have that prospect realized. If the acts are not also relevant to what he is, he desires but does not intend to realize that prospect. And if he is willing to entertain other prospects as possible objects of desire, he has not committed himself to the prospect he now confronts.

A man commits himself to realize comparatively remote ends. Such commitment is compatible with his intending a number of different and more immediate goals. The existence of a commitment is in fact underscored when an intended prospect is given up only for another which can also serve to realize some more remote objective. He, for example, who is committed to being a good player, intends to go to the game and play in it. Told that there is no game today, he turns about and goes to the gymnasium. Had he been sauntering toward the stadium without any intention of playing in the game, he would not turn back and go to the gymnasium on hearing that there was no game to be played. Had he not committed himself, he might have merely replaced his intention to share in a game by an intention to watch one on his television set. His commitment demands that he get ready to practice when he is prevented from participating in a game.

These brief characterizations of attention, desire, intention, and commitment do little justice to the difficulty and importance of these fundamental ideas. They do even less justice to the controversy in which the ideas have been embroiled, particularly in recent years. The acknowledgment of these private acts also, of course, cuts athwart the strong effort made by some thinkers today to avoid all reference to them. Some men have even urged the abolition of such terms as "intention" and its cognates on the ground that they do not refer to palpable observables. Others have been content to find translations for the terms, replacing them by names for moves and acts which terminate in some kind of satisfaction or equilibrium. Apart from the fact that dissatisfaction is an essential ingredient in the life of all who act, these efforts fail and must fail, for they all presuppose acts of attention. Behaviorists, like the rest of us, attend to what they would like to have occur. And once a place for attention is found, nothing in principle stands in the way any longer of the acknowledgment that there are intentions, or even wishes, desires, and commitments.

Not only do desire and intention depend on a power to deal with a possibility that is not observable in the sense in which these thinkers use the term, but without the power and possibility one cannot explain why a series of acts occurs, directed at the realization of that possibility. Without intention or desire there is no ordering of moves or acts to arrive at a result. At most there is only a linkage of them, established through repetition, and having a terminus which is arbitrarily taken to be a closure for that series of moves or acts. And unless one is also committed to an end which assures one of continuity in efficacious effort despite a change in intention or desire, one may produce only miscellaneous sets of acts.

A reference to commitment could perhaps be avoided by maintaining that moves or acts are so associated that one inevitably triggers the next. But then we will be confronted with what seems to be an insoluble problem: Why does x now trigger y, and later trigger z instead? Why does it end here and not there? Why, when we replace one ordered series of acts by another, does that other terminate where the first normally or probably does? Why is it that sometimes, despite the exercise of great effort, we act in ways which fail to bring us to the realization of our wanted objectives? Why can we sometimes arrive at a still more remote terminus along different routes? Why do we sometimes bypass obstacles, sometimes adventure in new ways, and sometimes proceed as we had, but only after considerable delay? These questions are not readily answerable on the associationistic theory.

The theoretical rejection of the idea of attention, with its reference to possibilities and their power to elicit moves and acts, cannot be carried out. But then there is little point in refusing to acknowledge some one of the related ideas, for they differ from it only in the way they specialize the structure and prospects characteristic of an act of attention. Let it be granted, though, that we could somehow avoid all reference to them. All we would have succeeded in doing would have been to provide replacements of them by other, presumably more observable, items. As a result our ordinary discourse would have to be altered, and would become more cumbersome. In a purely theoretical enterprise this might not be a significant consideration. But in connection with a practical activity such as sport it would be undesirable. It would be undesirable, too, in a philosophic study of sport which had as one of its goals the appreciation of phenomena in their full robustness, and which did not allow this to be sacrificed merely to avoid the use of all references to the mental and the private.

In realizing a prospect one fills it out, makes it concrete and present. This can be done in an endless number of ways, thereby realizing it in any one of an endless number of specific shapes. Different realizations give the selfsame prospect different concrete contents. We can, therefore, rightly say that what will be achieved is both predetermined and freely arrived at. It is predetermined in that it will be this prospect and not another that will be realized. But it is also freely arrived at, for it is brought about in an act which is then and there produced, giving the prospect a being that it did not have before.

The object of attention had some degree of definiteness, but not as much as the object of wish, desire, intention, or commitment. None of these, though, has as much definiteness as it will have when realized in fact. The athlete is a man who by bodily action freely makes present and substantial prospects appropriate to a sport.

Some of the ways of realizing a prospect are more direct than others. They get to it with a minimum of detours and hesitations. Some of the shapes the realized prospect assumes are more congenial or will prove more useful, perhaps, than their alternatives. Or they may have a coherence and a clarity, an intensity and complexity that allows for a greater fulfillment of one's promise. The best of the ways will be found if the player at once commits himself, intends, desires, and attends. A batter should commit himself to performing excellently; but he should also intend to hit the ball, desire to run rapidly, and attend to the pitcher.

It is often good for an athlete to attend to the crucial moves traversed by his act. A diver or a golfer makes it a practice to do this. In a silent, internal rehearsal he focuses for a moment on a pivotal move as an inseparable phase of an act, before attending to the next. Other athletes engage in somewhat similar rehearsals, though these are not usually precisely articulated, because the conditions of a contest are not so completely under their control.

It is the *dedication* of the athlete that marks him off most conspicuously from those who have the same commitment, intentions, desires, objects of attention, and inclinations. This makes him one who is not merely ready, but one who is in fact inclined to do, independently of the prospect, what the prospect now requires him to do. To the obligation which his commitment involves, the dedicated man adds a self-determination by which he supports that which he aims at with inclinations in that direction. The batter will not act superbly if he does not incline to do this rather than that, now, while he faces prospects he would realize.

There is a logic to dedication. By dedicating himself, a man at once accepts a prospect through attention, desire, intention, or commitment, and inclines to act so as to bring it about. If he has dedicated himself to an athletic life he is not only required to keep in condition, to play fair (which includes respecting the rights of others), and to resist the lure of other enterprises at the expense of his athletic achievement, but to tend to act so as to bring these prospects about. The intensity of his dedication is increased by making him attend to what it requires, thereby enabling him to live up to his implicit promise to himself and others that he will do all that is necessary in order that excellence be achieved by himself and his fellows.

Most men are not dedicated at all, or are dedicated only episodically or hesitantly, or are dedicated to something other than sport. To make a man dedicate himself to sport, we must make him sense something of great value that is to be obtained by his giving himself to it. He must resolutely turn away from other areas and see himself to be under the aegis of special conditions which mark him off from most of his fellow men. But a willful separation from the rest of men, particularly when it must be supplemented by self-sacrifice and self-denial, is not alluring. Men can be induced to want it only if it appears to be worth so great a price.

Even if it be true, as I have urged, that in the end men engage in athletics because it offers a fine way in which they can become as excellent as possible in and through their bodies, one must appeal to more obvious rewards if one is to keep their minds fixed on sport. The dedication must be kept alive, or be regularly renewed, by making the men aware, in the guise of models and tales of glory, of the nobility of the enterprise they have embraced. Otherwise they will risk being tempted by crasser goods. Sometimes, though, we can direct them properly through an appeal to their ambition or conceit, or by compensating for the fact that they may be afraid of failure and ridicule, may be unsure of themselves, or may be driven by strong, uncontrolled impulses. Occasionally an appeal is made to their loyalty, but it is questionable whether this is often efficacious.

Exhortations on behalf of team, town, or country may please those in authority, but they usually leave the rest unmoved, especially if they have been similarly exhorted before. Repetition tends to produce inattentive men who may manage to look alert, but little more. Those who wish to have athletes dedicate themselves properly must dedicate themselves to the ideal of having athletes see afresh on every occasion what it is to which they had given, and to which they should continue to give themselves.

Dedication relates the athlete to a set of values toward which he also leans. The inclination is encouraged by his union with his body, the situation, the equipment, and eventually the contest or game. These unions, to be successful, must be actively produced, and not merely allowed to happen.

A man can unite himself with his body passively, by allowing his bodily impulses to be exhibited without any or much control; or actively, by controlling and using his body to carry out what his project requires. The athlete embraces the active mode. He does not allow his body to react to whatever stimulus happens to be operative. But he also refuses to allow it to carry out the somewhat undistinguished, unsteadily maintained projects which he assumes in the course of daily life. Instead he attends to his muscles, controls his normal impulses, and bodily responds quickly and effectively as the occasion demands, all within the compass of a firm dedication.

A golfer tries to master a single swing by using different clubs, with different degrees of lift, so that he can carry out different tasks. He who has made golf his game finds that he never comes to the end of the work of perfecting his stroke. His is the perpetual problem of getting his wrists, fingers, arms, legs, shoulders, neck, head, and hips to function in harmony. He must make the body, in its parts and as a whole, be almost indistinguishable from himself. He must submerge himself in it, at the same time that he keeps it under firm control. Only because he has become that body for a while is he able to bring about the results he seeks.

Everyone of us, at least some of the time, accepts his body as himself. He is what his body does. It would be an error to suppose the acceptance is ever complete and perpetual. The supposition is not only unwarranted but it prevents us from accounting for formal knowledge, inquiry, religious faith, and duty. A permanent and complete acceptance of his body can, though, represent an ideal for the athlete. He will then have to be willing so to dedicate himself that he does not devote himself to mathematics, that he gives up an interest in an inquiry into the whole of things, has no hope for a salvation lasting beyond his bodily life, and does not feel the need to live up to ethical prescriptions. He would have to abandon all aspirations which are neither functions of the body nor related to bodily matters; it is doubtful, therefore, whether he could ever exercise his imagination.

A full dedication relates one to an obligating end, and accompanies this with inclinations toward what the obligation requires. The inclinations may, however, not be expressed in needed acts. Bad habits, awkwardness, and untoward circumstances may prevent the inclinations from coming into the open in an undistorted form. But if properly trained, the dedicated man will match the elicitations of a commitment with appropriate actions. This outcome is achieved by having the prospect, to which he is committed, prevent certain inclinations from being expressed, then allowing the commitment to favor some act and, following this, by inclining toward that act through the help of a dedication.

Appetites, impulses, and anticipations make a man incline in one way rather than in another. If he is to do what is required in order that his prospect be realized, he must occasionally avoid the carrying out of his normal inclination to favor certain moves or acts. The more emphasis he puts on his prospect, the more surely will he determine what is to be prevented. He must then be made to incline in consonance with that which his prospect demands. This is best done by allowing the prospect to dictate the selection of some one of a number of pertinent activities, as that which is now to be performed. This requires him to refuse to favor any of the alternative courses of action which are left over after a prospect has enabled him to eliminate undesirable ones.

Relaxation is the art of avoiding an inclination in any particular direction. If engaged in by a committed man, it permits a number of possible acts to be on a footing. The prospect to which one is committed is then able to provide the differential factor that favors one desirable activity over another. Unless a man can relax, he will occasionally do what does not necessarily cohere with what the prospect demands.

Sometimes it is said that we must make men play, but what is then intended is a reference to the necessity that they relax. We want them to stop taking themselves so seriously, and to begin to enjoy something, or themselves, for a time. If we wish them to play as children do, we must help them assume a position they once had in the past. But it is rarely that an adult can, without self-consciousness, retreat far enough back to recover the position where he can really play. And if he is self-conscious, he will not play as children usually do.

A man may cast off serious concerns and indulge his fancies, experimenting idly and at random. This will not make him a man at play, but at best merely exhibit him to be at ease or without a care. No one really plays who is not absorbed in what he is doing; he must for the time free himself from the vexations that characterize his working day, but the freedom itself does not yet make him a man at play.

He who is relaxed is not inclined toward any particular move or act. This state an athlete ought to achieve, so that what his commitment requires will not have to compete with inclinations toward other moves or acts. He will, therefore, tend to do what he is committed to do. If he can now go on to incline toward what his commitment favors, he will support with an emphasis of his own the emphasis his commitment places on some act. This is what he does, as was remarked, when he dedicates himself. Exhausted, weary, fatigued beyond endurance, the dedicated athlete continues to perform because he is not only free to carry out his commitment, but inclines to do what his commitment demands.

It is possible to incline for an indefinite period without doing anything. A dedication must be supported by an acceptance of an actual state of affairs as a beginning of the act which is to realize the objective the athlete has committed himself to realize. Some circumstance or piece of equipment must be provided which enables him to begin the actual realization of the prospect he is not only inclined to realize, but which his commitment demands. He must give himself to the action which is favored by his commitment and supported by the inclination that his dedication requires. The batter must be resolved to take this bat to be the bat which he is to grip, pick up, and swing. He must take a stand that this is where he is to begin.

Each type of act has a distinctive beginning. This is produced when a prospect, made the object of a commitment, elicits what one, because of a dedication, is inclined to do, at the same time that there is an insistence that the act be produced in these circumstances or with this equipment. Without the support of that insistence, a committed and dedicated man remains only one who may do and may even be willing to do, but does not, in fact, will to do what he ought to do.

The relation a man has to his future, whether it be through attention, wish, desire, intention, commitment, or dedication, can be made the object of study. That relation can be abstracted, and thereby denied some of its concreteness. It is then a *structure*.

A structure is a relation made the object of thought. It is of primary interest in mathematics and logic. Others are interested in it, mainly, when it does not merely lie between its terminal points, but makes one of those points relevant to the other, thereby turning them into a beginning and ending of a *unit* occurrence. The same structure can be found again and again in different units, all of which have beginnings relevant to their endings.

A structure can be treated as a guide. One then acts so as to produce a unit occurrence in which that structure is embodied. Treated as a guide which demands that we begin and end in a certain way, the structure functions as a *program*. We follow a program when we not only insist on acting now in consonance with that which our commitment requires and toward that which we incline because we are at once relaxed and dedicated, but when we want to remain for a time in accord with some impersonal demands. We then deliberately set ourselves to bring about a series of acts. If the acts we insist on are merely elicited—even if they are in accord with our commitments and dedications —they will not yet be *impersonally justified* acts. We will have done what we have perhaps pledged ourselves to do, but this may not be in accord with what others are required to do. We will then not be able, together with them, to live up to the demands pertinent to all of us. We will not be athletes participating in a sport.

Athletic programs usually embody principles and conditions whose violation does violence to the meaning of some sport. A boxer may knock out another by hitting him in the groin, but this is not the approved way to defeat him. The program of a boxing match condemns it. Were there no such program, hitting a man in the groin would be an inviting means for disposing of him quickly. The program, of course, does not merely endorse or condemn certain acts; it directs and makes demands. A boxing program requires the boxer to watch his diet, to punch the bag, to work with sparring partners, to plan a strategy, to avoid fouling, to take a long count, and so on.

Reflective men try to act only after they have acknowledged a program. They not only try to realize a prospect, but want their acts to be justified by having them in accord with what the program requires. Most men, though, act without ever isolating or knowing a program. They nevertheless exhibit its structure, usually learning what it is in somewhat the same way in which they learn a grammar or manners, through imitation and repetition. This is particularly true of athletes. They perform their tasks in consonance with some program, but rarely do so by taking account of what it requires. Instead, they allow the program to form the background of their consciousness. It is usually only when they criticize or correct themselves, or, more often, when their trainers and coaches criticize and correct them, that they bring the program to the fore and make some reference to it.

5.   the equipped body

THE athlete seeks to be a bodily tempered man for a time. By canceling out all interest in nonbodily acts and content, he centers himself in a well-coordinated and functioning body. This serves both as an outward boundary and as a localization and expression of what he has in mind.

Methods similar to those that are effective in helping the athlete accept and use his body are effective in helping him unite himself with his equipment, with the situation in which he finds himself, and with the tasks imposed by a contest and a game. Our next concern is with these unions.

Exercise and calisthenics enable a man to improve his acceptance of his body by making it use energy and carry out inclinations effortlessly and successfully. If his body is enabled to fit into any number of situations it is a healthy body, whose various parts cooperate to allow him to act well wherever he is.

A healthy man is able to be part of an endless number of situations. He is prepared to make the objects in them into continuations of himself, thereby extending himself by means of them, and making them function on his behalf. If he works with clubs, weights, bars, and other apparatus, he does something similar to what is done by those who make themselves one with sticks, bats, skates, horses, etc. That is why gymnastics can be counted as a sport, while exercise and calisthenics cannot. They merely get men into good shape; sport extends a man into the world about to make him a larger, more effective man. Though he may use gymnastics to enable himself to perform in some other public adventure, he has already prepared himself to be, and can make himself function as, an athlete just so far as he has continued himself into, and by means of, the gymnastic equipment.

In the civilized world, men enter into the public arena, not only habituated and often skilled, but in command of roads and vehicles, with cues and keys that enable them to function well in many situations. When they turn to sport it is necessary for them to master still other habits, cues, and keys. As a rule, they also make use of special equipment designed to enable them to do more than they could with their bare hands, legs, and heads. In some sports, shoes, gloves, rackets, or clubs must be used if the men are to perform; if they are to perform well, those items must be used effectively. Other sports, such as mountain climbing, require the use of much more equipment, the mastery of which demands considerable experience and knowledge. But no matter what the sport, the equipment it requires offers a challenge to a man, demanding that he not only accept his body but unite himself with items beyond it.

Like the body, equipment is part of a larger world, where it moves at its own pace, follows its own tendencies, and is subject to laws regardless of what men wish or do. But unlike the body, equipment is initially not within the individual's control. It is instead an integral part of an objective world. There it must first be met and isolated, and then be adjusted to, before it can be made into a continuation of a man.

Both the attempt to accept oneself and the attempt to continue oneself into one's equipment may end disastrously. A man may so neglect the life of the mind as to leave himself almost depersonalized, a body routinized and unswayed by fresh thought. His attempt to become one with some piece of equipment may depersonalize him in another way by involving him in a regrettable mechanization. Objects usually have careers that are too monotonous and repetitive to make it proper for anyone to accept them without reserve. And if there is to be subtlety, variety, or gracefulness, men will have to be in control.

Because equipment has a nature and a career of its

own, it can be united with an individual only at certain points, and then only after he has exhibited sufficient flexibility to allow him to remain in accord with it. Despite the fact that he and it are subject to different causes, have different promises, and go through different courses, the athlete makes it into an extension of his body, and therefore of himself. His equipment becomes a part of him for a time. He continues into it, allowing for no sharp break between his and its functioning.

Through constant use a man gets the feel of his skates and hockey stick. He learns their heft, their capacities and limits, and acts accordingly. He shifts the center of gravity from within himself to a position which includes himself and them. The shift is somewhat similar to that which he underwent in the course of his acceptance of his body. But where, in connection with the body, he had to do little more than undergo an internal change, here, in connection with his identification with his equipment, he must contour himself and his acts so that they accord with the equipment's structure and its functioning. Equipment always testifies to the fact that it is a distinct reality with which a man can unite, but which he can never completely take to be himself. But a man accepts his body even when he rests. He can never altogether separate himself from his body; all he can do is to change the degree, or way, he accepts it.

Ideally, the athlete eventually arrives at the point where he hardly notices his equipment. He acts with and through it, as though it were just his body extended beyond the point at which it normally is, or can function. The hunter hardly knows where his arm and fingers end and his rifle begins. It is barely a metaphor to say that a polo player is a centaur. The baseball player tenaciously insists on using a special glove, and sometimes even a particular bat, or a cap. There is more than a touch of superstition that accompanies some of the more insistent identifications, but none ever totally obscures the actual continuity that characterizes the well-trained athlete and his well-used equipment.

By using his equipment a man comes to use it well. Over the course of time he learns to accustom himself to it.

If, like a glove, it is malleable, it in turn will accustom itself to the shape of his hand and its movements. But it never accustoms itself to him so thoroughly that there is no need for him to act upon it in order to act more effectively by means of it.

The identification of a man with his equipment, his making himself one with it, occurs only when he is using it. The rest of the time he merely possesses it, or is prepared to use it. Since it always retains its identity and maintains some rigidity, he and it are never altogether united. He must consequently adjust himself to it, to some degree, every time he uses it. (Such equipment is, of course, to be distinguished from the common materials— basketball basket, tennis net, cinder track—which are used by the players as part of the game.)

These observations achieve a needed clarification when we stress the fact that any piece of equipment, or, more generally, any object that might be used in the course of an act, has at least six roles. It is in the world; there is an opportunity to unite with it and use it; it is an instrument or agency for the production of something else; its use is subject to regulation; it is the object of a decision to use it; and it is in fact used.

1) Only objects which are initially distinct from us can be used; only these can qualify as possible items of equipment. They are part of a world in which we, too, exist; we and they are subject to the same laws of nature. We *use* our bats, gloves, balls, nets, and headgear; we do not use, but only *make use* of, our eyes, ears, hearts, arms, and legs. Each used object has its own distinctive past; each has its own center. When a man becomes one with his equipment he makes it function in consonance with his aims, but only because he gives up aiming in independence of the nature of that equipment, and instead makes himself adjust to its presence and nature, while intending, desiring, being committed to, or dedicated to, what he can accomplish by means of it.

It is one thing to want to hit a tennis ball with one's hand or with a baseball bat; it is another to try to hit it with a tennis racket. And when changes are made in the constitution of the equipment, when, as has recently been the case, tennis rackets are made with more resilient and stronger materials, the athlete must make new adjustments. As a rule, this is not easy for him, and he is soon replaced by others who have had no opportunity to habituate themselves in the use of the now discarded equipment. The young take to the new more readily than their elders can, because they have so much less to unlearn.

2) A boxing glove in the store is not yet equipment; if it is torn, without stuffing, it is no longer to be used in a match; if made for a man, it is not equipment for a normal child; if designed for the training camp, it is not usually suitable for the ring. Equipment not used is equipment capable of being used only if it is available, in working order, and suitable to the individual and the situation. Even a barefoot runner on unprepared terrain meets something like these conditions. He must have the opportunity to run over that ground; it must not be too waterlogged or blocked by boulders; it must be flat enough to run upon; and it must be sufficiently free from animals and hunters to make for unhindered progress. Without these provisions, he will spend too much time struggling, evading, and protecting himself to be able to participate in a racing contest.

3) Equipment can be used without any significant attempt being made or signal success being achieved in the use of it. The result is awkwardness and often ineffectiveness. He who uses equipment properly makes it into a continuation of himself.

The athlete's body is adjusted to the equipment, usually in the course of practice, and eventually under the guidance of a prospect which he seeks to realize through its aid. By playing with his racket, the tennis player gets used to it; he gets the "feel" of it, knows how to manipulate it with skill. But not until he plays in a game does he normally learn how in fact to be one with his racket. It is then that he turns his attention away from it, to realize together with it a prospect beyond the power of either one alone.

4) An adequate program of sport states, among other things, what is permitted and what is not permitted to be done with equipment in the course of a game. One may not so swing a bat backward that the catcher is always knocked down.

Doing what is required qualifies one to be in a game. It does not mean that one performs well. A batter may do all that the rules demand of him; but this permits him to do much that he should not do, if he is to play well. He is permitted to bunt, but this may not be what he should then do. He is permitted, but it is not good for him to swing the bat so slowly that the ball is in the catcher's mit before the swing has reached its climax. There is a good and there is a bad permitted use of equipment.

Programs, because of their generality, cannot cover any and every conceivable use of equipment. Every once in a while some player does something new; his act must be assessed and ruled upon to determine whether it is permitted, and whether it is to be permitted in the future. There once had been no provision to permit or to exclude a forward pass in football. It was an innovation produced in the course of a game and subsequently ruled as permissible. Now it is a part of the standard arsenal of the quarterback. In this particular case, it is the ball that is the equipment, though unlike a tennis racket it is continuous with the body for only a short moment.

5) No equipment is used in fact unless there is a decision to use it. If the skates are not seen to be the skates which are to be put on, they are not skates which will function as equipment in the hockey game.

Decisions are also made in the course of a game. In basketball one must decide at almost every moment whether to advance or to retreat, to turn to the right or to the left, to jump up or to stand still so as to have a proper relation to the ball. But now the idea of the use of equipment undergoes a change; the basketball player's movements, though directed at the ball, do not end with his coming in contact with it. With this fact in mind, we can sharpen the earlier observation that contact is made with the equipment, to affirm that one must make contact with the equipment in the course of the production of moves or acts. If this correction be refused, a basketball and similar objects would have to be treated, not as equipment, but as common material, and the term "equipment" be reserved for what is in steady contact with the body. It is desirable, though, to make the change, for the basketball player, when he does in fact have the ball, deals with it as that which has an independent being but to which he is to adjust himself so as to function by means of it.

6) Finally, equipment is what is in fact used. It is an avenue through which one acts to bring about the result at which one aims. In that use the emphasis shifts to the situation and what lies beyond. It then becomes evident that the boundary of the individual extends to the limits of his equipment, and that he is primarily concerned, not with it, but with what he can attain through its means.

An act occurs only because there has been (5) a decision to do something here and now (6) with whatever agencies are (4) required or permitted by the program. That program is grounded in and is used when (3) one makes an attempt to identify oneself with the equipment in order to realize a prospect. But it is only because there are (1) real objects which are (2) available, suitable, and in proper circumstances that one is able to bring about that which he then intends.

An athlete assumes a *role*. He may do this with equipment or without it. In either case he takes up a position, momentarily or for a while, in relation to where other things are and what they might do. The role is normally adopted by choice. But even when it is not, when it is forced on him by circumstance or is assigned, it involves an adoption of a position which is not normal for men, not normal for that individual, or not normal in the circumstances.

A role defines a status and a function assumed for a time, requiring in different situations that certain selected things be done and others not. A first baseman covers a limited territory and catches, tags, and throws; a sprinter sets himself to run at full speed all the way, inside his assigned lane. All the while other powers and interests, other involvements in life and politics are forced into the background.

We speak properly of roles when we deliberately quiet other interests to concentrate on acting in accord with preassigned conditions. Originally, the term "role" was associated with actors who assumed the parts or characters depicted in the roll or scroll for a play. Athletes in their roles, however, act according to rules and not according to a script. This is true of the rest of us as well. Did we make our selections of tasks persistently and under well-respected limits, we would carry out a role at every moment. But though we stress some particular part of the body and use limited routes to arrive at limited ends, we do not then act out roles because we do not antecedently take those limits to define what we are to do. We move too episodically, too casually, too subject to whim and sudden decision to allow one to say that we always carry out some role.

By himself a man may assume an attitude. To have a role he must function inside a situation. This is a complex of items centered in him. Like equipment, the items have their own dynamics, and have a reality no man can entirely defy. A man must yield somewhat to their power and structure or move elsewhere. Only if he is willing to yield is he able to accept the situation as a continuation of himself for a while. By adjusting himself to the items, a man makes himself fit into the situation, thereby being enabled to engage in action which begins not with his body, but with his body as interlocked with other things.

An effective acceptance of the body, achieved through exercise and training, makes a man feel self-confident. An effective identification with equipment, achieved through practice and in contests and games, makes him feel masterful, a man in control. An effective carrying out of a role in situation after situation, where he is adjusted to whatever else is there, and is, thereby, enabled to perform with and through them excellently, makes him feel fulfilled, at home with himself because he is at home in the world, whether this be the world of common sense, or the more restricted and more sharply defined worlds of business, stage, or sport.

Since each situation is distinct, a man must act differently in each. And because no situation is entirely static in membership or structure, he is constantly forced to modify the way he is to try to become one with it. He would be lost in particularity and change could he not note and act in terms of common structures or meanings exemplified in a number of situations. This he does conspicuously when he enters a contest or a game. There he uses structures as rules, and at one and the same time conforms to constant and general conditions while taking account of particular objects and issues.

He who immerses himself too soon in the world will too soon get lost in particularity. He will be too ready to be contoured by what he confronts, and too lost in immediacy to know what else he has to do. When existentially minded thinkers insist on the importance of men involving themselves with other men and other things, they tend to forget how much is gained by first standing away from all involvements. One needs to stand away in order to get one's bearings and thereby make possible a re-entry as a man in control of himself, who tries to control other things as well, while allowing himself to be controlled by common rules. Athletes, despite their concern with quite definite things at each moment, remain steady and masterly because they enter situations as trained men who carry out roles in accordance with rules.

"Rule" and "regulation" have the same root. Sometimes they are used interchangeably. But on the whole a regulation is a structure imposed by an authority, while a rule is a structure accepted as a standard and control. Confusion sets in when we have authoritative prescriptions which are in fact accepted. Because the acceptance is so important for an understanding of sport, which is after all voluntarily engaged in, it is preferable to speak of any accepted prescriptions there as "rules," reserving "regulation" for authoritative decrees relating to what is permitted.

Rules are comparatively constant, the acceptance of which enables a man not only to fit into a situation, to escape from it, and to vary with it, but to remain selfsame from situation to situation. Because the athlete is rule-governed he can remain steady while a good deal fluctuates.

A man might be able to accomplish more occasionally were he to ignore the established rules. Sometimes we find those who have no knowledge of rules, and yet who, without violating any accepted rules, outrun, outthrow, outfish, or outskate all others. They are "natural champions." We take note of their records but do not normally include them in the annals of sport. There is justice in this decision, for what we want to know is what can be done by those who are rule-governed. Rules impose restrictions. A knowledge of them could conceivably limit one's achievements, giving an unfair advantage to those who perform "naturally" in ignorance of them.

Rules provide stable guides, and permit us to compare one performance with another. Here is another reason why we ought not to follow those who put an emphasis on winning or on aggression as the primary motives for athletic activity. That emphasis blurs the fact that athletes carry out roles in a plurality of situations while conforming to rules within whose confines other men also act.

Contextualistic theories, such as those advanced by G. H. Mead and John Dewey, and held by many sociologists as well, are admirably suited to describe the athlete in relation to his body, his equipment, his situation, or in a contest or game. But their very success points to a serious inadequacy. The theories are not able to explain how it is that some men are not well-adjusted to these, or why it is that they are unwilling to be rule-regulated everywhere. The athlete would like to be an integral part of various contexts, but he does not succeed in doing this as often or as excellently as he would like. And the non-athlete, though he would benefit from a submission to rules which make for easier and more successful behavior, often does as he likes. Contextualism is a theory about achievements, and not, as it supposes itself to be, a description of an aboriginal state of affairs, encompassing everyone—unless all that is intended by the theory is the harmless remark that no man is wholly sunk in privacy, and always has some relation to something else.

The athlete, with or without equipment, functions in accordance with rules. Only because he accepts certain rules is he able to have a role in the world of sport. Only by turning away from the ordinary world in somewhat the way in which a mathematician, scientist, or painter does, is he able to carry out his role.

The athlete may offer a fine illustration of social mobility, or of the effect of economic pressure. His biography or psychology may be considerably clarified by seeing him in political, social, and economic frames. But as athlete he attends to none—and we ought to attend to none—of these. His task is to carry out an athletic role. He may be made to represent regions, nations, or some limited portion of mankind; he may be used for a multitude of nonathletic ends. But these should not be allowed to jeopardize the truth that he is expected to live up to the ideals of his sport. Later, as a matured man, he will be able, perhaps, to return to the world as one who can lead mankind as well as follow, who can rule as well as be ruled, or who, while disciplined, creates in art or thought. But that is not his concern now.

It might be readily conceded by most men that there is warrant for a monk or a philosopher to hold himself off from the world for a while. The separation may be necessary if he is to be able to return to the world, fit to help those who remained behind. Enriched and ennobled, he may then be able to function in a manner that would not have been possible had he not for a time moved away. But not many will allow that such an adventure is appropriate to an athlete. They are, I think, mistaken. The refusal, though, does point up the fact that an athlete's achievements are not altogether comparable to those open to the religious or the speculative, and that he, even more evidently than they, is not living a full life. That does not mean that the athlete is wasting his time or doing what is only of minor value. It will always be noble work to become a body, and to unite that body with equipment and situations, and in these ways move to the position where one makes oneself a man.

There is no need to apologize for or to justify the athlete. It is a great accomplishment to turn a body from a creature of vagrant stimuli, insistent appetites, and poorly focused objectives, into one which is taut and controlled, and directed toward a realizable excellent end. It is a great accomplishment to have made oneself willing to see how to deal well with the obstacles and challenges that one's body, other men, and nature provide. It is a great achievement to make oneself ready and willing to discover the limits beyond which men cannot go in a rule-governed, bodily adventure. It is a great achievement to have found one way in which men, as possessed of finite bodies involved in finite situations, can become self-complete.

Athletes, of course, often fall short of these noble ideals. Sometimes they misbehave, not only outside the arena but within it. Too often they yield to the pressure of organizations, to slogans, and to the persuasion of raw power. Too often they are tempted by money and by what they think is fame and glory. The misbehavior of spectators is more common and conspicuous and, in one sense— the injury that it does to men and property—more serious than that characteristic of athletes. Not rule-controlled, spectators sometimes do not hold themselves within the boundary of a sport. They then but reveal that they are not genuine spectators, but are concerned with only a part of the sport, or with only some contestants in it. A true spectator, like the athlete, brackets all other interests and remains within limits, voluntarily accepted. His identification, in the end, is with the athlete as man epitomized, and not with him as fellow citizen, fellow worker, or fellow student, who is to win no matter how.

The athlete is a man apart. The beauty and grace of his body, his coordination, responsiveness, alertness, efficiency, his devotion and accomplishments, his splendid unity with his equipment, all geared to produce a result at the limits of bodily possibility, set him over against the rest of men. Mankind looks on him somewhat the way it looks on glamorous women, the worldly successful, and the hero. These enhanced themselves by reordering their minds and bodies, and thereby realized bodily attainable great goals. We sense in them a power which we also sense in their perverted forms—in the prostitute, the criminal, and the villain. They are at the end points of the spectrum of human promise; they define our boundaries, good and ill. The athlete has a particular fascination for most men because, in addition to his athletic prowess, he provides a conspicuous illustration of the fact that even the young can sometimes be superb. But this they are only if they back their training, their acceptance of their bodies, and their union with their equipment and situations, with a healthy spirit that enriches whatever they do.

6.   health

A DEDICATED athlete, at ease with himself, making decisions to act in ideal circumstances, performs as he should,
but perhaps not as well as he might. Although he does not
do merely what he had been trained to do, but also what
makes his training worthwhile, he still may not have a
satisfactory strategy, or employ the proper tactics in the
circumstances. Faced with unexpected problems, due to a
change in circumstances or because of the acts of others,
he will, more likely than not, act improperly.

Strategy is the art of envisaging an entire course of
action so that advantageous positions are made likely at
crucial times. Without it one leaves the development of a
contest or game, and eventually the determination of one's
acts, to the decisions of an opponent or to the play of luck.
If an illustration from a nonathletic venture be not too
misleading, we see something like this in international
chess play. The Russians refuse to make a definite plan in
the beginning; instead they await some decisive move by
their opponents and then plan their strategy from that
point on. In effect, they have two plans, one of which tells
them when the second is to be put in operation. This is
quite different from having no plan at all, or only a plan, if
one likes, to allow the opponent to dictate what the problem is with which one is to deal. But those who play with
the Russians are sometimes so discommoded by this twofold strategy that they give up their own and are forced to
play on terms set by their opponents.

Strategy is generalship; tactics is management. Strategy needs support from tactics, the art of ordering and using one's forces in the face of conditions then and there encountered. Both require adroitness, strategy demanding this in the form of an accommodation to an overall plan, while tactics requires it in the form of a flexibility in attitude and procedure to make it possible to take advantage of whatever opportunities are suddenly laid bare.

Players are neither taught strategy nor learn it. They accept it in the form of a plan, and make this concrete by adapting their activities to it. Tactics, though, is taught usually in the course of training. Fundamentals and standard moves are there faced and dealt with appropriately. Since no game goes according to the book, the tactics learned in training must be reshaped in the course of an actual playing; otherwise one will find oneself facing novel problems with devices appropriate only to old ones. The tactics practiced before the game could, therefore, be said to be but a blueprint of that to which men are subsequently to adapt themselves.

There is no strategy for parts of a game, any more than there is a tactics for the whole of it. Tactics is strategy divided into steps and specified in the form of particular acts which give the strategy body and vitality. Strategy envisages an entire enterprise. It refers one to the anticipated pace of the venture, and points up the vital joints in it. Tactics, instead, concerns itself with the producing of effective means for realizing the strategic plan. Since tactics are determined partly by the different situations in which one is, they must be constantly changed, but strategy needs to be changed only when it is discovered that it is making victory more and more difficult to attain.

Nonplaying captains and coaches are in the advantageous position of being able to make judgments in tactics, which take account not only of what both sides have done, but of what they can do and seem intent on doing. But it would be wrong for these guides to think that they should dicate not only the strategy but the tactics of a game. If they did, they would make their players into little more than puppets—a result sometimes produced by very strong-minded coaches. The danger is minimal in swift-moving sports, such as skiing, speed skating, lacrosse, polo, and the like, where there is little opportunity to convey anything to the players once they have begun to participate. In these sports all the strategy must be communicated beforehand, and the tactics varied by the participants without hesitation as the occasion arises.

Participants can see a game only from limited positions, but coaches—the term is used here to refer also to managers and others who decide the strategy—can take account of both sides, and note what seem to be their major strengths and weaknesses. Coaches, therefore, can have a knowledge that is available to no one else. If athletes are really to engage in their own struggles, that knowledge, where permissibly conveyed during the course of a game, should encourage players to freely produce their own tactical moves.

Game theory, particularly as developed by J. von Neuman and O. Morgenstern, is a theory about tactics and strategy. It has little pertinence to athletics because in good part it is appropriate only to statically defined problems—for which in fact it was designed. It depends, too, for its operation, on the assumption that every item of relevant information is known by the participants. Such a theory can at best offer a model which the actual tactics of a game—since it operates with an unknown number of unknowns—copies at some remove.

In actual competition, athletes must often act without reflection to take care of novel problems, presumably by making use of skills previously mastered. They would be in a better position to deal with the issues that arise if they had made earlier use of pseudo opponents, opponents who, like sparring partners, imitate the kind of opposition that might be reasonably expected, and therefore enable the athletes to be practiced in the performance of crucial moves and acts. Though they will then not know what in fact will take place, they will be alert to the places where signal changes in effort must be made.

Tactics dictates which actual detailed modifications are to be introduced in the course of an action, to make it effective and efficient. It gives an existential involvement an opportunity to realize a sought objective. Helped by quick responses and a dedication to the production of excellence, tactics is, at its best, supported by a high degree of awareness of what is actually, as well as what is incipiently, present. In it we can usually distinguish at least six components: A. judgment, B. rules, C. decisiveness, D. control, E. rhythm, and F. flexibility. Some of these have already been remarked upon, but they must be dealt with now as well, if the nature and role of tactics is to be clarified.

A) In some sports there are definite preassigned things the participants must do. Ice skating, gymnastics, diving, and dressage are conspicuous in their demands that the contestants go through a series of prescribed performances. What the athletes rehearsed they try to perform. New elements have here only a minimal role in comparison with what they have in most other sports. But even here there are new factors introduced in each contest or exhibition. The arena has an effect. The judges, the crowd, and the competitors impinge on one another, and thereby alter the nature of what occurs. The announcement of points and standing, of records broken, of the victories and defeats in other contests change the quality of the entire meeting. And sometimes the competitors are asked to show what they can do in "free," self-prescribed activities which, though well rehearsed, make the participants compete against the performances of others which they are unable to evaluate or to counter in advance.

Usually athletes are forced to make fresh judgments at every moment as to just what they are to do. Those judgments are practical, concerned with what is desirable in a given situation. Surely and quickly, a player must decide where, how, and when he should advance or retreat, emphasize or minimize, remain steady or change.

Good practical judgment is a habit of using good common sense—which is to say, a habit of making reasonable suppositions regarding what is and is to be, and consequently deciding what one is to do, and when and how.

The habit is acquired in large part during the course of daily living; it is accentuated in training and stabilized by practice.

The wisdom that the athlete needs is schematically present in him because of what he did in the past. By going through comparable acts again and again under controlled conditions, he builds up the power of quickly estimating what a situation demands and how he is to behave in it. Without the habit, he will be forced to spend too much time in deliberating or experimenting when he has to be right, fast.

It is possible to have good judgment without at the same time exhibiting much skill. That is how it is possible for there to be good critics, and even trainers and coaches who are not as capable as the men they criticize. The converse, of course, is also true. It is possible to have considerable skill and yet have poor judgment. An athlete may be well-adjusted to his equipment, his teammates, and his opponents, and yet fail to evaluate situations properly. As a consequence, he will skillfully do what is ineffective. Again and again, a hockey player may hit the putt correctly, only to have it countered by opponents whose movements he did not anticipate.

To win a race it may be necessary to slow down or to accelerate suddenly, or to cut in or out awkwardly, because there is no time to spell out one's energy under clear control. Both judgment and skill are then exhibited, but not without gracelessness or inaccuracy, and a possible frustration. And no matter how well the preparation has been, one may be defeated by unpredictable and ungovernable changes in circumstance. Automobile racers are sometimes undone by the unexpected appearance of a slick of oil. In an instant their outstanding abilities are turned into helpless accompaniments of a series of disasters. Good judgment helps but little then.

No one, perhaps, has made as many telling and lasting observations about the nature of practical judgment as Aristotle did. He remarked that it related to particulars and not only to generals, and that it made use of opinion, which is a reasonable belief, and not an hypothesis or theory. He saw that it is never adequately expressed or expressible in any situation, and that it can neither be precisely confirmed nor denied. I think that what Aristotle says here is sound; I find it persuasive. It is not clear, though, whether or not he thought that a man could acquire good judgment without having some initial aptitude in that direction. But without some aptitude, good judgment is beyond his reach. He can gain little from the best of mentors; no coach can do much with a pupil who has little sense. Fortunately, most men do seem to have the aptitude. As a consequence, good judgment is not too rare. But if coaches are to change men who have their bodies well controlled into men who control what they must in order that success be achieved, they need pupils who have more than ordinary judgment. They need men who can be decisive, controlled, rhythmic, and flexible.

B) Two kinds of rules are worth distinguishing. One relates the actual beginning to the actual ending of a particular game; the other defines a set of norms which is to be ideally realized in every game. In the one, a condition is provided in terms of which all the participants are to try to achieve excellence. In the other, a standard is set up which actual performances can only approximate. Had we only the first there would be no comparison of different games as better or worse; all those played in strict conformity to rules which relate their beginning to their ending would be equally good. Had we only the second, there would be no necessary reference to any actual game. Both types of rule are needed, the one to structure an actual game, the other to express the ideal in terms of which all games could be evaluated. In the best of games both play an effective role.

A game is to be produced in such a way that one moves as close as possible to what an ideal game requires. But it is possible for a man to play exceptionally well, approximating to a high degree an ideal performance, and yet play in a poor game because he is not supported by his teammates. It is also possible for a man to play poorly in a splendid game, where the ideal is approximated closely by a team which he does not support significantly.

In play there is only a minimal adherence to rules, with

a compensatory stress on spontaneity and novelty. Though one might play idly while conforming to rules and trying to live up to norms, play does not allow either of these to have a dominant role.

Many forms of idle play are repetitive, involving an almost mechanical adherence to rules. Children repeat verses over and over again; they go through the same movements many times, trying hard to avoid any variation in the rhythm. These repetitions, though, seem to be more like definitions dictating the nature of the play than like the rules which govern contests and games, for they demand no well-defined beginning or ending, and provide no explicit grounds for the formulation of objective judgments, or the recording of results. For those who, like Johan Huizinga, do not distinguish idle play from play in games, it makes sense to say "All play has its rules. They determine what 'holds' in the temporary world circumscribed by play." [1] But his view would be rejected by anyone who remembers that what occurs in play is freshly produced, and that any "rules" utilized there serve only to remark the boundary conditions, or to signalize the main turning points; in contrast, the rules of a game structure and control the whole. Huizinga himself is forced to admit that on his view "There remains, however, an extensive and very important domain [not accounted for, but] which in our terminology would come under the head of playing . . . to wit: matches and contests." [2] These do not properly come under the heading of mere play, because they are rule-dominated in a way that play never is.

To know a rule is not yet to know how in fact to carry it out. No statement of a rule tells just what must be done in order to exemplify or conform to the rule. Knowing a rule and acting in accord with it are quite distinct operations. Much has been made of this fact by the Wittgensteineans. But they exaggerated the distinction that should be made between stating a rule and acting in consonance with it, largely because they overlooked the role of intent.

If a rule terminates in an intended prospect, the prospect dictates that a rule-governed action is to be per-

1 Johan Huizinga, *Homo Ludens, A Study of the Play-Element in Culture* (Boston, 1955), p. 11   2 *Ibid.*, p. 30

formed. Because the batter intends to get home by going round the bases in a certain order and in one direction only, he goes from one to the other without hesitation. He had, of course, to learn what the stated rule about traversing the bases means in act, but he learnt this while intending, and under the guidance of, the desirable objective of getting home.

It is hard to live up to rules which define an ideal game. No matter how well trained a man may be, he may fall far short of what the ideal requires. His muscles may be tired, his attention may wander, and he may be intruded upon by persistent forces. He cannot always perform at his peak, making use of all the energy that he in fact has. He must, therefore, exercise a tactical discretion. If he is to be both maximally effective in a particular game and able to approach the realization of an ideal performance—each in conformity with rules—he must make use of his energy in different ways and at different times.

c) At every moment men are to do what will bring them closest to an ideal performance. Their aims and their actions should be in accord. This they will be if the performers' decisions follow the bent of their judgments. Without loss of flexibility they will then curb their impulsiveness; without loss of caution they will then overcome their hesitations and doubts. As a consequence, they will sometimes change their tactics and sometimes even their strategy.

Decisiveness avoids both unrestraint and constraint, to focus on the act that is relevant if progress toward an excellent result is to occur. Having to do primarily with the joints of an enterprise rather than with the joints of a body, decisiveness is practical judgment put to work in a particular situation so that maximum performance is assured.

To be decisive it is necessary to will. This means that one must face a number of alternatives and have both mind and body focus on one of them. Decisiveness, though, is more than an act of will. It puts the body to the work of producing a willed act, leading to the realization of that to which one is committed. A decisive man does what his commitment then requires.

d) Decisiveness presupposes that the body is under control, and that it, therefore, has to some degree already been accepted. In good part the control becomes a matter of habit, leaving over an area which is to be mastered only so far as one knows what the body can do and what the circumstances permit and preclude. That knowledge should also control what is done.

When there is genuine mastery, habitual control and control mediated by knowledge support one another. Neither is quickly acquired. It takes time, too, for the unity of body and mind to be solidified and stabilized. Many experiences and trials are needed before the body can become the locus and avenue for a mind and, as a consequence, do what is required. But only then is the body ready to spring into appropriate action, effectively answering to the conditions that prevail.

It is possible to have considerable control and yet be insufficiently decisive. One will then not be effective, but instead will blur, hesitate, or vary too much. It is also possible to be decisive but not have much control. One will then resolutely get in one's own way. Acts will be insisted upon which cannot be carried out effectively. That failure can be occasionally remarked in great quarterbacks. They have a kind of arrogance and willfulness which leads them sometimes to decide to do what is beyond the reach of their capacities.

E) In a successful performance, the body's natural pulsations, the objects' careers and circumstance, the dispositions of opponents, and the nature of the sought end are lived with and through. Gracefulness and skill are combined and thereby gain a distinctive and appropriate rhythm. That rhythm spaces what is done. It demands thrusts forward as well as retreats, and the interlacing of movements with rests. Sometimes it demands variation in speed and direction. Ideally, it keeps abreast of changes in what is being used and what is being faced. In effect, therefore, it is a sign of the degree of harmonization that has been achieved by oneself and expressed in activity.

Each individual has a distinctive rhythm as a consequence of the way in which he has incarnated himself.

That rhythm, like control, is also only gradually acquired. Over the course of his career, in training and on the field, the athlete constantly adjusts himself to his body, his equipment, his opponents, and his games, until he acquires a characteristic way of spacing what he does. He is to prevent his rhythm from becoming so dominant that it precludes his acting flexibility; but if, in fear of this eventuality, he tries to avoid having a characteristic rhythm, he will inevitably compromise his skills.

Often dramatic and exciting, a man's habitual rhythm may not mesh altogether well with the situations in which he finds himself. As a consequence, he will not perform as well as he might. He should modify that rhythm until it serves to synchronize his controlled body, equipment, and roles with the confronted novelties.

In such sports as the shot-put, the hurdles, the high jump, and the pole vault, a successful performance demands a series of moves and acts having not only a well-defined order, but a definite timing in relation to one another. Some, but not a great deal of attention must then be paid to the circumstances and the pulse beat of what goes on about. The individual will have to mesh with other items in the situation, but the dominant fact will be his rhythm. At the opposite extreme are such sports as lacrosse and football, where the rhythm of most players is made subordinate to that of the particular play that has been initiated. Most of the other sports fall somewhere between these two extremes. In some, such as crew, there is a well-defined cadence to which all adhere; in others, such as boxing, sometimes the individual and sometimes his opponent dictates the rhythm of the contest, although occasionally the two together make a single sequence with a distinctive tempo. But in all the sports each participant exhibits a rhythm all his own, hopefully in some consonance with what else occurs.

F) Too often, particularly in professional basketball, hockey, and football, athletes are trained to be ready for only certain types of situation. It is no surprise, therefore, that they are sometimes caught by surprise. Every situation is distinctive; some are so unusual that no provision can be made for them even in principle. Flexibility is needed if one is to be able to respond properly at a given moment. Agility and alertness must support it, the one making it more rapid, the other more appropriate to what must be done.

Flexibility is the capacity to meet new demands. It is of obvious importance in those sports where new challenges are constantly faced. Mountain climbing, automobile racing, and wrestling offer conspicuous examples of sports where flexibility is in much demand. But it also has a large role to play in tennis, football, squash, baseball, basketball, and similar engagements where problem succeeds rapidly on problem.

Flexibility is needed in every sport. It is not a prominent factor, though, in diving, gymnastics, or skating where one merely attempts to exhibit what one has already mastered in private. In these sports, of course, suppleness, the ability to bend and twist the body, is a necessity. (Minds are never supple, while bodies can be both supple and flexible. Minds can be flexible and accompanied by bodies which are not very supple, but this may be enough to enable a man to do what he ought to do in situation after situation.)

The alertness that supports flexibility has an import of its own. In some sports, such as bullfighting, in good part because of the dangers involved, alertness must be to the forefront. In other sports, alertness is not so persistently demanded. There are periods in almost every baseball game when both the participants and the spectators can allow their attention to slide off in other directions.

Every participant in a game must of course be alert at some times. He must be on the watch, keyed to attend to what is of significance. Otherwise he will not be ready to deal properly with what is confronted. His alertness is consistent with the biding of his time; it is sometimes copresent with indecisiveness and ineptitude. Without it one will not be sufficiently aware of the way things change and are best to be dealt with. But since it requires only a restraint on actions and a quick calculation as to just what to do and when, it does not preclude a lackadaisical performance.

I have now distinguished strategy and tactics, and have analyzed out of the latter the components of judgment, rules, decisiveness, control, rhythm, and flexibility. Earlier, I noted the differences which mark off attention, intention, wish, desire, commitment, and dedication. For some, this will prove to be a surfeit of distinctions. No one, it will be remarked, attends to many of them, either in training or in the course of becoming an athlete. This is true. They are like the parts of the body remarked upon in anatomy; few men know that they have some of those parts —until something goes amiss, and then it becomes important to know what they are and how they should function.

Athletes fail in many ways; they need to be helped on many different sides. A knowledge of their anatomy will help us learn what is wrong with their physiology. An understanding of the nature of the different elements which are essential to a fine performance should help the teaching of athletics and may promote their learning.

For some the foregoing distinctions will be taken to be insufficient in number or in detail. I think that the more important discriminations have been made. If something central has been omitted, or if the accounts of some are severely distorted, we have an excuse for returning to the task again, with corrections and amendments. In any case, some such set of factors appears to be part of the constitution of the true athlete, but, of course, only as unified and merged.

He who possesses all the essential factors in a vital unity is a man in condition, which is to say, in good health, where this is understood to mean not merely the absence of illness, undesired pain, defects, frustration, or regrettable suppressions, but the presence of a unitary and usable power to act properly. The healthy man is whole. "Whole" and "health" have, in fact, the same Anglo-Saxon root, and even today have close affinities.

To be healthy is to be at ease in oneself, in the situations in which one finds oneself, and in the work to which one has dedicated oneself. It is to be in possession of a full set of powers and agencies, to see things without distortion, and to utilize them without undue difficulty or waste.

This sense of health is rather close to that expressed in the General Confession of The Book of Common Prayer: "We have left undone those things which we ought to have done; And we have done those things which we ought not to have done; And there is no health in us." The Book of Common Prayer undoubtedly intends to make reference to the spiritual side of man, though I suppose it wanted the bodily and social sides also to be considered. An adequate characterization of good health would in any case give body, mind, spirit, and position significant roles.

A man is bodily healthy when his organs function in harmony. He has mental health when he thinks accurately and constructively. He has spiritual health when he has a good sense of values, knowing what is right and what is wrong, what is important and what is trivial, what a man ought and ought not to be and to do. If he accepts himself as a man equal in rights and dignity with all others, and works harmoniously with them, he is, in addition, socially healthy. He who is healthy in this quadruple sense may be in considerable difficulty; he may be involved in problems to whose solution he has no clue; he may be subject to great strain and may end defeated and spent. Were this not the case, we would have to draw the paradoxical conclusion that athletes are not healthy, or that difficulties, fatigue, and even clear defeat are not possible to them.

Health should be viewed as having a different content for different types of human endeavor. That will make it proper to speak of a lax athlete as a man not in good health, and of a well-functioning school teacher as a man who is in good health—with of course an emphasis on the spirit in both cases.

The fully healthy man does justice to the multiple promises he has. He lives fully as a body, a mind, a spirit, and a social being. This is an ideal result. Everyone is frustrated and defeated in the end, no matter how limited his goal, but he who would be fully healthy will be more frustrated and will meet defeat more often than others. He will inevitably fail to achieve an excellence in some one dimension, or perhaps even in all dimensions, for each dimension normally demands a severe concentration on one type of endeavor and will be sacrificed if a more general result is sought. That fact, though, cannot extinguish the truth that he may for a time approximate what a man ought to be. One who seeks to become a matured man, acting firmly and successfully to preserve and enhance whatever values there are, builds on the achievements of the past, and tries to contribute to the civilization that is about to be. This is a noble effort, but it prevents him from matching what an athlete can achieve with his body. The athlete, on the other hand, is not fully healthy in all dimensions, for he has neither the time nor the inclination to perfect his mind and social life to the degree that is ideally possible and desirable.

An athlete can, nevertheless, be treated as offering one step in a progress toward the state of being a full, matured, i.e., a completely healthy, man. Having achieved a bodily excellence, the athlete can go on to try to master the other dimensions of himself, and so eventually become excellent on every side. Occasionally we hear of men who have done this. But for most it is more than enough to achieve the state of being excellent in some more limited area. For the young man there is nothing he is likely to do as well as make himself be an excellent functioning body. And there is hardly a better opportunity for doing this than that provided by contests and games.

the athlete in action
speed

BOXING and wrestling are sports in which two contestants struggle with one another to determine which is superior. Most sports, though, have more than one man to a side. Even when, as in field events, they compete against the clock, or a situation, or another individual, the contestants are usually representatives of some organization, or are taken to represent some place, and in that sense are more than just individuals.

A contest is a testing with. It is part of every game. There can, though, be contests apart from games. Boxing matches are contests, not games, though they are part of the Olympic Games. Football matches, whether amateur or professional, are games, though occasionally they are called "contests" because of the struggle that goes on within them. The term deserves a steadier use. It will make for clarity, I think, if "contest," taken by itself, is reserved for those cases in which individuals struggle with one another, and if "game," particularly in the area of athletics, is reserved for those cases in which there is team play, or where men act as representatives.

Contests, whether they occur by themselves or in games, usually pivot about the performance of individuals occupied with demonstrating their relative superiority in five areas—speed, endurance, strength, accuracy, and coordination. Speed usually arrests interest more than the others do because it so conspicuously shows man conquering what is initially alien to him, and because it can so readily be understood as encompassing the other tasks as well. Also, unlike the others, speed may be displayed from the beginning to the end of a contest, whereas the others, instead, often start slowly from a state where their specific nature is not in much evidence.

A central question in many sports is how fast one can go over a portion of space or for a set amount of time. In other sports the question is still important, though not paramount. Throwing events allow speed only a minimal significance. In football or baseball it plays a telling part at times, but irregularly, and may contribute little to the final result. The pole vault and the running broad jump give it a larger role, but only as serving another end. It is only in races that speed is the main issue.

The primary meaning of the term "speed" is "success." That meaning we still preserve in such expressions as "good speed." A tincture of this meaning seems still to cling to its use in athletics. The fastest human seems to be superior to the most versatile, the strongest, the most agile, or the most accurate, in part because he perhaps is supposed to be incidentally superb in these other ways as well.

"Speed" is normally used to refer to the amount of time needed to traverse a definite spatial distance, or to the amount of space that can be traversed in a specified amount of time. In a race an effort is made either to reduce the amount of time that is used, or to increase the amount of space that is traversed—usually the first. Why? Is it not that time is felt to be in short supply, whereas space, despite its finitude, seems to go on and on? We want to cut down the amount of time used, but to extend the distance covered. (Sometimes, e.g., in endurance contests, we reverse our usual attitude toward time, and try to see how long something can last; and sometimes, e.g., when we attend to accuracy, we make a somewhat similar reversal with respect to space, keeping ourselves confined to a narrow region. But speed and its stresses seem to interest most spectators more basically than endurance or accuracy does.)

The different approaches to time and space characteristic of our interest in speed can be related. Having discovered that one can run a mile in four minutes, it can be asked how far at that rate one could go in five minutes, or how long it would take to run a sixteen-hundred meter race. Such questions are sometimes posed in the attempt to relate records that had been calibrated on different scales. The attempt is successful only so far as one abstracts from the fact that a difference in time or space may alter the quality of an athletic adventure. An extra minute or an extra number of yards cannot be added to what had been achieved, as though the whole were not thereby changed.

Even when it is planned to do nothing more than determine how fast a man or an animal or a vehicle can speed, other issues are also decided. It is always necessary for the contestants to exercise judgment in the face of unexpected hazards and obstacles. To go as fast as possible in a given situation, the various factors already distinguished—intention, dedication, rhythm, etc.—must be put into play. This is true even when the race is between greyhounds off in pursuit of a mechanical rabbit, for what the greyhounds do is primarily an extension of these factors as they occur in the trainers. Neither the trainers nor the greyhounds are athletes; treated as a unity, though, they exhibit features similar to those found in men prepared to race.

Where judgment, skill, and the other factors are no longer required, we have a merely mechanical exhibition of what had already been decided. A race between missiles was long ago settled on the drawing board, in the factory, and on the launching pad, subject to contingencies which confront them during their flight and the opposition which they might encounter. Once the opposition comes to the fore as a major matter, of course, the race becomes a contest, with the missiles serving as extensions of their makers and guides.

When obstacles are great and problems sudden and severe, what were only contributory factors in other efforts become preconditions for, and vital components in, achieving whatever result is to be obtained. Then judgment, decisiveness, or flexibility may turn out to be more important than speed.

Speed records normally ignore all issues but that of the amount of time involved in traversing a given space. This is also what primarily interests the participants and the spectators. The winner, on whom they focus, is the man who has sped the fastest, according to the rules. His ability to function in novel situations, some of them crucial, was, however, also tested at that time.

Ideally, a runner arrives at the end of a race completely exhausted, but only because the race had been so calculated that he arrives as one who had achieved the maximum speed possible to him. Yet the resolution of some such problem as to whether or not he should move into the lead may have been the primary question that he in fact settled at some particular moment while he moved toward the finish at full speed. The ability of others to outdistance him may have been hobbled by their refusal to take risks, by their failure to meet a challenge, or by their unwillingness to arrive exhausted at the finish. A victory well within grasp may have been lost because a runner took the lead too late or failed to change his pace, or because the lead had been taken too soon or the pace had been changed when it should have been maintained. The winner testifies both to his own abilities and the comparative abilities of the others, as well as to the manner in which all back their abilities with suitable tactics and acts.

In motorcycle, automobile, motorboat, airplane, and similar races with machines, what is tested is the ability to speed despite an increased probability of failure, injury, or death because of the state of the equipment, the prevailing weather, the conditions of the course over which the race is run, and a host of other matters which are sometimes lumped together under the heading of "just luck." An automobile race may be won by a man fortunate enough to have a car that continued to function when others broke down, or who happened to escape the collisions and accidents that plagued them. Though the superiority of his machine and skill, and his ability to decide correctly at some crucial turn, may account for his conquest of many of the hazards which overwhelmed the rest, there are usually some hazards which he escaped only because he was fortunate enough to be at a different part of the track at the time. He may be credited with a speed record, but this was achieved under unrecorded conditions.

Even apart from these considerations, a speed record is always more than the result of a movement faster than that exhibited by others. In addition to skill, judgment, and luck, it reflects the quickness with which one responds to a starting signal, the explosiveness of the initial move, the efficiency with which the body or machine is used, the strategy laid down, and the alertness, flexibility, etc., displayed. In many races the position one has at the start also plays a considerable role, particularly when the race is for a short distance, or when there are many turns to the track. "Speed," evidently, is but shorthand for "speed under such and such circumstances," many of which are unspecified or never mentioned.

Also unrecorded in many races is the time needed in order to achieve the acceleration necessary for speeding at a maximum rate. Ideally, speed records should refer to what can be done after one has arrived at the point where a race can be run at maximum speed for that distance. Foot races should be brought into closer alignment than they now are with contests where a preliminary accelerating period is allowed. In automobile trials, one is permitted to take a preliminary run up to the starting point, so that one can begin there at maximum speed. In the pole vault the participants run to get themselves into a position where a maximum leap is possible. Geoffrey H. G. Dyson remarks in his thoughtful *The Mechanics of Athletes*, "Other things being equal, the height cleared in pole vaulting is proportional to the square of the take-off speed."[1] The formula seems to be a little too neat to be able to encompass all the factors involved in a good pole-vault. Yet there can be little doubt that the take-off speed is a vital factor in the determination of the height that the pole vaulter can clear. No difference in principle separates such permitted acceleration before the vault and the acceleration that the sprinter must confine to the race itself.

[1] Geoffrey H. G. Dyson, *The Mechanics of Athletics* (London, 1964), p. 155.

It is difficult, and sometimes it would be foolish, to note all or most of the factors, other than speed, which determine the outcome of a race. It would be trivial to take account of the acceleration of a marathoner as he passes from rest to motion. But there is a point in noting those factors which make a conspicuous difference in the outcome. And this is sometimes recognized. In international competition no results are accepted if the winds blow at more than four and a half miles an hour. Baseball games are stopped when it rains on the field (though football games are allowed to continue even in rather heavy snowstorms). Our tracks today are fairly smooth, making it unwise to compare the records now made with those reported of previous times. Extreme heat and cold and unusually high or low altitudes also make a difference to the result that is possible. Bruno Balke's observation to the effect that "Work tolerance at 14,000 feet is approximately 75 per cent of normal performance," [2] does not cancel Dr. Jokl's conclusion that "although hot climate evidently represents a physiological handicap, it does not necessarily render the attainment of athletic success even at Olympics impossible," [3] for a 75 per cent performance by a great athlete may yield an outstanding victory.

As computers become easier to use in a wider variety of situations, it will be possible to come closer to making ideal measurements, in which every factor, no matter how slight its influence, is given a weight in the final result. A wind of three miles an hour, a wind even of a half mile an hour, blowing against competitors in one race and on competitors in another surely changes the import of what is achieved. Ideally, a normal set of conditions for a race is one in which there are no turns, no wind, no interference, no interval between starting signal and start, and no irregularities to the track—in short, no deviations from a standard situation.

2 Bruno Balke, "Work Capacity at Altitude," *Science and Medicine of Exercise and Sports*, ed. Warren Russell Johnson (New York, 1960), p. 341.

3 Ernst Jokl, M.D., *Medical Sociology and Cultural Anthropology of Sport and Physical Education* (Springfield, Ill., 1964), p. 107.

We can, perhaps, never preclude all deviations from a standard, but we can imagine their absence and take the pure case to offer a measure for judging all performances. This would be objective and impersonal, applicable to all races, regardless of the conditions under which they were run. Deviations from it could be treated as handicaps to be subtracted from or added to the achieved result in order to see what its value would be in the ideal case. What we now have, instead, is a series of records made under diverse conditions, the nature of which is not often indicated. Our comparisons between one performance and another, consequently, are all subject to qualifications by a number of unknowns. The newest record, showing a maximum speed over a given distance, may have been made by one who is, in fact, not faster than others but has merely been favored by the wind, terrain, and other circumstances.

A racer is occupied with the task of achieving a mastery of space, primarily under the limitations of time, with an objective which all athletes pursue—the attainment of excellence by means of the body. To understand his specific occupation with space, some knowledge of the nature of space is required. He may not have that knowledge; indeed, it is likely that he does not. But this means only that he does not altogether understand what is involved in running a race.

The space that environs us on every side is a medley of bumps and planes, of stretches of emptiness broken abruptly here and there by irregular solidities. It lies before, behind, alongside, above, and below us. As lived with, it is structured by us, our products, our work, and our interests; our geometries deal only with flattened, monotonous abstractions from it.

Apart from us space has a nature of its own, contoured and sustained by whatever things there are. It is an impersonal space. We learn what it is like in cosmological science. We can also learn about it by subtracting the difference we make to realities by our presence and concerns—a knowledge which must be possible if we can know that we do make a difference to the structure of whatever space there is.

Sport is a human product; the space with which it is occupied is an experienceable, not an abstract or an impersonal, space. Our bodies are at its center, defining what is near and what is far, what is up and what is down. The charging lion makes us attend to it because it presents a major threat to our welfare. The lion could, of course, be occupied with a horse or a deer. This, however, will not make it or them assume the center of our experienced space; our interest in both lion and horse turns them into parts of a single spatial area centered in us. Though oriented in us, the space is no creation of ours; it is the result of an interplay of the objective, impersonal space with our interests and interpretations, and our perspective.

The space in which the athlete plays is conditioned by what else is there, but it is centered and partly shaped by him. He is occupied with the impersonal and the distant, but as oriented with respect to himself. His targets and goals are at a distance from him, a distance which is measured from where he is expected to start to reach them.

Human institutions make certain places important and allow others to slip away into insignificance. The available transportation defines the major routes over which men are to move readily from position to position. Our possessions determine what directions are important and what are not. "There," "not-mine," and "objects," refer to relevant factors correlative to and almost coordinate with the "here," "mine," and "subject" of ourselves.

We live within a rather limited but not very well demarcated space. This is true whether we engage in daily pursuits or are involved in sport or other special activities. No man can locate himself simply within the physical dimensions of his body; his breathing, eating, and perceiving, successfully defy that attempt. He is impinged on from many sides and places; his involvement with equipment and situations prevent him from keeping his center within his body. The distant is pertinent to him whether he be active or passive. He is challenged by it; to get it into his possession he must act with judgment, flexibility, and decisiveness.

Since distant objects are distinct from us, with a reality of their own, we must be said to lack some reality, to be imperfect to the very degree that we are not identical with them. Some of the objects represent a possible danger; others promise a possible delight; all, because they have a being of their own, accentuate the fact that we are finite beings, limited in power as well as in position. If we are to reduce our imperfection, we must overcome the distance that separates us from whatever else there is. That act takes time. The more time that we need to reach one of these things the less time will be left over to spend on the movement and the mastery of the others. To cover a spatial distance in minimal time makes it possible for us to cover other distances within whatever larger time is available. We can, however, be said to save the time for other purposes only if it is necessary for us to go through that space. Were it not necessary to do this, we could save the time by occupying ourselves straightway with other matters.

If we are in danger, or if we seek to reach something of considerable importance to us, speed is desirable. In the absence of such needs, it is not necessary for us to concern ourselves with it. When men race, they are not expressing a need but, on the contrary, are occupied with matters which are best pursued when their needs have already been met. A race, like other athletic contests, is best run by those who are the masters of themselves, and not the creatures of something else. It is an event closed off from the world of appetites and drives, from pragmatic achievements and economic struggle, no matter how much these may have determined the initial desire to race, and how much they may condition the placing and the timing of the event, or give value to the consequences. Nor is any race a mere contest in which men discover only how fast they can go; it is also an occasion for discovering who they are in relation to others and with respect to some preassigned task or goal.

Distant objects can be reached by passing sequentially through a number of intermediate regions. This is only one way in which the space between us and them can be mastered. Sight and hearing put us directly in touch with something at a distance; they enable us to attend to that which is at a different part of space from that which our bodies occupy. The space between us and other objects, and the space they occupy, can also be known through reflection. Its geometry can be studied in mathematics; its contents can be explained by science; its reality and the reality of the objects in it can be made the topic of a philosophic inquiry. We can also deal physically with the intervening space without having to move through it. We can jump over it, throw something across it, shoot through it. We can insert various objects in it, and can shape it with works of sculpture and architecture. In some of these ways we will reach a distant region more rapidly than we could were we to traverse it by means of our bodies, or even by riding on some animal, or in some machine. But if we do use our bodies, alone or helped by animals or machines, we will not only be able to measure the distance covered, but will be able to test ourselves and thereby discover what we can do and therefore, to some extent, what we are.

Measurement requires the coincidence of a ruler with a portion of space. To measure a space longer than a ruler length, the space adjacent to that with which the ruler was previously coincident must be made coincident with the ruler, and so on and on, until the entire region is covered. A runner can, therefore, be viewed as a rapidly used ruler, the record of his race showing how long it took for him to measure the space by means of his unit strides. Since there is no time limit imposed on the use of a ruler in the normal measuring of a distance, it is not possible to reverse this account and look upon a ruler as a slow moving runner. And the runner's measurement of the distance, of course, is only incidental to his traversing that distance with speed.

A scientist might like to measure the speed of a planet, an electron, or a bird. Their speeds provide him with clues for the discovery of the kind of forces that govern their movement, and presumably that of a host of other things. A clocker might like to ascertain just how long it takes some horse to run a furlong. That information will help the owner decide when and where the horse is to be raced, or how to place a bet. A runner's interest in measuring his speed is different from theirs. Ideally, he wants to know what can be achieved when an effort is made to go at the fastest possible rate, and then for no further purpose. A race, like every other sporting event, is autotelic, essentially serving no end other than that of exhibiting man at his bodily best.

We are interested in knowing how fast man can run. Later, we may also interest ourselves in knowing the speeds of other living beings, in order to satisfy a scientific curiosity. Long before that time, a knowledge of the speeds of different kinds of beings is wanted in order to enable us to see how man compares and contrasts with other quickly moving beings. Directly or indirectly, we then learn what man is, in a way and to a degree that is not possible by other means.

In measuring speed, successively occupied portions of space are correlated with definite units of time. Speed, though, is never simply a question of such correlation; and this is true whether we are dealing with animate or inanimate beings, with projectiles or with men striving with all their might down their individual lanes, because judgment, flexibility, etc., as we have noted, also play a role. If we abstract from these factors, however, we can obtain a useful measure. Since objects differ in bulk and in the distance they cover in unit acts, and since we can conceptually correlate any space, no matter how large or small, with any temporal unit, no matter how small or large, we can come to know the speeds at which a wide variety of things can move, and evaluate these in terms of what we know of man, and man in terms of what we know of them.

Athletes are bodily successful men. We must look to them to learn what it is possible for man to achieve in and through his body. When the athletes give themselves to the task of finding out how fast they can speed, we learn from their performance about man's capacities and limits in one dimension of activity. A man may be able to speed faster under other conditions—alone perhaps, on a special kind of track, absolutely naked, in the middle of the night, downhill, pushed by a wind, or helped by drugs. But unless we make these the conditions under which a race is run, we are not much interested in knowing what they enable a man to do.

A race tells us, not the speed that is possible to a man, but the speed that is possible to him under such and such antecedently defined conditions and commonly accepted rules. It is thought (rightly, I would hold) that we can learn more about a man by seeing what he does under prescribed conditions than we could otherwise. We then take him away from the wide-open world and place him in a limited, controlled context, thereby making him contest in a cultural setting instead of letting him act like a brute struggling against whatever happens to occur.

A man may want to win a race. He may be anxious to beat all his competitors; he may find joy in running; he may expand when he finds that he can outrun everyone else. A precise formulation of the conditions and rules under which he performs will make it possible to state what his achievement means compared with what is done in other places and times. Learning that others have covered his distance in less time than he has, he will perhaps allow this to challenge him. He will then try to do better. Through the use of his body and what it controls he will then measure a distance, and perhaps discover, not only what he can do, but what for the present is possible to man. Whatever his motives, he will inevitably reveal what it is to be a man on specified occasions.

When we make dogs and other animals race, we learn something which may prove useful in improving the breed. But we will also be able to learn something about man. The speed, though the speed of animals, tells us what a man can do through their agency. The skill of a trainer, the concern of the owner, the ingenuity of promoters, and the like are brought into play to get the animals to run as they could not on their own. It is the animals that are being raced and even tested, but not without revealing something of man as a contestant operating under and applying rules. Apart from him, the animals are almost anonymous, mere carriers of numbers or signs, without individuality.

Even if we turn from racing dogs and similar animals

to horses, with their well-kept track records, their carefully documented genealogies, and their distinctive presence, we do not entirely escape a testing of men. There may be a drive and spirit which one horse displays, enabling it to outdistance the others, but this is qualified by the determination of trainers, grooms, and jockeys. The Greeks honored the trainers and owners, and not the jockeys, apparently because it was thought that the main work had already been done before the horses were mounted. The bias enabled the Greeks to overcome a bias of another order. Though they forbade women to participate in the Olympic Games, they gave some women Olympic prizes because the women had trained or owned the horses that won in the games.

When men race, their speed offers indirect testimony to the excellence of their mentors' character and pedagogy. When animals or machines are made to race, their speed offers indirect testimony to men's excellence as trainers, coaches, riders, and drivers, and thus primarily to an excellence in the ability to train, control, and judge. All competition of this kind—by boat, car, plane, or sled, skis, skates, or horses, dogs, turtles, snails—can be treated as the accomplishment of intending men. It is the men who define and control the competing forces.

Geoffrey Dyson remarks that the strongest parts of the body are the heaviest, and since they have the greatest inertia, their movements are the slowest. Consequently, the athlete should first make use of the strongest muscles which are near the center of gravity and follow this by using those in the trunk and thighs. Properly carried out, the movement should flow from the center of the body outwards, along a number of lines, ending at the extremities. Speed, he also observes, is a product of length and stride frequency which change their ratio from athlete to athlete, as well as in the course of a race. And because it is desirable to conserve oxygen until comparatively late in a race, the second half (say, of a mile) should be run faster than the first half.[4]

Athletics today is being made the object of extended,

4 Dyson, p. 196.

careful scientific study. As a consequence, we are learning how men can improve their speed, if only they would supplement their physical prowess with good training and a proper spirit. We are learning, too, to see more clearly the kind of role that endurance and strength play in making possible an increase in speed. These also have a value of their own—as do accuracy and coordination. All merit examination.

8. the athlete in action
endurance, strength, accuracy, coordination

THOUGH time is omnipresent, we do not understand it very well. Inevitably, we leave in some darkness our understanding of even such familiar occurrences as walking and talking. Almost everyone believes, of course, that time is mathematically divisible without end. Whatever magnitude we assign to it—say a minute—we can conceive to be broken up into shorter portions—say seconds—and these into still smaller ones—tenths of a second, for example. We can subdivide the last into tiny fractions—fifty thousandths of a second, fifty millionths of a second, and so on without end. Yet we do not thereby divide time itself into shorter and shorter periods. Not every mathematical expression has a factual counterpart. Because we can mathematically divide a figure for a temporal stretch into fractions as small as we wish does not mean that we can divide the stretch in fact. There are, there must be, unit times which cannot actually be subdivided.

A unit of time occurs all of a piece. When it occurs it is an extended, present moment. Were it not extended, there would be no extension to time. One consequence would be that last year would not now be distant from next year. Because the present is extended and quantifiable, mathematical fractions of its magnitude can be formulated, but because that present is a single, undivided unit, those fractions do not have their own corresponding temporal units. And since a present moment is a single, undivided unit, it can not come into being gradually, by first passing through an endless number of fractionated portions of itself.

A present moment is followed directly by another, without interval. If there were an interval between them the moments would be separated by what is nontemporal —in effect, eternal—and we would never be able to get from one moment to another.

A present moment is an indivisible extended unit which follows other units, without gap, and is in turn followed without gap by still other extended indivisibles. Because those moments succeed one another in this way, the impression remains that time is one continuous flow, though in fact it is a sequence of fixities displacing one another without interval. There is no time in which the displacement occurs; the displacement cannot, therefore, properly be said to occur quickly or slowly.

To ask how long it takes for the next moment to come is but to ask how long a present moment is. This is of unit length, a fact which can be expressed by means of some subdivision of a longish event whose measure is given by a conventional clock. It is because a present moment has a duration of, let us say, one second, as marked off by a clock, that we can say that what had just been present occurred two seconds earlier than what will immediately be present.

Time is a sequence of distinct, indivisible, extended units. An extended time without these units would be a simple continuum. We could not then legitimately speak of real temporal beginnings and endings, of genuine turning points, of crises in time. Every distinction said to characterize time would reflect only our interests and decisions; all would be arbitrary in the sense that they would have no necessary relevance to whatever distinct occurrences took place in fact. But we could not make distinctions in time, whether they answered to anything external or not, except in distinct moments of time. Whatever beginnings and endings, whatever turning points are imposed on a supposedly continuous time, are inevitably produced in the time in which the men, who make the distinctions, in fact live. That time has distinct, indivisible, extended moments, making it difficult to see how men and their time could occur in the same universe with the supposed continuous time. It seems more correct to say what in truth is easier; men and other beings exist in a common time which, apart from any interests or decisions, is in fact divided into extended, indivisible moments everywhere. Those moments are not of the same magnitude in every place. Some presents, as we shall immediately see, stretch over other shorter ones.

Time moves on in some independence of all occurrences. It has a nature and being of its own. We cannot increase our supply of time, and, strictly speaking, cannot waste it. There is nothing we can do to make it flow faster or slower. All we can do is to engage in lively or monotonous activities, do much or little within some temporal period, and use that period as a unit to measure larger or smaller traversals and other events. The quality of the temporal units, however, is affected by the occurrence over which they extend.

There are many differently sized units of present time. A swing at a ball occurs in one present moment. This is distinct from the present occupied by an entire ball game. Both the swing and the game are distinct, unit, present events; they have distinctive magnitudes which extend from their beginnings to their endings. The single present moment of a ball game, of course, stretches over a number of present moments such as that appropriate to the swing at a ball, as well as over others such as that of an inning or a rally. Similarly, a present moment of human life extends over a number of presents appropriate to the jumps of the electrons within the living body, and a present moment of a ceremony stretches over a number of presents appropriate to the pulses of life. Apart from all these acts, time would consist of a series of very minute units. It has many different kinds of units, not because there are men, or because men think about it, but because there are different kinds of events, each occurring in an appropriate present moment.

The shortest possible event occurs in a minimal unit of present time. The magnitude of that event is evidently a matter for scientific investigation. All other events occur in times which stretch over the shortest possible units, but it is not easy to grasp how this occurs. Some clarity, though, can be achieved by emphasizing the difference between "earlier and later" and "before and after." Each event and present, whether it be long or short, is a single unit whose beginning and ending are in a relation of before and after. But what is before need not occur earlier than what is after. The number six is before eight in the cardinal number series, but it is not earlier than eight. What is before and what is after, if they are the beginning and ending of a present event or moment, are copresent. The entire event or moment itself, however, is earlier than its successor, and later than its predecessor. A longish event or present will have shorter ones within its confines in a relation of before and after and not in a relation of earlier to later, though, as apart from the longish event or moment, the smaller ones will be related as earlier and later.

This topic has a special place in cosmology and metaphysics. A philosophy of history takes it to be of central importance. There, distinctive events, with their characteristic beginnings and endings, push forward the problem of whether or not there is a time independent of all occurrences, and whether or not the occurrences and their times have indivisible extensions in which we can find an order of before and after but not one of earlier and later. Here it suffices to observe that an athletic contest, like any other event, has its characteristic indivisible present moments of time. Innings, rounds, periods, and chukkers are occurrences occupying indivisible temporal units; they stretch over smaller present occurrences—striking out, feinting, hitting, or making a goal—without thereby becoming divisible into a sequence of those occurrences. In turn, they are encompassed by the still longer present occurrence of the entire contest or game. Each present is as ultimate and as indivisible as every other.

There is a distinctive color and dash to most temporal units and occurrences. Moves, acts, contests, and games are dynamic wholes with a beat and a quality that must be lived through to be known. But all of them can be dealt with in terms of a single measure. Some one occurrence and its moment can be used to provide the unit in terms of which all other occurrences and moments can be described as shorter or longer. This is what is done when we record the time that is taken for the completion of various events. We then abstract from the concrete occurrences and their characteristic indivisible moments, to attend to the results that can be obtained by using a watch or a clock.

The precise reports of the amount of time that elapses from the beginning to the end of certain events do not speak directly of those events, but instead measure them by units appropriate to a quite different type of occurrence, remote from human involvement. This is not surprising, for our watches and clocks are not constructed to accord with a sequence of vital acts. What matches the markings on a watch or clock is rarely something experienced, or even experienceable, by either spectators or participants in a sporting event. Calibrated to beat off some fraction of an astronomical transaction, our timepieces are only mechanical, repetitive agents, external and indifferent to the existence of human activities and their time.

If we wish to compare the times appropriate to a number of events we must abstract from the concreteness of those events and the indivisible present moments which characterize them. We can then take all of their unit times to be multiples of the moments which are marked out by a neutral, impersonal, astronomic time.

Though we never live in neutral time, we can use that time to measure and eventually compare the temporal stretches of our acts. We are thereby enabled to compare one duration with another in communicable ways. And because we are all willing to govern our comings and goings by reference to such an impersonal time, we all can arrange to meet together, even though we individually live through our own distinctive lives and their associated moments.

A neutrally measured time yields readily to quantification. The resultant quantity can be used to give numerical value to the speed of a runner. The quantity can also be used to state a limit beyond which no one lasted at some given task. It is this idea which is germane to the endurance tests that men undergo. Sometimes, as in mountain climbing, men are unexpectedly called upon to exhibit their capacity to outlast unfavorable circumstances. But sometimes they deliberately enter into contests to see just how long they can walk, run, hold up a weight, fight fatigue, sit still, and the like. In both types of test they show how much they can endure.

The question, how much can be endured, is not altogether unambiguous. It could be asking how much work can be accomplished without a man becoming tired or without becoming completely exhausted. It could be asking how long a man can keep himself engaged in a certain type of act. It could be asking how long he can willingly remain in unusual circumstances, without any stimulation, for example, or without sleep, or motion, or food, or water. It could be asking how long he can or will continue to perform a certain type of act despite such and such restraints, or under certain limiting conditions, such as being chained down, without adequate covering, in freezing water, etc.

We come closest to the common meaning of "endurance" when we take it to refer to the length of time a man can continue against great obstacles—which can be taken to include pain, hunger, and thirst. If endurance is made the object of a contest, we try to determine who can outlast the others and by how much. Rodeo offers such a contest. That rider wins who can maintain himself on the bucking bronco for the longest time. His success, of course, depends on his judgment, his flexibility and suppleness, his dedication, etc., as well, but what is recorded is the length of time he retains his seat. In other endurance contests there are recordings of analogous attempts to persist in the face of conditions so unsatisfactory that others no longer continue.

We attend to the problem of endurance when we ask how long a man remains at some task, no matter how. He may stop after a time because he lacks sufficient determination, nerve, or courage. We normally ignore such considerations to attend solely to the question as to whether or not failure occurs at a point beyond that which others have reached. If it does, we are content and do not probe further. What we want to know is how long a man lasts, not why. Yet a man may have continued, not because he was able to resist the pull of pain or the feeling of fatigue longer than others, but because he did not feel pain or fatigue when others did. We do not ask if this is so, being satisfied to note that he does or does not outlast the others.

The winner of an endurance contest may merely have a higher sensitivity threshold than others have. He may have no pain where others suffer unspeakably. We could conceivably test him in other contexts to see if he is pained when and how others are. We might ask him to report to us just when disagreeable feelings begin to dominate. But we will still not be sure why it is he continued in a given contest. Despite his pain, he may insist on continuing, or without pain, he may have to fight boredom, or fear, or even the honor of being successful, in order to be able to carry on after others have stopped.

No one is altogether sure just why one man persists while another does not. We tend to avoid the problem by first supposing that all men have about the same degree of sensitivity, and then ascribing the ability to outlast others in an endurance contest to superior stamina, courage, or determination. Because this double supposition is not checked, and may be unjustified, it is desirable to take endurance contests to report only the time that elapses before a man stops at a task. We can then avoid asking whether he is like other men in sensitivity, and whether he stops because he is weary, bored, or afraid.

We read with awe of explorers, climbers, sailors, and trappers who kept on acting, or just living, despite extreme thirst, hunger, injury, disease, cold, and enemies, both natural and human. While engaged in some other activity, they incidentally revealed maintaining himself for a while against the background of a remorseless time. Because we want to know at what point failure inexorably arrives, we take note of such unusual cases of endurance, even when some other result is the main issue. They tell us what man's ultimate boundaries are. The results achieved in a contest will normally fall far short of what these heroic figures accomplished, but the contest will teach us something that these men could not—what men can do in well-defined situations, governed by impersonal rules and a presumably humane set of conditions.

Swimming and life saving are sometimes taught in order to prepare men to face unusual demands. There are occasions when some men face as their major task the keeping of their heads above water for a long time. Shipwrecked, capsized, or out of reach of help in a flood, they try to remain afloat, and sometimes are rewarded by a rescue. Endurance here is at once practical and important. The object of an endurance contest, in contrast, is far less practical, and in one sense far less important than is the attempt to survive under severe conditions. A contest has importance only in the way in which art or thought has importance—when we seek not to preserve life but to enhance it.

In an endurance contest men are pitted against one another to see who will be the last to stop, thereby showing how man can continue to be man under conditions which are at once unfavorable and prescribed. Even if one sets up normal conditions, the fact that endurance is being tested requires one to carry on for such a period that those very circumstances become unfavorable, militating against continuance in the activity. And though it is inevitable that unanticipated contingencies will arise, complicating the situation, the contest will be concerned with the meeting of the prescribed conditions. It is these which permit of a comparison of man with man, and therefore enable us to know what it is that man can do, not in life, or no matter what the situation, but inside a limited area where the achievement acquires a definite structure, a distinctive quality, and a place in the history of sport.

Endurance is a factor in every sporting event precisely because there is always a need to push oneself close to the breaking point, and to continue there until one has completed the task in hand. A sprint, a broad jump, archery, and diving demand endurance, as surely as do weight lifting, marathon running, and tug of war.

Exhaustion is a limit which every athletic program sets before men; ideally, it is to be reached by all at the end of a performance. Before that point is arrived at, the athlete becomes fatigued, a state not easily specifiable. According to F. J. Kreuzer,

Fatigue may be defined as the reversible decrease of the functional capacity of an organ or organisn, resulting from activity. Unfortunately, there is no method available which would permit the quantitative measurement of fatigue in man. The symptoms of fatigue include: slowed and uncertain motor actions, disturbed muscular coordination, increase of effort and reaction time, loss of incentive, decreased physical and mental power. Fatigue cannot be attributed to any single factor, but is based on the combination of several physical, chemical, nervous and hormonal processes.[1]

Fatigue and exhaustion can be postponed by proper training. Weight lifting offers one way this can be done. Though Bannister, in his preparation for breaking the four-minute mile, did not practice with weights, it is commonly accepted today that weight training not only promotes an increase in strength, but an increase in the capacity to endure.

A number of writers have remarked that endurance is specific to a particular type of sport, making a transfer of the power only partially possible.[2] Yet if there is justification for weight lifting exercises, now more and more employed in order to prepare men for running, football, and other sports, we must conclude that either some significant transfer is possible, or that the muscles developed in weight training are also being used in other sports.

Surprisingly little is known about the human body. We are not sure just what it is that is improved when a man is trained. It is not even known whether or not the long jump and the high jump cause damage to the pelvic muscles, or whether or not a mile race overtaxes the cardiovascular system of women.[3] How strange it is that we

1   Ferdinand J. Kreuzer, *International Research in Sport and Physical Education*, ed. Ernst Jokl, M.D. (Springfield, Ill., 1960), pp. 328–29.
2   *Ibid.*, p. 334; Ernst Jokl, M.D., *Physiology of Exercise* (Springfield, Ill., 1964), p. 40; *Conditio Humana*, ed. Walter von Baeyer and Richard M. Griffith (New York, 1966), p. 121.
3   Ernst Jokl, M.D., "The Athletic Status of Women," *British Journal of Physical Medicine* (Nov. 1957), 4.

do not yet know how long a man can continue in any number of distinct and well-defined tasks.

It would be good to know how men compare in different activities, in high, low, and normal temperatures, and under other clearly specifiable conditions. It would be good to know how long a man can withstand some specified pressure, or how much pressure he can stand at a given time. (The former question can be turned into a variant of the latter, for in asking how long a man can maintain himself at a specified pressure, we but ask if he can withstand a given pressure for a unit of time.) It would be good to know how long a man can continue despite fatigue, or when he is denied the normal protection of clothing, tools, weapons, or companionship. But we have no right to make any man suffer, nor to want him to suffer even for the sake of making clear just what the limits of human capacity are. We have no right to induce any of these undesirable states nor to lure men to submit to them, even voluntarily, for we then infringe on their right to be healthy. The laws against injury, mutilation, murder, and suicide make evident that there are acts which a man has no right to perform and which others have no warrant to try to induce. Instead, we should try to see what men can achieve despite the presence of forces that normally prompt them to stop, in situations where they are in firm control and are benefited rather than hurt.

What we seek to learn in sport is not what men can possibly do, but what they can do when subject to rules, under controlled conditions and on specified occasions. Our endurance contests should, therefore, not demand that they be asked to push beyond the limit of what their flesh or spirit can bear. The exhaustion they are to reach at the end of a performance should be momentary and without ill aftereffects. We must be content with the fact that some of them can continue to live or work after all others stop, without hurting any of them in the process. This will be enough to let us know how well a man can perform for a period of time.

He who endures more than another is thought to be stronger than that other, even though he may not be able to lift weights as high, or does not have muscles as big. Endurance and strength are evidently closely allied. One is tempted to identify them. But they are really distinct, and deserve to be distinguished. According to Lucian Brouha,

> Gain in absolute strength, that is the power of one contraction, does not always mean a greater endurance. A strong man such as a weight lifter can perform work against greater resistance. But a man with less powerful muscles such as a miler can produce a much greater amount of work over a given period of time.[4]

> Exercises of strength produce mostly a hypertrophy of the fibers, whereas exercises of endurance increase the number of capillaries.[5]

And Ernst Jokl, in his discussion of exercise in rehabilitation, states,

> Strength relies primarily upon structural determinants, more particularly upon skeletal structures and the bulk of striated musculature. Endurance depends primarily on the functional efficiency of the cardio-vascular system, of respiration, and of metabolic process.[6]

Thomas K. Cureton tells us that "sprinters are relatively stronger and react faster than the endurance swimmers."[7]

The ideas of strength and endurance can, however, be brought together with the recognition that strength is exhibited in unit periods, and that endurance can be viewed as repetitive acts of strength exhibited for a length of time. Still, the two require different trainings and stresses, and are practiced for different reasons.

Strength can be used to support speed. There is then an insistence making possible the use of less time or more space than is usual. Strength can also be used to reduce an opposing insistence. This is evident in wrestling, boxing, and judo. In these, strength, or the power to overcome, is

4 Lucian Brouha, "Training," *Science and Medicine of Exercise and Sports*, ed. Warren Russell Johnson (New York, 1960), p. 405.   5 *Ibid.*, p. 404.

6 Ernst Jokl, M.D., *The Scope of Exercise in Rehabilitation* (Springfield, Ill., 1964), p. 5.

7 Thomas Kirk Cureton, Jr., *Physical Fitness of Champion Athletes* (Urbana, Ill., 1951), p. 4.

used to support endurance, the ability to outlast, in part by reducing another's capacity to continue.

Living beings insist and resist. We speak of their strength when we wish to emphasize the fact that the ability to resist and insist is equal to or greater than that which is normally available. It is the degrees above normal that we usually note when we speak of strong men. We can also attend to comparative strengths, strengths in relation to one another, without regard for any base. In the human realm comparisons have been made of the strengths of girls, boys, men, and women, and of the members in each group with other members of it. Though there is a wide range of strength exhibited amongst the members in each of those groups, the members are usually treated only as intra-competitive. We do not, consequently, find many trials of strength set up between girls and boys, boys and men, men and women, even though it is evident that some girls are superior to a good number of the boys, and that some boys and women are superior to a good number of the men. Fortunately, it is possible to state precisely not only what the members of each group can do, but how they compare with all the others, no matter in what group they are.

Like every other athletic endeavor, a contest of strength is ideally open only to men who are well-prepared to exhibit the limits of human attainment. Everyone, of course, from childhood on, has, and ought to have, opportunities for determining the amount of strength he has. Athletic activity is not to be restricted to men, or only to those who have some hope of coming near the limit of human attainment. But the ideal case offers us a paradigm for all the rest.

Strength can be expressed in radically diverse circumstances. Differences in temperature, environmental conditions, equipment, and competition will make a difference in the result. The expression of the strength may be modified by the introduction of drugs or stimulants. Or the strength may be brought out violently, brutally, without regard for anything but the demonstration of a power to overwhelm. Rarely in any of these cases is there a matching of the results that are obtained by well-trained men, using good judgment and expending their energies with delicate control.

Violent action is a function of animal spirits. It exhibits brawn and muscle explosively. The violent man hacks, but a controlled one seeks out the joints. The violent man keeps pressing, while the controlled one shifts his position again and again, and even at times retreats in order better to advance. Controlled action exhibits strength in subtle ways, allowing one to take advantage of whatever openings and weaknesses there may be, and of whatever opportunities the unfolding of events provides.

If the test of strength is the overcoming of opposition, he evidently is strongest who overcomes most, even when he intersperses his resistance and insistence with retreats, yieldings, and restraints. If another, without exercising these controls, makes out better in a given contest, we remain confident that he will not continue to do so for long. Should he continue, we are confident that he would have done better had he trained. This confidence underlies athletic education. Native strength, we are convinced, can be made more effective and its power increased through training.

If a violent man succeeds where a controlled one does not, we are nevertheless inclined to accept the record made by him because it does tell us something about what a man can do. But training, we think, would have enabled him to achieve even more.

A trained man can use his strength suddenly, and in a concentrated form, but he will do this only if that is what it is best then to do. He does not engage in such a display where it is not necessary. This is most easily seen in karate. One of the lessons that a student of that sport must learn is how to conquer without injuring. Both novice and master know how to avoid some injury to themselves, but it is only the master who knows how to use his strength so that even the opponents are not hurt. Sailing, surfing, and judo, also, more evidently than most other sports, emphasize the fact that strength without subtlety is usually strength reduced, unable to accomplish all that the available energy permits.

The slugger is weaker than the boxer who escapes from being hit and yet succeeds in landing blows when and where he likes. Were the slugger able to hit the boxer properly, he could perhaps win the bout with a single blow, for he has greater strength in reserve than the boxer has. But to have strength in reserve is not yet to exhibit strength. It is not yet to be strong in fact or to give public testimony of the amount of strength one has.

Just as speed offers one way of meeting the challenge of an obdurate space, and endurance offers one way of meeting the challenge of a relentless time, so strength offers one way of meeting the challenge of an inescapable causality. There is an inexorable sequence of cause and effect in nature. Though it takes place regardless of man, a man can qualify it, add to it, redirect it, and become an integral part of it, not only as a part of nature, but as a being with a judgment and an objective of his own. He is no mere place through which the cosmic course of events moves on its way; he is a pivotal point and a creative source who redefines and gives new import to the process.

As a natural being, what a man does has causes and effects; as a being involved in organizations, conventions, and more particularly contests and games, he continues to function as a natural being, but one who is now so reordered that he arrives at some desired goal in accordance with accepted rules. When he exhibits strength, he returns to the world the energy that he derived from it, but tamed, compliant, and humanized.

The control that strength, speed, and endurance demand can be isolated and itself exercised and put to a test. This is done when we try to find out how accurate we can be—which is not the same thing as discovering how much skill we have, or how gracefully we can perform. Skill is the acquired ability to accomplish an act with minimal waste and delay. Literally, it sets one apart. Gracefulness is a quality adorning smooth, harmonious movement. It pleases. Accuracy, in contrast, is a willed arrival at a selected target. It is an achievement.

A man can be accurate without having either skill or gracefulness. He might hit a target after having gone through wasteful motions, or after having jerked and twisted in the course of a preparation, aiming, and moving to it. It is also possible for him to be skillful without being accurate or graceful. He might be betrayed by circumstance—high winds, poor terrain, misinformation—or he might imitate the motions of an expert, but with a skill that has not yet been made part of himself, or which is forced and artificial. It is possible for him to be graceful without being skilled or accurate. His movements might be a delight to watch, but they may not be altogether appropriate to the task in hand, and may fail to get him where he wanted to be.

All three, accuracy, skill, and grace, can be combined in various ways and degrees. The athlete is then well coordinated. This characterization is in accord with Anna Espenschade's observation that coordination is present wherever there is any movement and a well-controlled rhythm.[8] The ability is clearly evident in the bullfighter and the marksman. But it is always present; a good athlete is a well-coordinated one.

Coordination can be supplemented by speed, endurance, or strength. A sprinter emphasizes the first. He not only uses his energy in such a way that he ends with nothing to spare, but he starts with the gun and keeps to a straight line, moving his limbs and arms with skill, but sometimes sacrificing gracefulness in order to better his position. A marathoner puts greater emphasis on skill. He knows when to hang back and when to pass, how to allow another to protect him from the sun or wind, how to conserve his energy, and when to make his final bid for victory. He, too, may not have much grace, but he must make accurate judgments and use his body effectively. A discus thrower is strong; he also emphasizes grace, though only as supported by accuracy and skill. His is a single fluid movement carrying out an attempt to place the discus where he wants it to be.

Accuracy is promoted by taking care. If no effort is made to do something right, a man may arrive where he

8   Anna Espenschade, "Motor Development," *Science and Medicine of Exercise and Sports*, ed. Warren Russell Johnson (New York, 1960), p. 428.

intends, but he will not do it accurately. Accuracy is, therefore, not identical with correctness, which can be attained accidently or mechanically. A first down can be correctly made after a fumble has been recovered; but had the ball been passed correctly, the fumble would not have occurred. A golfer may correctly hit a hole in one because of a fortunate set of circumstances, but he still may not be an accurate player for he may not be able to make the play all his own.

The attempt to achieve accuracy is triggered by a concern to dominate some distant position in space, time, or causation. In contrast with the runner, he who seeks accuracy above all will ignore intermediate spaces and times. In contrast with the shot-putter who tries only to cover a distance, he who is concerned with accuracy tries to arrive at a position.

In most sports accuracy has to do only with a gross result. The basketball player must get the ball into the basket; it makes no difference whether it touches the rim or not. But in some sports exactitude is demanded—accuracy in the small. The diver and the figure skater, the marksman and the mountaineer must try to be exact.

Unlike tests for speed, endurance, and strength, which report a relative excellence, having reference to one's competitors or to a successful passing beyond previous achievements, a test for accuracy can be stated and met without reference to what had been done in the past. The accurate man treats a definite place, a predesignated moment, or a specific link in the causal process as that which he is to make determinate in some accepted way, and thus become a master of what is now distant. His accuracy reflects his ability to impose precise determinations on what is reachable but outside his direct control. What he accomplishes can be something absolute—perfect accuracy. Such accuracy has been achieved in shooting, golfing, and bowling. No one can get closer to the center than a bull's-eye. No one can make a hole in less than one stroke. No one can knock down more than all the pins in all the frames. These are instances of accuracy in the large. They are not instances of complete accuracy in the little, or perfect exactitude. That would require an accuracy in the very last detail, and this cannot be obtained. Bull's-eyes vary minutely one from the other. Holes in one differ in the precision with which the ball arrives at and falls into the cup. Pins are knocked down in bowling from various angles, and are hit with varying finalities.

Accuracy allows for perfection only within certain somewhat arbitrary limits of precision, and for limited periods of time. It cannot be absolute down to the smallest detail. It cannot be absolute when combined with a demand for endurance. He who reaches the limit of endurance can no longer continue to be as accurate as he had been before; we can therefore define the limit of endurance to be at the point where accuracy can no longer be maintained. Following this lead, one can also take the limit of endurance to be at the point where one moves slower than some designated speed or can exhibit no more than some specified strength. But definitions in the reverse are not possible. Accuracy, strength, and speed cannot be dealt with in terms of endurance, though, of course, they are possible only so far as there is still some control or some strength or energy in reserve.

Though a man may be concerned with showing his superiority over all other men inside a world of sport, and therefore as subject to special conditions and rules, he cannot entirely escape the influence of natural forces. No matter what he does he must take account of these. He can never wholly or forever withstand them. Whether he speeds, endures, or only meets a test of strength or accuracy, he will fail to gain more than a momentary victory over the forces that in fact exist. No matter how big he is, puny he always will be. Success in sport is but a moment held over against an implacable, powerful nature.

The athlete is not a "natural" man, a mere object pushed and pulled by impersonal forces. He stands away from nature when he thinks; he adds to it when he acts; he enriches it when he creates. He stands away from, adds to, and enriches nature when he participates in a game. The world which he then inhabits is located inside the cosmic space, time, and causality within which all particular activities occur, but it is a world with its own boundaries, within which distinctive occurrences are produced.

The athlete is always an individual. He performs as an individual even when he plays with others. Speed, endurance, strength, coordination, and accuracy are to be attributed to him. But whether he engages in an individual event, or struggles with as well as against others, he also carries out a role and represents something bigger than himself. This fact obtains considerable clarity from an examination of the nature of play, sport, and game.

9.   play, sport, and game

THE language of athletics changes rapidly. It must, to
keep abreast of new rules and new types of activity. But
even where these remain steady the language often undergoes rapid transformations. Reporters, writers, and sports-
men exhibit considerable ingenuity in their creation of new
expressions. They are not held back, as sport is, by a desire
to conform to tradition. Their linguistic fecundity ef-
ferveses into a multiplicity of terms which sometimes enjoy
considerable popularity, though rarely for more than a
short span. Spurred by a desire to be forceful and dramatic, these men change the language at a pace which
often outdistances the innovations that are made in sport.
Yet the subject needs a rather fixed vocabulary if it is to do
justice to those constancies that are to be found in almost
every age and in many cultures. It should be freed from
the ambiguity that now haunts its central terms. "Sport,"
"game," and "play," at least, deserve fairly constant
meanings.

"Sport" has no clear, commonly acknowledged use. It
is reasonable to suppose that it covers whatever is dealt
with in the sports pages of newspapers and magazines. But
these also contain reports on bridge and chess, which it
would be odd to call "sports." We need a better guide than
the coverage which periodicals offer. Unfortunately, the
usage of the word by officials is of little help, varying as it
does from place to place. In the United States, for example,
"sport" is almost equivalent with "athletics," or with an
"athletic activity or game," but in England and in the
Olympic Games, "athletics" is used to refer only to field

and track events, and has no application to other "sports."

"Sport" comes from "disport," to divert or amuse. It has now moved far outside the limits of its origin. Mountain climbing and weight lifting are sports; but there is little diversion and sometimes no amusement in them, either for the participants or for the spectators. A good deal of sport, of course, is pursued for no other reason than the pleasure that it gives. There is a delight in moving one's limbs with grace and skill; there is joy in testing oneself and one's opponent. Pleasure is rarely absent from any sport, even when one has pushed oneself almost to the limit of human endurance. This fact should not lead us to overlook the large measure of self-sacrifice and self-denial that is also demanded. That is one reason why it is not easy to get a man to the point where he wants to devote his life to sport. Even in the sports in which most seem to enjoy themselves—diving, swimming, golfing, and tennis—there is so much tension involved that it prevents us from considering pleasure to be more than a subordinate phase. "Sport" both needs and deserves a steadier meaning than it has today.

"Game" also has many different meanings. Sometimes it is interchanged with "sport." Today we speak indifferently of the game or the sport of football. Sometimes it is treated as having reference to any idle conformity to rules. It is in this sense that we speak of "children's games," "card games," and "word games." Sometimes it is used when men are subject to tests which make evident their defects of character or disposition. We follow this usage when we speak of the "game of life," or of "the games people play [on one another]." "Game" is also used to refer to the locus of idle play; children and some adults, we say, play games of parchesi, tag, and tictactoe.

"Play" sustains an even greater cluster of meanings than either "sport" or "game" does. Kittens and puppies, babies and children are said to play. But we also speak of men playing strongly contested, rule-bound, refereed games, in which none of these others can really engage. Soccer and hockey are played in ways which differ radically from the way in which kittens play with a ball of yarn, or children play with a top. And of course, "play," as referring to a distinctive act in a game, has still another meaning, not to speak of the meaning it has when used to refer to a work for the theatre.

"Sport," "athletics," "game," and "play" have in common the idea of being cut off from the workaday world. This leads some to use one term for all of them. Johan Huizinga, in his influential book, calls all such activities "play," which he describes as "a free activity standing quite consciously outside ordinary life as being 'not serious.' . . . It is an activity connected with no material interest. . . . It proceeds within its own proper boundaries . . . according to fixed rules."[1] Yet animals and infants play without rules, and some activities, such as whittling, even when they conform to rules, are not spoken of as "play." Play also can be serious—as Huizinga later admits [2]—though not serious in the sense in which ordinary activities are.

Roger Caillois offers, I think, a more reliable and interesting guide. Play, he says, is *free, separate, uncertain, unproductive,* and governed by both *make-believe* and *rules.*[3] He understands these terms in ways which will not always meet criticism. But they do offer handy pegs on which to hang some crucial characterizations.

In referring to play as free, Caillois means that it is voluntary, dependent on the individual to begin and terminate. This, however, is not a necessary feature of play. Children can be sent out to play; they can be made to play in games against their desires or express intent; they can be made to end their play. Play, though, must be freely accepted even when it is not freely entered into or freely ended; it is free in the sense that it is carried on by the player only while he desires to engage in it. Made to play, he nevertheless plays only while he willingly does what he must.

By "separate" Caillois means that the play is limited

1   John Huizinga, *Homo Ludens, A Study of the Play-Element in Culture* (Boston, 1955), p. 13.   2   *Ibid.*, p. 45.
3   Roger Caillois, *Man, Play, and Games,* trans. by Meyer Barash (Glencoe, Ill., 1961), pp. 3 ff.

in space and time. But this is a characteristic of every human activity, and will not, therefore, serve to mark off play from any other activity. Play is separate, though, in the sense that it is autotelic, bounded off from the daily pragmatic world.

A quite common view takes the play of a puppy or a child to be a preparation for later life. Everything, it is thought, has a purpose, and the purpose of the young is to get ready for the time when they will be older. We have here a variation on the discarded theory of preformation, which holds that what will be is already present in a compressed or inchoate form. The variant deserves to be discarded as well. Puppies and children extend themselves when they play; they explore, discover, experience, and grow. But they do not have these as their objectives; discovery, growth, and the like are but by-products of an absorption in play. When children assume the role of doctor or nurse, parent or fireman, and attend meticulously to what are then taken to be essential parts of the role, they not only do not then prepare themselves for an adult life—why otherwise are not all adults doctors, nurses, etc?—but they firmly hold the activity away from what they ordinarily do, as a separate domain needing no justification.

In order to play it is necessary to bracket the activities of daily life and attend to a more restricted and sometimes a better controlled world. Even the small child must go through this process of bracketing. It has, to be sure, little to do with the concerns which characterize daily living; its turn toward play demands of it little more than a holding in abeyance its usual attitudes toward eating, talking, pushing, pulling, crawling, and walking. These are normally at the service of some goal beyond themselves; made part of play, they are cut off from the activities involved in satisfying the child's hunger, curiosity, or sense of security.

The child's daily activities, like ours, take place in a comparatively wide open world where most of the objects are more powerful and insistent than it is. When it plays it shifts its attention to a sphere where it is in charge, mainly through its reinterpretation of what objects are and do. As it grows older, its earlier flickering separation of its moments of play from its moments of occupation with the satisfaction of its desires in a world of imperious men and things, is replaced by sharper and sharper divisions which become harder and harder to break through. The child gradually becomes caught up in responsibilities; it may have to work; it cannot avoid all plans. If it is to play it must make an effort to break away from its daily routines and tasks. Not only must it shift its attention, but it must carry out a new role.

Ordinary life is intruded upon from many angles by many things. Those things make diverse claims, eliciting lines of action which are effective inside a narrow range but are loose and largely ineffective outside that range. In turning from ordinary life a man turns as well from the larger world that environs it. He then begins to live inside a tighter world where he may be somewhat relaxed. Both ordinary life and play have strong components of tension and passivity, but in opposite corners. Daily occurrences force a man to remain attentive to what will affect his welfare inside a larger world which appears to be loosely held together, but when he plays he moves in a structured world inside of which he can be somewhat more at ease.

We are seriously involved with the particulars of daily life; in play our seriousness is directed at the entire scheme which we have taken to be bounded off from all else. We see daily life inside a somewhat amorphous setting toward which we have a vague and receptive attitude, whereas in play we take such an attitude mainly with respect to what happens inside a whole that we have momentarily held apart from all else.

Play is not only separated off from daily life; it is separated off from the fields of religion, art, and inquiry as well. These have as part of their meaning an intent to achieve a desirable result with respect to some ultimate reality. They are serious in somewhat the same way that daily life is serious. Often yielding great satisfaction, and sometimes denied pragmatic significance, they nevertheless involve one in controlled activities set inside a larger, not yet mastered whole. But in play what is mainly controlled is a demarcated portion of time, space, and causality, with subordinate areas and activities left open to spontaneity and free interpretation.

One may play in order to refresh oneself, to be a good companion, to use up some time, and the like, but once the step has been taken from an involvement in serious activities to an acceptance of a bracketed domain in which one is to be at comparative ease, all the initial reasons are left behind. He who wants to be refreshed through play must forget about refreshing himself, and just play.

By "uncertain" Caillois intends to call attention to the fact that playing is a process subject to the unexpected. This is certainly a large factor in play; it is, of course, not altogether absent from other types of activity, even the most monotonous and serious. No process is ever reducible to a pattern; the dynamic always adds something not expressed in any structure. Whatever we do has its element of unanticipatable contingency, spontaneity, and unexpectedness. But more room is left for them in play than elsewhere. Play invites improvization and imagination because it is serious with respect to the domain it bounds but not with respect to what is done within it.

Politics, war, and art also have much of the improvizational about them, and their course is often governed by decisions then and there made. Yet we do not speak of them as forms of play. Where play requires decisions which may promote self-expression or vitalize a contest, the others require decisions which promote a desired outcome. One might like to come out victorious in some adventure at which one is playing, just as a politician, general, or artist might like to be vitally unstructured. But victory in play and spontaneity in politics, war, and art, are to be kept subordinate to self-expression and successful achievement, respectively, if the character of these different activities is not to be distorted.

By "unproductive" Caillois intends to refer to the fact that play is not directed toward the production of economically viable goods. I think he is right; the very bracketing off of play from the daily world makes it nonproductive. Professional players, of course, earn money. Gamblers sometimes find it profitable to play with cards, "to play the horses," and "to play at roulette." They are then rewarded for shrewdness, guessing, or for their skill in doing something which does not increase the number or value of material goods. Play is equally unproductive, differing from the activity of professional athletes and gamblers, though, in its lack of concern for what its outcome means in the world of daily living. A professional athlete or a gambler may ignore the consequences of his activities, but they nevertheless qualify what he does, and come sharply to the fore as the play comes to a close.

By "make-believe" Caillois intends to refer to the fact that one who plays puts himself in a position to engage in activities for a while without actually identifying himself with them. He is making an important point, though I think he spoils it somewhat. A good deal of identification takes place in all play that is dramatic, or into which one enters with some enthusiasm. Play is make-believe in Caillois's sense, though, in that it requires one to assume a role known to be a role, and to assume it for no useful end.

Play is often subject to rules. But it can be carried on without making any reference to them, and even in their absence. This is the play referred to when athletes are told to stop "playing around," and instead to attend to the game, with its conditions and rules. It is only when play is rule-governed and well controlled that one can be said to play in a game. Such play is engaged in by those who, for the moment at least, have detached themselves from an attempt to achieve something in daily life or from the pursuit of some career, to attend instead to the rule-controlled demands of an activity requiring bodily excellence and a union with equipment in situations which challenge and test.

These various characterizations can be summed up in the idea that play is a distinctive activity carried on with no intent to do anything other than follow out the created rationale of a controlled area, arbitrarily bounded off from the rest of the world. Any serious activity can, therefore, be made into a world for play, once it is seen to allow for a free assumption of nonutilitarian roles within its confines.

The root meaning of play is "to bestir oneself." Despite this, it requires one to be loose and free of responsibilities. If engaged in for the sake of health or money, play ceases to be play at the point where these objectives dictate what is done. Exercise is not play, but a game of tennis can be. Exercise is directed at a particular objective, the improving of the muscle tone, but in tennis one need do nothing but play.

The athlete has many responsibilities and too little time to interest himself in idle activity. As a consequence, he plays less than most other men do. If he is to play in a game, the one thing he must do is not play the way a child does. Instead, he must assume the role of a player and carry out a task responsibly, without considering what is needed elsewhere. Daily life, economics, politics, religion, art, and science are not permitted to impinge.

When a child plays it adopts a posture and sets itself a task that allow it to use its imagination and often its initiative to a degree it otherwise cannot without risking serious criticism or injury. It usually plays because there is no better way for it to be a child, unfocused, unselfconscious, inexperienced, with few habits and no plan. All other activity demands that it direct itself toward the responsible realization of some presumably socially significant project.

Play may have many by-products, not all of them good. There can be too much time spent in fantasy, in following one's whim, in staying inside a bracketed world. All play and no work keeps Jack from becoming a boy. It is playing as a child which makes it possible for him to become more mature. He who concentrates on being fully what he is, is best enabled to become what he is not yet.

After childhood has been left behind play may still provide an opportunity for the exercise of imagination and initiative, or it may be used to absorb surplus energy, to forget some heavy responsibility, or to escape from routine. Man's play may prompt him to adventure and to learn truths about himself and things daily life partly obscures. But he could conceivably do something better. It is when a child plays that it usually is most a child, but a man is normally most a man only when he stops playing and tries to do some justice to his responsibilities.

A child is at its best when it plays. A mature man who plays is always less than what a man might be. The young man is in between. It is all right for him to play some of the time because he is not yet able to do more important things; it is not right for him to play all the time for there are other, more useful or noble things he could do. He matures, as does a child, in the course of his playing, but rarely because of it, or to the degree possible to the child. But through his play he is able to perfect himself as a body to a degree not yet possible to a child.

Play is not always joyous. Children are frequently intense and anxious when they play. They may make-believe, but they never make believe that they are making-believe. About that they are serious. They are serious, too, about the game that is played, but not serious enough to want to persist in it for its own sake. As a consequence, children stop when they are tired, bored, or when they become interested in something else. In contrast, the athlete is serious about continuing a game. He takes a game to be not only an event which is bounded off from all else, but one which he wants to have exist until it has run its course. That is why he tries to remain in it, despite tiredness, boredom, or the lure of other activities.

Only if one submits to rules can one play in a game. Only if one submits to a game as having its own rationale, which is to be made manifest by an actual living through its prescribed beginning to its prescribed ending, does one play a game. And only if one makes a concerted physical effort, involving exertion to the limits of fatigue, can one be an athlete playing through a game.

Play is all-absorbing, both for the child and the athlete. For the one, it is little more than a sequence of spontaneities, requiring little or no preparation, while for the other it is an occasion for the exhibition of the skilled use of physical energy. Play allows the child to discover where it stops and the world begins, but the athlete, by keeping his activities confined within the accepted frame of a game, goes on to learn who he is and what he can do.

Though the athlete is rarely playful, he often has his moments of innocent exuberance and pleasure; his primary tonality is satisfaction for having done what he ought, and not, as a child, for having done what he wanted to do. The child's play is subject to custom and runs along inherited grooves, but it expresses no tradition and realizes no ideals. An athlete, intead, performs inside a well-established tradition that is preserved in formulations of what is required and permitted, as well as in records and histories. Children play the same games, recite the same verses, make the same moves generation after generation, but they have no sense of history, accumulative, causal, and explanatory. Few athletes, of course, are aware of the history of their sport, but they live in an historic moment, as their consciousness of previous achievements, of the teachings of their coaches, of the presence of referees and judges, makes amply evident. And before them there is always the ideal of becoming complete men who have reached the limits of physical achievement.

It is a rare child who does not destroy what it has made. With one sweep of the hand it knocks down what took considerable effort and sometimes a great deal of time. Looked at as a single act, the destruction seems wanton and foolish. Treated as a supplement to its constructive efforts, the destruction shows itself to be but one of the ways by which a child discovers just how much power it has. An athlete may pommel his adversary; he may hurt him badly and may even be the cause of his death; but what he tries to do is to achieve, not to destroy. He does not seek to discover how much power he has, but how effectively his power can be used to bring about a successful outcome under established rules.

Through play a child learns what it is. Through both its constructions and destructions it comes to see that it is a limited human being capable of controlling the functioning of only a certain number of things. An athlete, instead, finds out through his play how much of a man he is by discovering how close to the limits of human performance he can come. Something analogous to a child's discovery of the limits of its power, however, is learned by an athlete in the course of training and practice. When he enters into a contest or a game he already knows fairly well what he can and what he cannot do. He is, therefore, free to learn in the contest or game how he meets various tests, what it is that perfection demands, and what man can bodily do and be. Because an athlete is a player he plays, i.e., keeps within the confines of a demarcated structured world; but the way in which the child plays precludes it from being a player, i.e., one who wants a game to be.

In root, "sport" means to divert oneself. This meaning it still rightly bears. However, we tend to think of diversion as primarily occupied with amusement and relaxed enjoyment, or as offering a relief from regular work, particularly when this is tedious, arduous, or unwanted. This meaning is only at the fringe of the idea of sport as we use it today. Men do divert themselves from work in order to engage in sport, but they then do not disport or frolic. They submit to rules which ask for effort and attention far greater sometimes than that required in daily work.

A sport is a set of rules instantiated in games. The rules may be set down all at once quite arbitrarily, thereby suddenly bringing into being a new sport. Usually, though, the rules of a sport are the product of a slow evolution. Whatever their origin they must be adhered to if one is to participate in the sport.

A man can climb a mountain in a hundred different ways. He can allow himself to be hauled over different crags; he can be pulled part of the way by machines or animals; or he can make use of explosives so as to force holds and routes where no progress is otherwise possible. He will then adventure and struggle, perhaps even test and find himself, but he will not be accepted as a mountain climber by the community of those who treat this as a sport. A sportsman who climbs a mountain is tested within the limits set by established rules.

Hockey demands bodily exertion. Like every other sport, it tests what a rule-abiding man can bodily be and do. Though chess also has rules, and these have a history, and though a masterly game makes considerable demands on the stamina of the players, chess is not a sport because it does not test what a man is as a body. Mind and body more or less reverse their roles in these two cases. In hockey judgment and determination are subservient to bodily achievement, but in chess the body is used only to make possible a more effective judgment and determination.

Puss in the corner demands physical exertion. One might conceivably play it under rules well publicized; it might have its referees and records. Even then it would not be called a sport, for it does not offer a test of how bodily excellent a man can be. Sport is a traditionalized set of rules to be exemplified by men who try to be excellent in and through their bodies.

The rules of a sport are like legislative enactments. But unlike such enactments they are not backed by brute force. Players, in contradistinction from themselves as citizens, voluntarily abide by the rules for an end to which they freely dedicate themselves. One can, of course, conceive of men being forced to play in some game, but they will then not be men engaged in a sport, freely seeking to achieve excellence, but instead will be men who are working at athletics. One can also conceive of men gladly obeying laws in order to promote the public weal, but they will not then be citizens of a state but philosophers living in harmony.

The rules of a sport are more like international laws in their present guise than they are like the laws of a particular state. Both rules and international laws are rendered ineffective by the refusal of men to heed them. Unlike international laws, though, the rules of a sport are exemplified again and again, and the outcome is accepted or at least submitted to by the participants of a game, and by others as well. Once international law arrives at the state of respectability possessed by the rules of sport, there will be more promise of peace than there is today, though there is no evidence that sport, itself, on a national or an international scale, helps promote even elementary good will. It is painful today to think of Baron de Coubertin's hope that the Olympic Games would prove to be a means for promoting the peace and unity of mankind; they have succeeded no better than any other agency.

A sport does not have a single unified history. It is a structure for a series of games, each an episodic, unitary, present occurrence. The games embody common rules which in turn define those games to be instances of a single sport. Normally, the rules are changed in formal meetings, but on occasion they may be modified in the course of a game. They are then left dormant, awaiting another occasion when they are to be used.

All who play in games sustain (and help create) the rules of a sport, just as all those who carry out the affairs of a nation have a share in making its history. To set up rules, however, does not mean that a new sport has been added. Otherwise one could create hundreds of sports in a few hours. The rules must be accepted by men who willingly and bodily participate in games.

A single game of a particular type is not yet part of a sport, for it is not yet part of a history of games; a sport needs more than one occasion when its rules are exemplified. Those occasions must resemble one another. When they differ markedly they are games in a different sport. Sport, as we know it today, is, strictly speaking, little more than a hundred years old. The sports of the Greeks came to an end with them; what followed after a long interval were games the Greeks never played. Even our Olympic Games have many new events; those events that are like the old are subject to novel conditions; they are competed in by men who are rather different in social class and aim from those who were allowed to participate in the days of the Greeks. Our records are made under rules and circumstances of comparatively recent origin. Sport, as we know it today, is about as new a field as sociology and anthropology, both of which are the products of nineteenth-century thought. Yet, even where there is no political or national history, games are played, exemplifying a set of inherited rules. In some form sport has had a place in every culture which has a tribal memory. But apart from some awareness by officials or by players of previous exemplifications of the rules, a sport exists only as a tradition sometimes does, i.e., as a set of possibilities which, when realized in the present, are thereby necessarily related to all past realizations, and eventually to the first, while still allowing for further realizations in the future.

When James Naismith invented basketball in the eighteen-nineties, he did not invent a sport—if a sport is recognized to have a history. What he did was to formulate a set of rules, and offer an opportunity for exhibiting them. By itself the first exhibition of those rules was only an experiment; it was not part of the sport of basketball.

At the beginning of the history of basketball, the baskets were different in shape, size, and placement from what they are now, there was no headboard, and the players did not have to face the penalties that are now in effect. Nevertheless, those games and the present ones are games in a single sport. The rules Naismith formulated and the quite different rules now followed structure a gradually modified sport of basketball; all basketball games, including the first, are part of one history. But there may come a time when the game that is played is so different from those games played yesterday that only indifference or habit will allow us to call both of them "basketball."

"Play," it will be recalled, originally meant "to bestir oneself." The root meaning of game is "to leap joyously." Since an exertion is presumably made on behalf of some possible good and since a joyous leaping requires looseness and irresponsibility, "game" and "play" have evidently interchanged their meanings in modern times. A game has an insistent objective of its own, which those who participate in it are to respect and try to realize. Like play, a game is cut off from the workaday world. Like play, too, but unlike a drama or a dance, it has no script and is therefore subject to contingencies produced in the course of its development. It is a bounded event, with a prescribed beginning, a prescribed course, prescribed divisions, and a prescribed ending.

A sport lays down the conditions which participants must carry out if there is to be a true game. A true game exemplifies rules that enable a sport to be exhibited. The rules to which the game is subject are highly general, to be filled out by actions which can have any form, providing they promote a test of what men are and can do.

Children's games, card games, newly invented games, games in which rules are changed as one goes along, and games whose rules are broken without penalty are not games of a sport. All of them offer islands of activity; all are separated off from economics and politics and whatever else is of importance to the welfare and prosperity of society and civilization. All of them enable one to learn something of man's ability; all of them provide occasions for comparing oneself with others, or for seeing what one's comparative good fortune is. They exemplify rules, but they fall short of being part of a sport because they either do not stress bodily activity or have no stabilized, historic set of rules. None of them is the kind of game with which we are here concerned.

It is a rare game in which there is not considerable expression of spontaneity, but the spontaneity is normally kept within the confines of the rules. If freshly forged, the game is still kept in consonance with accepted rules. Because there is spontaneity in a game we are justified in saying that a game is "played." Play, though, puts its emphasis on the spontaneity, and not on the rules.

Because a game offers a challenge to the body, it demands preparation and invites exertion. A man's success in it depends on his ability to lose himself in a strenuous effort. Because a game is structured and stabilized it offers a man an opportunity to see how excellent he can prove himself to be.

From the perspective of a game, neither it nor its participants is to be understood to have an existence outside the confines of its rules. Where its rules begin, there the game begins; where its rules end, there the game ends. When the game is over those rules are left behind. One is then free to engage in some other enterprise. This too could be called "a game." As a consequence, one will be able to think, with Wittgenstein, of every intelligible activity as a game, and of ourselves as being involved in a plurality of distinct games, each with its own vocabulary and grammar. But he who is willing to call daily life and daily discourse "games" must be willing to say that men leave such games in order to enter into others which have no practical import, and which are established by, are carried out in accordance with, and terminate as demanded by arbitrary, voluntarily accepted prescriptions. When the men once again return to the world of daily life and discourse, those prescriptions are no longer in operation. Why say, then, that the men continue to play in some game? It is not good analysis to lump together a multitude of different activities and term all of them "games."

Somewhat like a train ride, a game is begun and ended by one who moves out of and into a different setting. When we ride on a train we conform to various conditions and regulations, such as going to the proper platform, having a paid ticket, sitting in a coach, getting off at the station for which we have paid fare, and the like. But we ride the train in order to be, not merely to arrive at our destination. A game, of course, is not a vehicle carrying us to some place, but we do end it in such a way as to enable us to be somewhere else than at the game, even when we do not leave the playing field.

Rules for riding a train operate only within a larger setting where one does something other than ride the train. From the standpoint of a train ride, what is done before and after the ride is of a different order, even if before and after we merely ride on another train. Just so, what is done before and after we participate in a game is of a different order from it, even if we play a double-header and immediately follow game by game. Sooner or later we will leave the game to engage in a task too loosely governed by rules, too unstructured and unbounded, too irregular, and too strongly swept by contingencies to be properly taken to be part of a true game.

We can imagine a culture where all activities are severely bound by arbitrary rules, and where men are called upon to exert themselves so that they embody those rules in an exemplary fashion. We would not be inclined to say that they then played a game, because that requires that there be a separation from daily life. In our imagined culture a time could be set aside in which the members engaged in games. Those games, unlike ours, would not be more tightly controlled than what was done before and after the games, but we would call them games nevertheless, because they would involve a departure from the patterns characteristic of daily activity. Our daily activity has many degrees of freedom, but even if it had none, we could have a game only if we subjected ourselves to different demands.

Men enter a game armed with attitudes, personalities, bodies, and equipment. Not one of these is entirely suited to the requirements of a game. Each must be altered or manipulated until it is appropriate. The alteration may involve nothing more than a shift in outlook, or an abstraction from the many possible uses to which the items can be put, but either of these will be sufficient to point up the fact that entering a game is more than an act of going on a field. A bat is a piece of wood, a baseball diamond is a flat surface, a player is just a man—until they become part of a game. When the game is over, they usually recover their former guises or become only a potential bat, diamond, and player.

Bullfighting constantly, and other contests incidentally, seem to force us to take some of the occurrences in them to be in fact occurrences outside. The injuries and killings that result seem quite clearly to occur in our daily world. Hospitals, insurance claims, and the law take over and make the injury and death their concern. If a man is badly injured he is forced to stop playing; if he is killed his death usually brings a game to an end. Yet we cannot, I think, avoid affirming that the injuries and killings, even when forbidden by the rules of a game or when made the concern of the police, take place in the game. Sometimes the participants even act in terms of them, and perhaps even invite them.

The player who is severely injured and the player who is killed are defined by the game to be no longer fit to continue in it; so far, the men are on a footing with someone who is penalized or, more accurately, penalized twofold. He who is injured or killed is obviously disabled for the game and also for the workaday world. What happens to him is regrettable in the one, but it is tragic in the other.

Sometimes a child plays a game. That game may have been made up on the spot. It could have firm rules, and these could require the child to exert itself physically, and even to compete with other children. But the child will not be prepared to participate in the game with skill and mastery. It will show little inclination to obligate itself to live up to the rules, or show much judgment in the way in which it embodies those rules. It is not an athlete.

For an athlete a game is an event that unfolds in a prescribed order, and is directed toward a well-defined end. A certain number of points are to be made, a time limit is set within which to show what one can do, or some obstacle or condition is laid down that must be met in some designated way. Energy is there restrained and organized. Since a game always allows for some expression of unpredictable ingenuity, and even of invention and restructuralization, the restraint can never be complete—nor should it be—and the resultant organization is, as it should be, somewhat loose jointed.

It is obvious now, perhaps, that play, game, and sport have in common the fact that they are cut off both from the daily world and the worlds of the arts, sciences, and humanities. Play, sport, and particularly the game, all deserve still more detailed examination. Notice should be taken of the time, place, and dynamics of games, of the role that ceremony has, of the meaning of team play, of the way in which even violent games differ from war, and of the part played by luck and good fortune. These topics are dealt with in the next two chapters. Their import will possibly be a little more evident, however, if we attend for a moment to the distinction previously made between a contest and a game. Contest and game are not everywhere sharply distinguished, but they differ sufficiently to necessitate a separation of them in theory and in discourse. The one is primarily a controlled struggle between individuals, the other is a structured event produced by interlocked teams or representative men. While a game allows one to see what man can do, a contest, instead, offers an occasion for a self-discovery. There is, of course, structure and a proving of man in contests, and there is some struggle and self-discovery in a game, but these are subordinate to a self-discovery through struggle and a structured proving, respectively.

Boxing, wrestling, and marathon running are not usually spoken of as "games." They are contests. They offer occasions for men to demonstrate some control over themselves, some superiority over others, and sometimes (as in skiing) a mastery of quasi-natural situations. Because a contest puts primary emphasis on struggle, it is usually more concentrated than a game. In a game there are normally various plays for the participants to go through, and some release or relaxation normally takes place between these plays. Games are well-bounded, noninstrumental, rule-abiding, unitary events, having a number of distinct, interrelated parts, engaged in by representative men, or a team. Inside the game men usually contest, i.e., struggle with one another, to determine which is superior. If we spoke with utmost precision, however, we would say that despite the contesting there are no contests in a game. Men struggle in a game while cooperating with others, even those with whom they compete. The main effort is to bring the game from its official beginning to its official close in such a way as to reveal how excellent a man can bodily be.

We speak of the Olympic Games and not of the Olympic Game, because there are many unitary events in it (only some of which are games) and because, even in the contests that it allows, the participants are all accepted, not as individuals, but as members of and representatives of some nation or other. In the Olympics and elsewhere, however, most men compete as individuals. Sometimes some of them are unattached and represent no one. We, nevertheless, take them to participate in games because we see them as representing some group, or at least some region or place of origin.

A contest demands that one complete a task rather

than fill a role; it rarely provides pleasure or fun. A game instead has tasks defined by roles, and allows for periods of relaxation. It is the individual, though of course as manifesting various skills, who is prominent in a contest. It is a role carrier, though of course as expressing a distinctive judgment and commitment, who is prominent in a game.

Eleanor Metheny exaggerates, I think, when she writes:

The concept of "the good strife" is implicit in the word competition, as derived from cum and pedere—literally, to strive with rather than against. The word contest has similar implications being derived from con and testare—to testify with another rather than against him.[4]

A contest is a con-test, a testing or testifying with. This "with" includes and supplements an "against." A contest involves strife, conflict, and an effort to be victorious, but with others who acknowledge the same rules and grant one the right to be treated fairly. When the competition is severe and the struggle strenuous, we tend to forget that the justification of contests is their provision of opportunities to find out who one is in relation to other men in a bounded situation. Violations of rules, underhanded practices, deliberate attempts to injure, all testify to the magnitude of men's passions and their desire to be victorious— and to their failure to keep focused on the athletic event.

4 Eleanor Metheny, *Connotations of Movement in Sport and Dance* (Dubuque, Iowa, 1965), p. 40.

10.

GAMES and contests are carried on inside a distinctive time, space, and causality, under the aegis of rules accepted by the participants. To make men alert to the distinctive nature of contests and games, and perhaps to make their attitudes more appropriate to them, the beginnings and endings of these events should be signalized. We do this by framing them in ceremonies.

A ceremony accentuates the fact that a game or contest is a bounded event. An established form for marking the importance of some place, object, or venture, the ceremony is typically formal and solemn, dignifying what it introduces or closes. It consequently has a role on most state occasions. The sobering character it is then supposed to have is also intended when it is used before the start or after the end of a contest or game.

Before the game begins one salutes the flag, stands at attention, sings the national anthem, shakes hands, etc. These are opening ceremonies serving both to hold the game away from the daily world and to direct one into the game. If the occasion, the surroundings, and the attitudes of those present support and are supported by the same intent which sustains the ceremonial acts, that intent is kept alive or is renewed, and the interest is kept within clear bounds.

The introductory function of ceremony is underscored in the East. There the ceremony also separates one off from the daily world, but its emphasis is on signalizing an intention to respect the rights and dignity of an opponent. This type of ceremony is an essential part of karate, without which the contest becomes little more than a series of remarkable exhibitions in the controlled use of the body instead of, as it in fact is, a sanctioned struggle which demands that one have a pronounced respect for oneself, one's opponent, and the contest in which one is about to engage.

Because a ceremony is solemn and formal, it can be readily reduced to a series of empty gestures. Baptismal, confirmation, and marriage ceremonies sometimes have no effect beyond that of making the minds of the participants and spectators wander from the signal event to which the ceremonies should have directed them. It is not likely that a salute or a snatch of song will do much to raise the spirits of either players or spectators, even when as is the case with football, the spectators, too, join in the initial ceremony. We then do not have the most effective opening for a game. At their best, ceremonies make one aware that something important is to take place.

A ceremony is designed to invoke respect. The awe it sometimes inspires is that respect heightened and enriched by wonder and fear. Usually it invokes awe only when it is part of a religious service. But something of a religious aura clings to it, even when it serves merely to mark off some such secular event as the laying of a cornerstone, the opening of a road or a bridge, a graduation—or a sport. It is not too difficult, therefore, for a ceremony introducing any one of these to support a tendency to look upon what follows as having a religious import.

An athlete once was, and still can be, treated as a sacred being who embodies something of the divine in him. He is credited with the dignity of embodying a supreme value. While functioning as a single, organic being, self-contained and well geared toward the future, he is seen, through the help of a ceremony, to be adjectival to a more remote reality. Religious men acknowledge that reality in an act of faith; romantics use intuition; metaphysicians make use of speculation and dialectic. The athlete and those who attend to him are content to accept the fact that he is an unusual man, exhibiting and achieving what most men do not.

The ceremonies relating to sport are today predominantly secular. They pivot about national songs and symbols, and are expressed in conventionally approved gestures. If they solemnize an occasion, they do the work that is required of them. Should they instead turn a game into an instrument of propaganda, they load it with meanings which are at best irrelevant and at worst injurious.

Whatever values accrue to a game from religion or politics dignify its activity and participants. But a game, dignified or not, is self-enclosed; it has no purpose to serve other than that of exemplifying a sport and providing men with the opportunity to show what bodily excellence is and does. If the participants or their achievements are treated as counters in national affairs, games are thereupon transformed into exhibitions, showing us not what man can be and do, but how some limited group would like itself to be viewed.

The spectators in an international meet understandably want to identify themselves with the representatives of their nation. An increase in excitement and drama is theirs when they ally themselves with those contestants with whom they have had some connection, even if this be only in the guise of geography or copresence at some other occasion. And wherever they are faced with men they do not know, speaking languages they do not understand, and following flags and gods different from their own, all have a need to affirm their union with those with whom they are most closely affiliated. The affirmation helps them to establish their significance and to extend their identities.

We enrich our individual natures by identifying ourselves with others who do what we think is splendid, for we then accept as our own values that we cherish. It is better, though, for us to identify ourselves with those who are superb fellow citizens rather than with friends, or members of a club, a region, a sex, or a college, for the wider the group represented by the men with whom we identify ourselves the greater the range of approved values and the more nobly human we take ourselves to be. That very reason makes an identification with the leaders of civilized mankind even better than an identification with fine fellow citizens.

Religion and ethics lead to an identification with every man, whether base or noble, but athletics disdains the inferior. The reach it permits to an identification is determined by the spread of a concern for excellence. What it loses in numbers it makes up in quality. It accepts only a few but takes them to represent all.

Sometimes ceremonies serve to close off athletic events. If those ceremonies are made to point inward to the game as well as outward to the environing world, they will stress the fact that what had gone before was a distinctive, significant event which all are to leave for other tasks and other places.

There is something amiss when spectators leave before the end of a game. Even when the score is lopsided players in a real game continue until the end. Spectators should follow their example. But minor athletes do not merit that consideration; they are more like men in rehearsal, to be watched only as long as we like.

Before closure time arrives players and sometimes spectators normally go through various rituals. These are prescribed forms of action serving to equalize conditions, to renew the acknowledgment of common ends or values, or to endorse some entrenched custom. Football teams interchange their positions at the end of each quarter; wrestlers start each try from a set position; baseball spectators stretch at the seventh inning. These practices, so far as they involve the players and are rigidly adhered to, are something like the practices which conform to the rules of a game. They differ in that a ritual is usually begun and ended by an official, and that an avoidance or distortion of it either cancels the game or entails no penalty. It is one thing to accept a game as a distinctive domain, which is what ceremony and ritual underscore, and another to act inside the confines of a game, which is what is done when one conforms to the rules of the game. The acceptance is an all or none affair; rule-abiding action has degrees measured by rulings and penalties.

When Baron de Coubertin revived the Olympic Games —or more accurately, when he created Olympic Games for modern times—he saw to it that there were ceremonies not only at the beginning but at the end of the games, and that there were ritualistic acknowledgments of victories throughout. Despite the fact that he was most anxious to give the games an international or non-nationalistic character, however, he left them with an apparently indelible nationalistic import. Today they are overwhelmingly nationalistic in tone. Not only are men permitted to compete in the Olympics only if they are sanctioned by a country, but they parade and are honored at the games as members of particular nations. Scoring, to be sure, is not kept on a national basis at the Olympic Games, but the omission is amply compensated for by the press and in the way the awards are given.

Only citizens of a country are eligible to wear the colors of that country in the Olympic Games. It is not permissible for a competitor having once worn the colors of a country in the Olympic Games or World or Area Games or Championships to wear those of another country in future games. The exception to this rule is when his former country has been incorporated into another State, or if he wore the colors of the former country because his native land had, at that time, no National Olympic Committee, or after he has become naturalized and a period of at least three years has passed since he applied for naturalization, or in the case of a woman, when she has taken new nationality by marriage.[1]

Every game, like every dance, theatrical performance, and historical event, has its own distinctive time, space, and dynamics. It is a unity with distinguishable divisions, each occupying a unit of time, covering a portion of space, carrying out a unit causal process, and serving to bring about the realization of some prospect. It is a single occurrence in which there are a number of parts, any one of which can be designated and even held apart from the others in thought and sometimes in fact. No one of these parts is a game, any more than a part of a horse is a horse. But each separated part, like the whole, occurs in a distinctive present unit of time. That they are produced by going through a number of moves and acts in sequence does not affect the fact that each has an indivisible, unit, temporal

1   *Quadrennial Review*, Period of 1961–65, U. S. Olympic Committee (Washington, D. C., 1966).

span. Before the separation the parts, like their contained moves and acts, have no time of their own; they are then contained in a larger unit present.

A round in amateur boxing is two minutes, in professional boxing three. In those minutes blows are interchanged, and a man may be knocked down and get up a number of times. The blows occur one later than the other; the man must get up before ten seconds pass. Each occurrence takes place in a present moment, the only time when anything can occur. But because the round is itself a present occurrence, it too must take place in a present moment, stretching over the interchange of blows. The round itself, in turn, must exist both in its own present and in the present of the match. It has a relation to the entire boxing match similar to that which the interchange of blows has to it.

A number of short present occurrences are ordered as parts inside a single present contest or game. The fact is not widely acknowledged because we time our athletic events, as has already been remarked, by watches which have no particular pertinence to what happens in a game, geared as they are to the passage of astronomical bodies.

He who attends only to the parts will never come to know the whole. To be sure, if he does not attend to the parts at all, he also will not come to know the whole. Knowing a game is knowing the parts in the context of the whole, where they are related as before and after one another.

Each of the occurrences is a distinct, indivisible unit when treated apart from the encompassing game, but loses its distinctness when it has the role of only a part in that game. Within the indivisible present of a game the parts take place in a sequential order. Those that precede condition and offer a background for those that succeed. Conversely, the succeeding parts are anticipated by those that precede. What is not yet is only a shadow, but it casts that shadow over what comes before or is actually earlier than it is.

Each game is a unit in a history of sport. That history is built up, not by going through a series of acts, but by adding game to game. Each of the games has its own tonality, affected by but not necessarily mirroring the character of the activities that occur within its confines. The activities or the game, both or neither, may be dramatic. If the activities are vital and arresting the game may still be dull, and conversely. Whatever tonalities characterize either the activities or the game may also be experienced in the same or modified forms by the participants. The spectators, meanwhile, may experience something similar or something quite different.

Players and spectators rarely know the whole game as it exists in fact, any more than those who produce or watch great historic events grasp exactly what occurred. To know what happened it is necessary to reconstruct an occurrence by converging on it from many angles, balancing the different reports and evidences with one another. It takes a sensitive reporter to sense what in fact occurred. But the players and some of the spectators see something the reporter often does not—what the game is for one deeply involved in it.

Innovations in rules are sometimes made in games and are later sanctioned and codified. Football, as was remarked, once did not make provision for the forward pass. The first forward pass, therefore, had an indeterminate status until the throw had been ruled upon by officials. They could have penalized the innovator; they could have allowed the pass; or they could, as they did, give it a place in the sport of football. Ruled to be legitimate, the forward pass became a regular part of the sport. The throwing of the ball, of course, takes place only in a game. An innovation in the game, and an occurrence only there, it is an act now permitted by the rules which define the sport of football.

The parts of a game and the acts in it not only take time to occur; they also cover a space. That space is distinct from the field in which the game is placed. The field is a bounded portion of space used for a game; the rules of the game turn it into the space of the game. The individuals and the teams intensify and restructure that space by their play. The space of a game, consequently, changes in geometry as the game progresses. At every moment and in every region it has a distinctive buckle and tension, a peculiar curvature affecting the action that takes place in it. We do not, therefore, know what is taking place if all we see are men spread out on the field and interacting with one another there. A proper grasp of a game requires some understanding of the way the participants contour it by making it the locus of many lines of force and the source of multiple radiations from themselves.

Each team has its own space. Neither severally nor together are the spaces of the teams identical with the space of the game. That space is distinct from the space of either and of both, being inseparable from the game's characteristic, indivisible, present moment in which the teams interplay.

The space of a team is the space which the members together constitute by their attitudes, expectations, actions, and reactions. The members of a basketball team are interrelated in a continuously modified space which relates them intimately to one another, even when they are at different parts of the court. They constitute a spatiotemporal group in which the members are more closely together than they are to the members of the other team, who may in fact be physically closer to them.

The space of a game like the space of a team, has a distinctive geometry in which distances are measured in terms of the relevance of acts to one another, and not by means of a ruler marking off feet and inches. A yard to the goal post is a different kind of yard from a yard at the center of the field, even apart from the fact that it permits of only some of the moves that would be appropriate otherwise.

Were there no time and space characteristic of a team (or a game), particularly when it is playing, its activities could be treated as the distinct acts of individuals which we later recollected in tranquility and there gave a single name. We would then have to say that there had been no team play—indeed that nothing in fact was done. The only reality would be an infinitesimal moment in an infinitesimal space which was filled by an infinitesimal state, quickly followed by another, and so on. All that we saw and enjoyed would have to be called an illusion. It seems perverse, though, to take games to be illusions, while treating infinitesimals as genuine realities. The one is evident and experienced, while the other is experienced by no one, and could conceivably have no existence.

The special talents and achievements of individuals on a team are subordinated to the work of all. Individuals are there pulled outside themselves and made to function within a larger whole. They may continue to be as fast or as strong as they had been, but what they do and can achieve will depend in part on what the others on the team do and will do.

A man may go out on a golf course and play a round by himself. He will then either be practicing or will be assuming for himself the role of an impersonal referee. If he is merely practicing, he may repeat a stroke, be careless about the score, nudge his ball a bit, or refuse to try an easy or a difficult shot. If he is not practicing, he will be as strict with himself as he would be were he in a contest where he would be judged impartially, and the result reported without question. And since he will, even though living through his problems as a man alone, have in mind the powers and defects of other golfers, he will also in effect be playing with them while he is playing by himself. But he will not be playing on a team. This requires him to be in direct, coordinated interplay with other men.

Alone, a man usually makes his activities turn in a circle about himself. When he plays on a team he carries out a role in relation to the roles others assume. As a consequence, he functions on behalf of all the members of his team. Not until he actually plays with others as part of a team, however, does he face up to what they can do, what they are doing, and what they will do. The response and even the presence of others involves contingencies no one can entirely anticipate.

Each player must keep within prescribed confines, but in such a way that his activities continue to be appropriate. The sonnet's tight demands make the poet call on his reserves; a similar result is produced when a player carries out his role. That role both enriches and limits. It lifts him up into a context of traditions, obligations, and ideals, thereby transforming him into one who is now to live through a new, distinctive career.

A role is an intersection point between receiving and giving, between rights and duties, acceptances and demands. It entrains functions that have a place in a totality of tasks which all the participants together are to carry out. The tasks and their place are usually stated in the description, and in the rules and regulations, of the sport. A first basemen ordinarily does not tag a batter who is running to the base, but a third baseman usually does. Each acts in terms of the way in which others have already acted and are expected to act out their respective roles. The third baseman does not merely catch the ball; he catches it to tag and to throw.

Each member of a team acts in terms of, as well as for, all the rest. No individual can, therefore, ever rightly be said to be solely responsible for a team score. The players together constitute a team which, with the other team, produces the unit occurrence, a play in a game. It would be foolish, of course, to deny that in many a game we see serious blunders and spectacular saves. A man might drop a crucial fly; he might commit a cardinal error; he might happen to hit the puck at the right time.

No team can ever rightly be said to be alone the cause of what happens in a game. It is equally wrong to deny that all players, even the great stars, are sustained by others on their team, and that their acts are produced in interplay with those on the other team. We chalk up failures and achievements against or for individual players, but what they do is only at the forefront of a host of other acts, produced by the members of both teams, all of which are essential parts of the game that is in fact being played. The final result is the issue of an interlocking of acts on the part of a number of men, each engaged in carrying out his role in the light of the way others carry and are expected to carry out their rules.

If some role, play, or individual is remarked upon at

the expense of the others, what occurs is misconstrued and the nature of sport confused. Writers, commentators, and spectators too often make this error. In effect they repeat the mistake characteristic of those political columnists who, for the sake of drama and the arousal of interest, speak as though the operation of a state was due solely to the head of it. Yet the most complete dictator has to allow decisions, even those of major importance, to be made by others. He has not the information, the time, the opportunity, or the experience to decide most questions, even those which he publicly takes upon himself to answer. For somewhat similar reasons, the greatest of stars must be supported by teammates. If he insists on himself he not only falsifies the situation but will soon find his performances qualified and sometimes nullified by them.

There are gifted athletes who do not function well as members of a team. They listen to no one and proceed at their own pace. There are also mediocre players who are excellent teammen. But the first must fit in to some degree, and the second must do something on their own. Ideally, a player must be at once an individual, with a distinctive pace and flair, and a member of a team meshing with the rest.

No matter how thoroughly a role is practiced in private it will be carried out in a novel way under the novel conditions produced in the course of an actual game. A role supports and is supported by others; what is produced by all is lived through by each, and what each does contributes to a single result for all. In team play, speed, endurance, strength, and accuracy also find a place. The test that team play offers, though, is not of skills, but of the power of each individual to be a whole man while functioning as part of a moving congress of men, producing through their several unrehearsed acts the single event we call a contest or a game.

Some teams are tightly organized; the members of a college crew and of some college football teams eat and live together for the entire school year. Other teams emphasize the overall effect, without compromising the fact that they are made up of individuals carrying out distinctive acts.

Crew and tug of war submerge the individual almost entirely. But there are teams that are fairly loosely knit; the members of college baseball teams are rather independent of one another. But all are teams in which individuals have a place, and where all the individuals must be seen as together constituting the game and its characteristic parts.

Ideally, in every game each player functions on behalf of all the members of his team as well as in terms of the positions and actions of all the playing members of the opposing team. Team play is the outcome of an adjustment of each to all. In it the self-awareness which the presence of opponents provides is overlaid with the awareness of the roles they assume and how they fill them. At the same time, there is an awareness of what the individual is supposed to do and of the relationhip he has to the others. Leonard Koppett, in his perspective book, makes these points evident again and again.

Assume that I [a fielder] am properly placed and the ball is hit to me. Assume that I handle it flawlessly. What must I do with it? I'm supposed to know: 1. The speed of the batter going to first. 2. The speed of all base runners. 3. The needs of the strategic situation; must a potential tying run be cut off at home? at third? at second? Is a possible double play more important than a lead runner? Is the chance of throwing out the man going from first to third good enough to risk the batter's reaching second? 4. . . . where will my best play be if the ball is hit slowly? sharply? to the extremities of my range, right and left? How much can I get on the ball throwing off balance? 5. The capabilities of my teammates. . . . What base do I cover? What sort of help can I give to some other fielder? [2]

Similar observations are made by him with reference to the other positions on a baseball team. Analogous studies could be made of other sports. There should be "A Thinking Man's Guide" for them as well.

Each game has its own dynamics. There unit act is followed by unit act. Those acts exist only in the game. The parts of the act are inseparable from it though they

[2] Leonard Koppett, *A Thinking Man's Guide to Baseball* (New York, 1967), p. 71.

can be conceptually separated out, and even learned and practiced as moves and acts having indivisible unities of their own. A bunt is a single occurrence involving a tap of the bat and a run to first, and a player who snaps up the ball to throw it. That bunt can be a cause of another act involving the next batter, a man on base, and any one of a number of relevant plays.

In sport the largest present is the present of the game. In this we can isolate plays and moves only conceptually. The bunt and any other play is an organic, integral factor in the present indivisible whole of the game. The plays are, of course, also distinct units—as are the moves they encompass—each with its own present. There is no more mystery here than there is in the fact that I am an individual with inalienable rights and duties, and also an integral part of a family having its own rights and duties.

Spectators live through a game in one way, and players in another. Sometimes there is an interaction between them, but on the whole it is what the players do that helps determine how the spectators will behave, rather than conversely. If the spectators interact with the players and therby affect the course of the game, the game cannot, of course, be treated as the production of the players alone.

The earlier parts of a game force a player to do one thing rather than another later. In addition, what his opponents now do and are about to do dictates how he is to proceed. Since each player assumes a particular role and internalizes all the other roles within himself—a point forcibly made by George H. Mead [3]—each blurs the distinction between himself and the others as helping produce the game and as constituted by it.

While they are playing a game, players are effectively outside the grip of their coaches. This does not mean that the coaches have nothing to do during the course of a game. In some sports, such as baseball, coaches constantly shout instructions. In others, such as football, though they are not supposed to intrude themselves or their advice, it is

3 George H. Mead, *Mind, Self, and Society: From the Standpoint of a Social Behaviorist*, ed. Charles W. Morris (Chicago, 1934), p. 151.

a common practice for them to use replacements as mes-
sengers. Some of the coaches even manage to signal their
desires surreptitiously to the players. Yet no matter how
much advice they give, and no matter how much they try
to influence the nature of the playing by their observations,
criticisms, signals, and replacements, what they do is at
best only suggestive and remedial.

A game is played through by the participants, leaving
the coaches to be more like spectators than players. Unlike
the spectators, of course, the coaches have an effect on the
strategy and tactics, the composition of the team, and
sometimes on what in fact is done. But only the players
play, and thereby make both themselves and a game. As
the spectators often do, the coaches, however, may lose
themselves in the game. But the game is exactly where the
players find themselves.

Much of what takes place in American games, particularly on the college and professional levels, becomes a
matter of record. Sometimes records are also kept in high
schools, in clubs, and by individuals. The practice is occasionally taken to be a consequence of a distinctive American belief that each man has an equal right with every
other to show just what he can do, while acting as a
surrogate for all the rest. This cannot be correct. We have
only very recently broken down the color bar in team sport,
and thus have only recently been willing to see what an
American, no matter how complexioned, might do. Nor
should we forget that other nations, some rather undemo-
cratic and anti-American, also keep good records. Granted
that Americans are more record-conscious than others—
which is far from being evidently true—it is tempting to
attribute the practice in part to the pressure of publicity
that we put on every great achievement, and in part to the
fact that it helps satisfy a democratic need to gossip. A
more plausible reason takes more account of the nature of
records. They have a definiteness and a finality to them
which a casteless society might need in order to make
evident who is superior and who inferior in native gifts and
promise.

Records enable us to compare athletes; by pointing up

their comparative strengths and weaknesses the records make it possible to correct and improve their plays. More important: all of us have a desire to know and fixate the supreme achievements of those whom we take to represent us, and this knowledge our records provide. But it is possible to over-emphasize the value of records. This, particularly when combined with a focusing on individual members of a team, can lead to a perversion of the meaning of team play. We run that risk in baseball. There each player is dealt with as a unit beside whose name is placed the number of times he has hit successfully, the times he has helped put a man out, the times he has made an error, and so on. Despite a reference to assists, runs batted in, and other team plays, the impression is conveyed that baseball is produced by eighteen players, each of whom plays and is judged as an individual. But each player in baseball, as well as elsewhere, ideally acts in terms of the others, both on his own team and on the opposing team.

Action alone does not make one a participant. He who merely runs down the field after a ball does not yet play soccer, rugby, lacrosse, or football. He does not score even if he gets the ball to the goal line. His action must be in accord with the rules of the game. In a true game, as has already been noted, rules guide and are embodied in the actions by which the game is brought from its beginning to its end.

No matter what their source or how learned, rules are exemplified in the form of commands obeyed, conditions met, and options and permissions accepted. They tell referees and other officials, the players, and the spectators how a game is to begin, how it is to proceed, and how it is to end. They may have been initially learned from books or by imitating others. Sometimes rules are mastered in the course of playing games, but the well-trained athlete usually has come to embody them through practice, well before he enters into serious competition.

Rarely does an athlete enter into a game without first having tested himself again and again in private, to see just how well he compares with himself at a previous time, and with others, past and present. In those private tests he usually controls many of the factors that are outside his reach when he engages in a public struggle with opponents who at times take the initiative and respond in ways he cannot altogether anticipate.

A game is rule-dominated and tradition-laden, demanding dedication, an appropriate set of skills, and, ideally, considerable training and practice. In it men are tested together with others. Each, acting against opposition, there offers public witness of the degree to which he has mastered himself, situations, rules, and other men. It is there that he discovers what his powers and limitations are, ostensibly as a body but in fact as a man. It is there that he makes evident how excellent he can be under circumstances not altogether under his control, and subject to a public evaluation by acknowledged judges.

A public struggle entrains a public evaluation. The prospect of that evaluation challenges the athlete in ways that he had not been challenged before. He may, therefore, falter; or he may extend himself to a degree that no one thought possible. Sometimes he does both. As a consequence, he performs unevenly, occasionally falling below and occasionally going beyond the kind of performances he previously produced. Some of the fluctuations he can avoid by good planning, based on an understanding of what kind of situations he might be reasonably expected to encounter. In advance of a participation in a game, he might find it desirable to become familiar with the terrain and to rehearse the weaknesses and strengths of his opposition. If wise, he will give thought to his own typical weaknesses and errors. There is some advantage gained by him if he is able to imagine the effect, on himself and the rest, of the crowd, of its cheering and jeering, and even of the tensions and pressures that might develop in the course of a well-conducted game. He will not, of course, thereby be able to anticipate every move and every act on the part of others; he will not even know just what he himself will do, particularly if the game is severely contested.

We do not, we cannot, know what others will do, in part because we do not know them well enough and in part because they act with freedom and spontaneity, both in initiating actions and in reacting to ours. We, in turn, are unknown to them; we too act with freedom and spontaneity as initiators and in our reactions. They do not exactly know what to expect of us. This double indeterminacy produced by both of us is compounded by the contingency of untoward conditions, by inaccuracy in play, by errors, and by dramatic saves. All conspire to make a game a sequence of unexpected crises.

A report of what occurred is necessarily abstract and set within a linguistic frame. A score is just some numbers. To know what happens in a game one must see it, live through it, be part of the process by which indeterminacies and contingencies are used to produce single, definite plays.

Young men can use their excess energy in many ways. If they properly participate in games their energy is spelled out effectively, in part along the lines they had been habituated to follow and in part along the lines which good play demands. Before that time they can be put through their paces under conditions which simulate those of an actual game. Boxers use sparring partners who imitate the style of the expected opponents; a first team can be opposed by a second, assuming something of the postures of the first's next opponent. But there is no escaping the decisiveness of the public contest: here and here only is where the game is played.

What is tested is not what a man abstractly is and can ideally do, but what he is and can do in a game. It is quite possible that he may perform poorly in public. It is quite possible that he may perform better, and even be a better man, when not participating in a game. But what we want to know is how good he and his team are when publicly tested, what happens when they act in a not wholly predetermined set of situations. He who does not measure up in public to what he has shown himself to be capable of doing in private frequently exposes a defect in himself. Usually it is a defect of character. His failure may, however, reflect only a mistaken judgment or a misconception of the nature and acts of the opponent. Sometimes all that it testifies to is just bad luck.

Not everything is allowed in a game. Provisions are made to eliminate many possible indeterminacies, by requiring field, weather, and men to meet certain requirements before the game can proceed. Records, since they record what happens in public and not elsewhere, consequently tell us, not what the best possible performance is under ideal circumstances, but the best possible performance under certain specified conditions.

We take it for granted, as we do in most practical affairs, that in a limited number of games the laws of chance will conform to the mathematical formulae appropriate to a great number of items in the long run. We believe that "bad breaks" will be matched by equally fortuitious but favorable opportunities, if not in that particular game, then in another, or over a series. There is no logical warrant for this belief. It has only the sanction of the practical judgment that if the laws of chance do not operate in this way, there is a bias in ourselves or the situation toward some particular outcome. Our readiness to accept the results of publicly contested games, despite their inescapable unpredictability, testifies to our conviction that all chances will have their day, and as a consequence that the play of luck cancels out any advantage or disadvantage after a while.

A single game does not often allow a man to show all that he knows, all the skill he has mastered, all the judgment and flexibility that he has in reserve. It is not often that he can there make use of the whole of his experience or every bit of his energy. When the opposition that he faces is not too taxing, he may be able to perform superbly without being superb. Occasionally, he may be given opportunities to display a brilliance and a power which no one expected that he had. But over the course of many games and over the course of his career, he is identified by himself and by us with what he does. What he exhibits himself to be in games is what he is as an athlete. Outside the game he is at most an athlete of promise; in this or that game he may be ill-used or a prey to bad fortune. As athlete he is nothing more and nothing less than what he has manifested himself to be over the course of his career.

Even if one were to reject the assumption that a long enough series of games will necessarily exhibit the chance distributions which a mathematical formula presents, one can accept the games as a test of a man as an athlete, since he is an athlete only in the games that he plays. Should circumstance or bad luck prevent him from doing all that he conceivably might, we could say of him that he might have been a better athlete than he has shown himself to be. But we cannot rightly say that he in fact is a better athlete than he has proved himself to be, for it is only in the proving of himself that he shows what kind of athlete he is. And it is only in the games in which he participates that his proving occurs.

The particular perspective which an athlete or his team has on the game makes it difficult for either to grasp just what happened there. It would be too much to expect participants to see what things look like from the position of the opponents or even from a position that is neutral to both sides. Fortunately, though, the game has an objectivity and a rationale distinct from the men, the teams, or the plays that help constitute it. The objective reality, presumably, is what the appointed officials report.

Since competitors cannot wholly see or wholly grasp the objective nature of what happens, no matter how fair-minded and reflective they are, there is always something amiss when they dispute with the officials—except of course where this is part of a ritual or a way of calling attention to correctable mistakes in judgment. There is, perhaps, an element of pleasing the crowd in some coach's angry protestations at unfavorable or close decisions. Such exhibitions of real or feigned anger sometimes make players feel that the coach is deeply concerned with their success, or at the very least, is interested in seeing that justice is done. Sometimes a protest offers a number of players an opportunity to express themselves as a united group. As a consequence of a protest a team may exert extra effort, being buoyed up by the defense or by a momentary exhibition of solidarity. Occasionally, too, players see something the official referees miss; like everyone else judges also make mistakes.

I do not think that the benefits justify the violent questioning of those who have been placed in the authoritative position of ruling on just what public, objective result has been achieved. Ritualistic objections should not be allowed to obscure the nature of such important acts as official decisions. Crowd pleasing is, after all, the task of an entertainer, and not of a player, coach, or other mentor. Players can surely be stimulated and encouraged in other and perhaps more effective ways than by getting them to bait the umpire, or by having their coach do it. As a matter of fact, in baseball, where protests are common,

Even if one stands in the front of the dugout instead of sitting down, unless one gets up on the top step, parts of the field will not be visible. This fact, known to all, seriously undermines the position of a manager or player when he argues with an umpire.[4]

Few disputes ever end in a change in the referee's decisions. In any case, the very nature of the sport and the meaning of judge are jeopardized every time there is a real argument, or even a sincere protest against an unfavorable decision. One should take toward the decisions the kind of attitude that one takes with respect to the luck of a game. One should assume that the bad judgments by officials will eventually balance, and that in any case what is being discovered is what a man can do in the conditions which in fact prevail, whether these conditions be shifts in weather or the fallibility of judges.

One of the glories of college sports is that its participants rarely argue with judges, referees, or scorers. Spectators, however, too often protest, and then violently. They thereby reflect their identification with one side or the other, and their consequent lack of objectivity with respect to the game. Men's reputations, and in professional sports their livelihood, depends on their records, but there are professional sports, such as basketball and football, where this fact is not thought to be inconsistent with the acceptance of official decisions in silence. If accurate statements of what did in fact occur are to be provided, and if objec-

4 Koppett, p. 131.

tive resolutions of the conflicts of judgment that arise between contestants are to be obtained, it is necessary to ignore the spectators, and to acknowledge and preserve the right of appointed judges to make the final decisions for both sides.

All officials have the duty to interpret and to defend the rules, and the right to refuse to listen to protests. Coaches, ideally, are also officials. They are not merely in charge of one set of contestants. They are representatives of all. It is their privilege and obligation to be living symbols of the objective rationale of a game.

Both sides should be judged by the same criteria because, from the perspective of the game, all are on a par. Indeed, the teams are supposed to be evenly matched. This, of course, is paradox, for it is one of the objects of a game to make evident the superiority of one side over the other. The paradox can be overcome by supposing that the game brings a hidden superiority into the open, or by supposing that the game adds a condition which enables one to differentiate between those who otherwise would be equal. On the first supposition, the game offers a means for making finer discriminations than were possible before. On the second supposition, the game provides a new factor in terms of which new distinctions are made.

We are offered a choice here between holding that individuals and teams are fully determinate, apart from the game—though our ignorance may prevent us from knowing how they differ and by how much—and holding that individuals and teams are partly indeterminate but are to be made more determinate in the course of a game, where they will produce the desired differences in merit. The alternatives seem to be exclusive, but it is possible, I think, to combine them. Men and teams are less determinate than the first supposition allows, but more determinate than the second does. Something happens in a game; there men and teams are made, reconstituted, redefined, but a game also reveals skills, talents, and powers that are actually possessed by the participants. Hidden superiorities come to light at the same time that new ones are produced.

Sometimes men, who have proven themselves to be superior to others, fail to exhibit that superiority in a particular game. A side, which has shown itself to be superior on other occasions may, in the course of becoming determinate through the playing of a particular game, reveal itself to be inferior to the other at that time. An upset occurs. Without exaggerating the importance of a victory, we must grant that a victorious team, by its victory, proves that it is superior to the other.

To leave a game it is necessary only to be free of the game's conventions and rules. When the victors (and vanquished) leave the game they do not go through an activity which is a mere reciprocal of what had been done to enter it or to share in it. But if instead of merely leaving the game, they end it, they go through a reciprocal of what was done to begin it. The ending occurs, not by stopping to conform to the conditions set down for the game, but by fulfilling the requirements for playing in the game. Whether they leave or end the game, the players of course move from it to a domain where the rules of that game no longer prevail.

A player can leave the field, without leaving the game. That is what a baseball player does when he returns to the dugout. One can even be pulled from a game, as a hockey player sometimes is, and be made to sit in a penalty box. So long as the player remains in that box in a prescribed way, he is a participant in the game, as is evident from the fact that he is required by the game's official to stay in the box for a certain amount of time, and that, during the penalty time, he is forbidden to behave as some spectators do.

Participating in a game is evidently not the same thing as conforming to its rules; nor is it identical with being active in the game. He who sits on the sidelines of a football game neither participates in nor is active in the game. Yet he conforms to some of the game's rules. A penalized hockey player is not active but does participate, while one who is active but does not participate is just movng in the area reserved for the game. Periods of rest and periods in which players are excluded because of some infraction of the rules are like the silences which separate the sounds in a musical piece; they are constituents of the whole, serving to space what is active and focal.

The objective of a contest or game cannot be separated

from the time, space, or causality, or from the kind of acts in which the individuals and teams engage. The objective differs from sport to sport, but not from contest to contest, or from game to game. In baseball it is "more runs than the opponent," in hockey it is "more goals than the opponent," in sailboat racing it is "the fastest possible time." The objective is particularized by the individuals and the teams in each contest or game, to become an objective that is appropriate in the circumstances that prevail.

Games are concrete "therefores," in which a series of decisive acts yield a specific realization of a particularized objective. To realize that objective the players must try to be victorious. That fact brings us to one of the most controversial issues of sport—the place that the desire to win occupies in the athlete's motivation and activity.

11.   the urge to win

A GAME incorporates an "agon"—hence our "agony,"—a struggle. It entrains fatigue, sometimes exhaustion, and almost always some discomfort. The emotions it involves are subject to control and are not, as they sometimes are in ordinary life, allowed to come out explosively. But they are expressed with comparatively little modulation, and consequently not so sensitively as they are in the creation of art.

Victory is what is normally signalized at the close of a game. This seems to be characteristic of games in every epoch and in every place.

The romantics exaggerated and thereby falsified the Greek outlook on sport; they supposed that the Greeks viewed victory in a spirit quite different from our own. Nothing base or vulgar was supposed to cross the Greek mind. The victors, we were taught to believe, were content to receive a mere wreath; the spectators also behaved admirably, applauding all those who won fairly in a clear exhibition of excellence. But as Erich Segal has observed,

The single aim in all Greek athletics was—as the etymology (from athion, "prize") suggests—to win. There were no awards for second place; in fact losing was considered a disgrace. . . . It is generally believed that wars were suspended so that the Greeks could hold their Olympic Games. But no Greek historian ever mentions such an armistice, nor is there any evidence that fighting abated during Olympic years. . . . The ancient Olympic victor may have won merely a simple wreath, but when he returned to his home town, gifts were lavished upon him, and he usually received an income for life.[1]

1   Erich Segal, "It is Not Strength, But Art, Obtains the Prize," *The Yale Review*, LVI, No. 4 (June 1967), 606, 607, 608.

The cry, "It is not the winning, but the taking part, not the conquering, but the playing fair" [2] (attributed to Baron de Coubertin), is not the ancient view. The Greeks found room for and apparently approved of trickery and cunning. [3] What the Greeks practiced, we practice in a muted form. Like theirs, our athletes also strive to win.

If a player would win, he should try to win, should strive to win, should want to win. To obtain maximum results in a game, he must give himself to it. He can then sometimes come close to getting what he desires. And this he will do if he is a true athlete.

The athlete must have a strong urge to defeat his opponent, and must carry out that urge in the form of actions which will enable him to outdistance all. This requires him to be aggressive. Man's aggression, as has already been remarked, is thought by some to exhibit in a vigorous but harmless form an inescapable but dangerous aggressiveness characteristic of us all. Aggression, on this view, is part of man's very nature, rooted deep in the unconscious, in the history of the race, and in the early experiences of the child. It is always and inevitably expressed; mankind is fortunate in having found ways for releasing it without much injury to anyone.

So much aggression seems to be expressed in games that to many an observer a game appears to be like a war, that outstanding example of aggressiveness. Though some sports seem to have been invented to promote physical fitness, skill, and dexterity, or for the purpose of using up surplus energy enjoyably, others—archery, fencing, shooting, judo, evidently, and conceivably boxing, wrestling, dressage, running, weight lifting, and the relay—have instead a military origin or a military objective. These, and perhaps others, refine and promote activities which are parts of the art of war. The fact has tempted some to think of games as a substitute for war. If they were, hopefully they might some day usurp the place that war has assumed in what we like to call "the civilized world." Unfortunately, it does not appear that there is much ground for

2 *Ibid.*, 608. 3 *Ibid.*, 606.

that expectation, in part because war and game are quite distinct in nature, and in the role they give to aggressiveness.

Both war and game aim at victory. Both usually end in a clearly evidenced superiority of one side over the other, though draws and stalemates are not unknown. Only games *must* conform to rules, though in modern times we try to make wars conform to them too. But it is paradoxical to expect both sides in a war to submit to common rules. Each side seeks to annihilate the other; it would be foolish for either to allow its efforts to be restrained or blocked by an effort to conform to rules it has agreed, with its enemy, to abide by. A genuine war is a ruthless affair, paying for victory with the lives of men and the destruction of property and works of art. Omnivorous, it sweeps away for the time any meaning to a common acceptance of any rule, and jeopardizes every civilized value. If the antagonists could agree upon anything one would expect them to agree to stop the war; when advantage is thought of in terms of what life is and what gives it value, war is evidently to the advantage of neither. It is because they can find no basis for agreement that they go to war seriously, with the intent to render the enemy impotent and sometimes even to destroy him utterly. Wars begin with a disagreement precluding the acceptance of common rules.

Men poised to destroy one another cannot, except foolishly and futilely, agree on conforming to certain rules. There is no punishment which the violators of rules need fear. If they win no one will punish them, and if they lose their loss is inseparable from whatever punishment they thereby suffer. The loser could be punished, over and above what is normally the case, because of his violations of a supposed agreement made in happier days, but since the punishment is meted out by the victor, as he sees fit, it is arbitrary to claim that a closer adherence to the rules would have resulted in a less severe punishment. Only where it is the object of a war to restrain or warn is there much point in keeping to common rules.

It is possible, and it may even be desirable, to act aggressively toward others in a game, but one must, to play with them, act with good will. An intent to cripple and destroy goes counter to the purpose of a game. The aggressiveness exhibited in it is an aggressiveness which conforms to rules, or one is doing violence to the game.

The soldier seeks victory. He must be aggressive. Of course, without a strong desire to defeat his opponent, no athlete can have much hope of victory either. He, too, insists on himself. But there is too much self-sacrifice, humility, team play, together with an acceptance of official neutral decisions and a conformity to objectively stated and applied prescriptions, to make the expression of aggression represent the primary or essential goal, or the motive for athletic activity.

The Geneva conventions and the Red Cross offer limits beyond which one is asked not to go. He who accepts them does so, more likely than not, because he fears retaliation. He then lives through a rule-dominated, traditionalized, conventionalized interlude in the life of mankind, and so far participates in a game which, like a bullfight, takes crippling and death to be prospects not alien to its intent. Nevertheless, a war cannot be taken to be only a game. War and game are distinct both in fact and in theory. The two have different times, spaces, causalities, objectives, and tests. Their origins, procedures, and intentions rarely coincide. Both may accept common rules and follow agreed-upon conventions. But if they do, they do so for different reasons.

The time of a game is cut off from the rest of time to make it the sequential measure of an island of occurrences, having little commerce with the main. The time of a war is a special time, entraining a host of new issues and occurrences, but it is a time which is nevertheless continuous with the time of normal politics and the interaction of various nations. War, it has rightly been said, is politics continued by other means. But a game is only a game.

The geometry of a space is constituted by the kind of roles, positions, and functions which the men and other items in it carry out. Forwards and goalies constitute one type of space; lieutenants and privates constitute another. And each type of space is traversed by its own distinctive time. The space and time of a war differ in nature from those characteristic of a sport.

The causality characteristic of a game is intended to stop at its borders. Awards, injuries, reports, and records outlast the game, and have resonances outside it, but they do not carry the causality of the game outside the game itself. But the causality of a war has an effect on what takes place after the war is over; the actual fighting that goes on, the deployment of troops, the carrying out of a particular strategy all have effects outside the war. Where the one remains within a distinctive, causal, bounded domain, the other has a bearing on the rest of life.

We could, of course, speak of a game in economic, propagandistic, or heuristic terms. The causality begun in the game would then exemplify a causality characteristic of a larger process. Conversely, we could deal with a war as an isolated event, and see the causality characteristic of it as contrasting with the causality that dominates the peaceful world. Even then there would be more in common between the causality in and outside the war than there is between the causality operative in a game and the causality outside it.

A game's causality contrasts more sharply with the causality that environs it than does the war's, because the game, even when started without much thought or preparation, is the product of a deliberate bracketing and the imposition of commonly accepted rules, whereas a war, even for a nation at peace, without an army, suddenly assaulted by one bound on destroying or enslaving it, is continuous with daily life, both before and after. Bracketing and convention disconnect work and game; life and property connect peace and war.

The objectives and tests relevant to a game are different from those which characterize a war. What is sought in a game is a victory judged impersonally under agreed upon rules. What is sought in a war is victory in fact, expressed, not in some judgment given by an official, but in acts of submission to the victor. The objective of a war is a defeat of the enemy somehow. The objective of a game is the production of results acceptable to both sides. The road to victory in war is through the subjugation of men by injury or destruction, and the breaking of their economic, social, and political power. The road to victory in athletics is through the exhibition of excellence in men, even in those who are defeated.

At least one, and perhaps both sides involved in a war, stumble into it inadvertently, but a game is entered into deliberately by all the participants. Both sides in a war may have been prepared for it, but they enter into it at the same time, not because they agreed that this was most suitable for both, but because the actions of one compel a reaction by the other. A war has an aggressor who forces a response, but an athletic event is begun by both sides together. A game is entered into deliberately by all the participants, even though one side may have taken the initiative and challenged or provoked the other to participate. Were nations to agree to start a war together they would have agreed to share in a game where destruction of lives and property were hazards or objectives.

War has its strategies; it is best fought when there are plans. Nevertheless, it proceeds step by step from unpredictable result to unpredictable result. A game, in contrast, is organic, controlled in its movement by rules which dictate what is to be done so that men will be able to show how good they can be.

In a war there is constant improvization, but in a game improvization is limited by what the rules allow. There are generals who fight according to plans adopted from previous wars that were waged with signal victories, but those generals usually fight badly, following old practices that are unsuited to new conditions.

Wars are carried out against an enemy, and therefore against one toward whom it is proper to express hatred and to act with brutality. Games, instead, should begin and be carried out with a concern for the rights of others. Everything is allowed in a war if victory thereby results; a victor in a game is to be denied victory if there has been a failure to abide by some essential rule.

Defeat of another is the object of war. But victory of the better is what is to be sought in a game. A belligerent may gain little and in fact may suffer more than his enemy, but the surrender of the enemy is sufficient to define the other as the victor. Were a side in a war to refuse to yield to the demands of the other, it would so far not yet be defeated, even if it says that it has lost. But in a game, if officials decide that a side has lost, that is the end of the matter, whether it admits defeat or not.

War thrives on the possession of advantages in supply and power. A game, instead, demands an equilization of advantages. In order to bring about an equilization, the advantaged is sometimes handicapped just before the game begins. Sometimes an effort is made a long time before to equalize the strengths of the competitors. In professional baseball and football, teams at the bottom of the league are given the right of a first choice of new players in the yearly "draft," in an attempt to place the inferior teams on a footing with the others. There is no desire for and no attempt at such equilizations in war. One side might have been forced to fight in self-protection; it might fight desperately without hope of victory, content if it can stave off defeat for a while or inflict some punishment on those who harass it. Each side would like to have a better opportunity to come out victorious; neither cooperates with its opponent to make the war possible. No one sees to it that the two are given an opportunity to be on equal terms. A great power, of course, may help smaller ones to be in some equipoise with reference to their traditional enemies. It does this, though, to forestall a war. Were a war to begin, it would try to see that the advantages were on the side of those smaller powers which it then favors.

Normally, each of the warring sides believes itself to be possessed of signal virtues, powers, or deserts, warranting victory by it; it does nothing to make possible the emergence of the other side as victorious instead. But in a game, though one wants to win and tries to prevent the other from being victorious, it is desired that the other be strong enough that a victory by it can be reasonably expected. In a war opposition is to be crushed; it is only to be momentarily overcome in a game.

The victor in a war decides what to do with the defeated. But in modern times at least, the victor in a game does nothing to the loser. When defeat in a wrestling or jousting match can have death as a subsequent penalty, we no longer have a game but a special case of war. Death here is unlike death in a bull ring or during a boxing match, for in these it occurs as part of the contest; treated as a price to be exacted from the loser, it is exterior to the contest in the same way as the awarding of a medal or the election to some hall of fame is to the winner.

The victor in a war wants to keep the enemy in an inferior state after the war is over. But the victor in a game does not see the defeated as an enemy; he is not, therefore, to deal with him as an inferior after the game.

The structure of a war is constituted by sides in opposition; the structure of a game determines what the sides can be and do. A war is produced by antagonistic opponents, a game by cooperating opponents. In war each side states its own conditions and moves at its own pace, but in a game there are conditions to which both sides submit even though they may not be to the liking of either.

In war men are sometimes heroic. They are sometimes more noble there than they are anywhere else. Their heroism and nobility is a product of the exigencies of the war. It is not something striven for. We would that it were not necessary for such heroism and nobility to be expressed. But in a game this is what is wanted. The virtues that are displayed in it are the very virtues which the game is supposed to arouse, promote, make provision for, and sustain.

There are war games, and there are games that are warlike. A past war can be recaptured in a study and used as a model in teaching. Men can engage in sham attacks and repulsions. The models and the sham fighting are not parts of a true game; they are parts of a preliminary session, offering one opportunities to practice and to rehearse for the serious war business ahead. The most warlike of games, on the other hand, with its hard-fought victories, spontaneities, and improvizations, is not yet war. Men contest there not to see how much they can destroy, but to see how well they meet the test of being fulfilled men who have accepted their bodies, identified themselves with their equipment, and acted as representatives of all others.

Even if we are inordinately considerate in a war, we will not make it approximate the shape of a game. Nor will the most belligerent of players make a game approximate a state of war. The one is a serious enterprise casting its shadow over the whole of life; the other is a serious enterprise encapsulated by rules which bind and define an isolated domain.

It is possible to speak, with some benefit, of a game as a battle carried out in another way, provided only that the differences between the two are not then blurred. Yet such blurring will most likely occur if we are not exceptionally alert to the great difference there is between using material advantages according to one's will, and having matched competitors follow out agreed upon rules, and if we to not attend to the even greater difference that exists between those who aim to injure or destroy their opponents and their property, and those who seek to determine who is the better, and therefore the representative of a better man.

Even the defeated gain from a game. They benefit from the mere fact that they have engaged in a contest, that they have encountered a display of great skill, that they have made the exhibition of that skill possible or desirable, that they have exerted themselves to the limit, and that they have made a game come to be. New technologies are sometimes produced under the pressure of war; possible dictators may be given pause; law and order may be reinstituted with considerable effectiveness as a consequence of a resounding victory. The results of war may benefit both sides eventually, but it will take a long while, if ever, for these gains to overbalance the irreparable, irreversible loss which the war produces in men, creativity, inquiry, and sheer joyous existence.

Games are desirable, but war is regrettable. A war hurts even the victors. They too must pay in some loss of life and property, and must turn away from their primary task of promoting civilization through the encouragement of art, science, and commerce, to deal instead with what they take to be obstacles in the way.

A good deal of sport can serve as an attractive means

for preparing men to become warriors. Our service academies see this; they take athletics to offer an opportunity for
training men to meet that final, crucial test which war
provides. Sport does promote physical fitness, and physical
fitness is an almost indispensable precondition for success
in battle, particularly when it is long drawn out and hotly
contested. But no one really knows whether some other
kind of preparation would not have been better; nor is it
unreasonable to suppose that there are advantages, beyond
that of promoting fitness, which sport gives to the prospective officer.

There is just as much plausibility to the argument that
the service academies' involvement in sport has no particular pertinence to the activities in which their men will
participate as there is in the argument that the sports of
other institutions have a special relevance to a possible
warrior's career. When the service academies compete
with other institutions they in fact show the same fine
spirit that the others do. They are then no more aggressive
or warlike, and are just as considerate toward their opponents as those who do not take themselves to be preparing
for, substituting for, or imitating actual combat. The service academies rightly encourage their men to know mathematics, poetry, and philosophy, not because this will make
them better able to fight or even to lead, but because these
subjects presumably contribute to the making of better
men. The same reasons suffice to justify their encouragement of sport.

What is desirable to learn in order to be an officer is
not necessarily that which anticipates a participation in
war, but whatever enables a young man to achieve a rich
maturity. Sport seems to contribute to that result. But
neither its history nor its present use in the service academies warrants the conclusion that sport makes use of
similar powers, proceeds along similar lines, feeds on similar motives and drives, or aims at goals which are similar
to those involved in war.

These differences do not make altogether invalid an
attempt to look at a game as an opportunity to express
aggression in a harmless way. But the aggression, it must

then be remembered, is only one factor; there are other factors as well, all of which have distinctive meanings when they are exhibited within the confines of a game. Sport is not aggression controlled and harmless. It is a constructive activity in which aggression plays a role together with dedication, cooperation, restraint, self-denial, and a respect for the rights and dignity of others.

A game, it cannot be too often insisted, is an event cut off from the rest of the world, though every occurrence in it may have effects in the world outside. Practical concerns are put aside by one who truly plays a game. That is why he is able to concentrate on the production of the game in accordance with accepted rules. But a game is like every other production, practical or otherwise, in that it cannot be entirely prepared for. It is never what it was imagined or predicted to be. Within it there are unforeseen variations, most of which are slight, though some may be very large.

Some of the minor occurrences in a game may prove to be momentous outside. A player may catch the fancy of some woman or businessman and as a consequence may have his entire life changed. Or he may play unaware of some injury which later festers and spreads. It is also possible for a momentous occurrence in a game to have little import outside. A crucial save might merely exercise a muscle or an eye. Deaths and cripplings, though, are momentous both inside and outside the game. As we saw, inside the game they bring some action to a halt, but outside it they have repercussions on relatives, the hopes and prospects of the family, the dealings of the insurance company, on hospitals, doctors, nurses, and so on. They have countless reverberations, but these are not *caused* by the actions as occurring in the game. As taking place in the game, even the most momentous occurrences are caught up in a causal nexus which is different from that which governs them or their effects as part of the world of daily life.

Because no one can be specifically prepared for all that happens in the course of a game, and because victory is so ardently desired, it is inevitable that athletes and others

will credit part of what takes place in the game to luck—
which is to say, to fortuitous, unpredictable forces operating to bring about a favorable outcome.

The meaning "luck" originally had, it still retains.
Luck refers to what bends together, to what is fitting. He
who believes in it, believes that there is a trend in the
course of events which will produce the results he desires.
(Used to refer to misfortune, "luck" is evidently short for
"bad luck.")

The silent prayers, the incantations, the ritualistic gestures of gamblers are supposed to be means by which the
gamblers are opened up to a trend in the world that will
issue in the occurrence of a desired event. If the agents are
thought to produce that event, they will, paradoxically,
have to be said to preclude the presence of luck. Any
symbolic device which can produce or sustain cosmic
forces is magical. A magic produces; luck simply appears,
though sometimes only after certain preparations have
been made. Luck can perhaps be cajoled; it can never be
controlled.

Like ordinary men, athletes make a daily, unreflecting
allowance for luck; in addition, during their athletic careers, they exhibit an abiding interest in it. Because of the
high stakes they take a game to involve, because of its
climactic character and, most important, because of the
prominent role that contingency plays in the course of a
game, they are inclined to find a larger place for luck than
most of us do. And to their occasional magical practices,
designed to promote the appearance of a lucky event, they
add a set of strong superstitions which are thought to
accelerate or underwrite the process. But luck is the
chance occurrence of the desirable; it is not the caused
appearance of a blind producer of what we want.

Gamblers put much more stock in luck and associated
superstitions than either ordinary men or athletes do. Like
athletes, they often have considerable skill and judgment.
They, too, match their wits, knowledge, courage, and flexibility against others. The great, successful gamblers add
to these a good understanding of human nature, and back
this with a capacious and accurate memory, all put at the

service of a successful outcome. But unlike most athletes, gamblers are men completely alone. For them, luck is not a grace note, an addendum to what they are or do. It is an integral part of their lives and of their performances. Sometimes they have a long run of bad luck. Since they see themselves to be blessed ones, children of good fortune, they still remain confident that good luck will eventually take over. To themselves they are luck subjectified, luck incarnated, luck's natural and proper beneficiary.

Living in a world which is governed by luck, the gambler takes little interest in the affairs of men. He has no interest in ends; he commits himself to nothing. It makes little difference how long he engages in the activity of gambling; he rarely learns anything about himself in the process. Having taken himself to be a chosen man who needs all his skills and knowledge solely to place him in the position where he can make an appropriate provision for the presence and for the use of his luck, he can then do little more than hope and wait for the inevitable to occur. Somewhat like a simple religious man, he, too, believes that he is a favored child of great powers which will sooner or later come to his aid.

If this be a world, as I think it is, that is governed by ineluctable laws, the gambler must be said to be one who does not understand what the world is like or what relation it has to him. Not that there is no luck in this world, or that there are no men who have more luck than others. Desirable things occur through the action of powers not in our control. But this is not yet to say that the luck has favorites, or that there are devices by which it can be promoted.

Good fortune is a steady run of luck. The gambler believes in his good fortune. He is confident that the universe has a unique predilection for him. When he is favored he takes that fact to testify that there is something distinctive about him which makes him worthy of being good fortune's child. He tends to associate this predilection with some virtue in himself. He has, he thinks, some mysterious power or feature which makes him be chosen as an object of good fortune. With Jack Horner "he puts in his thumb, pulls out a plum, and says, 'What a good boy am I.' "

The athlete tends to treat luck impersonally, as that which he is "lucky" to be favored with. Having dedicated himself to a cause, he hopes that he will be sustained by circumstance. Aware of his ability, conscious of the fact that he must make a great effort, luck can be for him only a supplement, a support, which assures him of the success he deserves in the contest. Because what he achieves is primarily due to efforts he deliberately made and carried out with practiced skill, it cannot be credited purely, or mainly, to luck. The gambler, though, even when he knows that he has made some blunder, never altogether blames himself. The issue, he thinks, has a cosmic root, which no blunder or failure can tap. What he achieves he credits to luck or magic, though in fact it is but a consequence of the play of law-abiding contingencies.

A defeated athlete knows who he is even more clearly than one who is victorious, since the latter provides a measure for the former, but not conversely. But neither the defeated nor the successful gambler knows himself; his self-knowledge is blocked by an unbreakable confidence that he has a virtue which the cosmos will surely reward.

Nevertheless, the gambler has a more philosophical spirit than the athlete, for he is oriented toward a universe and not toward some conventionalized segment of it, cut off from the rest. He does not benefit from this larger perspective, because his idea of the universe is awry. The athlete is better off since he has a clearer sense of the tiny world that he occupies than the gambler has of the larger one.

Because he is a cosmic oriented man, the gambler cannot be said to play in any sense similar to that characteristic of children or even of athletes. The ventures in which he engages are not separated off from the rest of things; they are but concentrated portions of the whole. Were he to rectify his outlook, he would become a player and see his card games, horse races, baseball pools, etc., as activities bounded off from all else—or, with the rest of us, he would take them to be places where the laws that govern all occurrences can also be found.

The athlete puts himself in a position in which he could be found wanting; the gambler does nothing more than present himself. The one attempts, the other accepts; the one treats the result to be definitive of himself, but the other does not, for he has characterized himself to be one whom luck will sooner or later favor.

A gambler sees his own errors as slips, merely forestalling the inevitable successful outcome. Luck is an inseparable part of his being. The athlete sees his luck as desirable, but neither revelatory of himself nor guaranteeing an eventual success. He knows that it appears adventitiously and will not inevitably make him successful. That is why the athlete exerts himself and tries to win. We are able to sympathize with the losing athlete, for he is a man who has put himself to the test. It is hard to sympathize with the gambler, for he sees himself to be a man who is and has whatever luck decrees.

A gambler who is not confident that luck is on his side, is no true gambler. In this respect, as well as in others, he is different from an investor, even one who takes chances. An investor may put up money on the outcome of some game, but he does this only when he has an "edge"—some built-in reliable basis—in the form of inside knowledge, manipulated odds, a stacked deck, etc. Like one who puts his money in stocks or real estate, the investor in a game tries to improve his financial situation. If he believes in luck, it is not as the gambler does. With the athlete he strives to win, and hopes that luck will sustain his deserved and well-prepared-for victory.

Luck for the investor is a welcome addition, which will make him successful in his effort to increase the value or decrease the risk of his investment. With the athlete, he shares the view that luck may provide him with a desirable support or supplement. Unlike the athlete, he does not exert himself physically and, normally, has less control than the athlete does over the factors that make for success.

When an investor succeeds he often has the gambler's feeling that he is shrewd and charismatic, and that luck is the cosmos' response to the signal nature that is his. But it is money that he wants, and for which he in fact works, never supposing that he *must* win, sooner or later. A gambler might also want to make money, but this is for him, in the end, only testimony that he is a distinctively favored man. It is because he is not interested in having money but in winning it, that he is so ready to spend and even to waste it.

Success satisfies the investor as it does the athlete; for the gambler it is but one of an endless number of possible evidences that can be and will be provided by an infinitely fluid, omnipresent, but episodically operative luck that is particularly attuned to him. Even in the face of persistent failure, the gambler continues to believe in his luck, confident that it will sooner or later find him. And because he is not content with success, even with a series of successes, he is ready, again and again, to enter into challenging situations which might bring great losses. Luck, he feels, has a singular bias toward him. No matter how often he wins or loses, it is, he thinks, waiting to benefit him.

A gambler seems to be convinced that he will come out on top at the end. But it is possible that he is really uncertain about that of which he appears to be sure. Though he never loses his confidence, he also never is content to rest with it. He seems to need constant reassurance that what he firmly believes in is so in fact, that he is favored and can win. Like a true and steady believer who wants his God to manifest Himself again, again, and again, the gambler knows that his luck will surely make itself evident and yet he wants it now to prove that he is right in having confidence in it. Like a jealous but devoted lover, he suspects what he believes, and fears while he hopes, trusting and not trusting all evidence, both that which sustains and that which challenges his confidence. Unwillingly he suspends not only belief, but disbelief; willingly he surrenders each to the other, sometimes in rapid succession. No athlete is so unsure. Each is aware that he must give himself to his sport, and not expect the cosmos to make things right for him. He knows that he is to be so well prepared that the luck he wants and even needs is only one factor in the totality that makes it possible for him to be victorious. And he knows that there will be a time when he will no longer succeed, let luck be as it may.

There is always an element of luck in every game. But it would seem right to abstract from it, if the game is to be ideally what a game should be. To fault a man merely because he has a poor draw, the wind against him, or has been unnerved by a serious accident to a fellow player seems unfair. With even more justice, it could be argued that luck is but a way of describing the overall effect of the contingencies which are essential to the very existence of a game. The athlete is to show what he is and can do in a game as it actually unfolds, peppered with the unexpected. And for those who sit in the stands, it should not matter that some man has had a run of luck, because it is not the individual or even the team with which they should be concerned, but with man in a world that is not in his firm control. It is man who, in this guise or that, shows what is the best that can be done in a game where contingencies play a vital part.

It is impossible to avoid the presence or the influence of luck. But whether it be present or absent, it is only the game, contested and refereed, played out in public in conformity to established rules, that provides the final test of what an athlete has done and therefore what he bodily is. If he has an urge to win he will do all he can. If he is lucky, he is one who is enriched gratuitously. In any case, he is whatever he shows himself to be in his games.

SOME men make sport their job. They are professionals who are paid. Some are paid very well, but most are not. A few get a good deal of publicity and acquire considerable social weight. If they had been underprivileged, they find that they have moved up in the social scale. Not surprisingly, a number of underprivileged men take up professional sport as a career.

A rich man does not need to become a professional player. Since he has more leisure time than most, he also has more time to devote to sport. As a consequence, he may become an amateur athlete. Though there are many amateurs who have little money or status, and though there are many professionals whose earnings are fairly modest, by and large the line between amateur and professional is mainly a line between the unpaid members of a privileged class and the paid members of an underprivileged class.

Very successful professionals arouse admiration. In part this is due to the fact that we respect those who have either money or status, even though we may be poor in both. But admiration is also awakened by amateurs. Even when the amateur is not well off, we honor him if he is outstanding, because he seems to us to have voluntarily and nobly made a great effort, and subjected himself to an arduous disciplining when he could have been lax or indifferent. We like to see a man give himself to an activity with full spirit for no other purpose than that of putting himself to the test, showing what he can do, what he is at his best. We like the idea of a man enjoying himself, or being free to do all he can to be as good as man can be, regardless of any further benefits, economic or otherwise. The amateur, we think, like a game, is bracketed off from the rest of the world; he is simply, solely, a man who exists in the game.

It is consonant with our view of young men that they should give themselves wholeheartedly to whatever they do, without regard for consequences. It seems proper for them to be amateurs. Since they have not yet assumed the responsibilities of the mature, they can readily adopt this position. Many young men, too, are able to avoid the question of receiving money for their sport activities because they are supported by their families or their society. Still others have not yet had experience enough to warrant their being accepted into professional ranks. Whatever the reason, most of our amateurs are young, inexperienced, comparatively well off, and not yet subject to the entire quota of obligations that hedge in their elders.

Today our admiration of the amateur is somewhat qualified. The large incomes and the wide publicity of some of the outstanding professionals not only give them something of the status enjoyed by those who have inherited their wealth or position, but also the appearance of experts who are being well paid because they well-deserve it. In baseball, football, hockey, tennis, and golf, the amateur often is treated as though he were an unpaid apprentice professional, one who wants to, but is not yet qualified to earn large sums through his activities in the sport.

These observations make steady sense only if author and reader have tacitly assumed common definitions of "amateur" and "professional." But in fact there are no widely accepted definitions of either. The oldest and easiest definitions are that an amateur is an "amator," "a lover," one who gives himself to an activity without reserve and for no further end, whereas a professional engages in the activity only to make money. These definitions overlook the truth that many professionals love their sport, and that many an amateur has money in mind. More important, perhaps, is the fact that no one ever gives himself absolutely to any one type of activity; if he did, he would have neither time for, nor interest in, food, sex, art, or social affairs. Nor, for the same reason, can it be said that anyone lives solely for the sake of making money, since this would preclude an interest in his work or his collaborators, or in other preconditions for making money.

For some, amateur means one who is never tainted by any economic considerations. The Olympic International Committee, for example, thinks that an amateur participates and always has participated in sport solely for pleasure. It wants him to see athletic activity as a form of recreation entraining no material gain. It denies eligibility to those who have participated for money or for merchandise prizes easily converted into money, to those who have been paid for training or coaching others for organized competition, to those who have capitalized on their athletic fame, to those who are participating as amateurs to enhance their commercial value, and to those who have neglected their usual employment in order to engage in competitive sports.

These rules are not only arbitrary, unfair, and ill-conceived, but are unenforceable. Is it possible to know whether anyone has *always* participated in a sport *solely* for pleasure, or for recreation without material gain *of any kind?* What merchandise is not easily converted into money? What is disreputable about training and coaching others for organized competition? How does one know whether or not men are participating as amateurs in order to enhance their commercial value? Those who participate in Olympic boxing contests are surely not unaware that victory will make possible a professional career under good management; it is a rare boxer who has not made a decision to become a professional, should he win a resounding victory. And must not anyone who earns a living have to neglect his employment if he wants to compete in the Olympics? It was something like the spirit of these regulations that once led Olympic officials to strip Jim Thorpe of his records and awards after it was discovered that he had earned a small sum playing baseball some time before.

For others, amateur means simply one who does not receive money for any activity which might be thought to stem from his success as an athlete. This is how some societies for amateur athletics construe the term. The Olympic Committee has something like this in mind when it tries to deny eligibility to those who capitalize on their athletic ability. But it is hard to see where a line can be drawn between those earnings which do partly depend on, and those which are entirely independent of, a career in sport. Though it is comparatively easier for a man to sell insurance in certain circles if he is a well-known, highly successful athlete, no amateur athletic society denies him this right. May he work in a sporting goods store? May he not teach any sport, even as part of his duties in a small college? Must he refuse a promotion given to him after he has successfully competed? No principles are offered by the Olympic Committee in terms of which these questions can be answered.

For still others, an amateur is one who does not play with those who earn money at the sport. Yet golf, squash, and tennis have "open" tournaments where amateurs are permitted to compete with professionals. In these sports, evidently, an amateur can play with those who earn money at the sport.

It is sometimes held that an amateur is one who willingly plays in a game without compensation, even though money had been earned by that player in some earlier game. The Golf Association holds this view. That is why it was possible for Babe Didrickson, who was a professional golfer, to be reinstated as an amateur—the very change denied to Thorpe.

College athletic associations defend one of the most stringent definitions of amateurism. Overlooking the fact that many a college baseball player plays for money during his vacation, they hold that anyone who had been a professional in any sport whatsoever is automatically a professional in every sport. To earn money is for them something like a mortal sin, unexpungeable by anyone but God. But it is not clear whether or not they think that a man is still an amateur if he receives a trophy and then pawns or sells it for needed cash. Amateur boxers take such a privilege for granted. Is one an amateur if he is paid for expenses incurred in training and traveling? The Olympic Committee seems to think so. Is entertaining permitted; may one be accompanied by one's family if, by taking poorer accommodations, it can manage on the normal allotment for an individual? No clear answer is given. Should it not be possible for any athlete to participate in any game, no matter how distant; if not, will we not in effect be penalizing those who are unable to afford the trip? Is one an amateur if he has a patron who relieves him from the necessity of earning a living or supporting his family? If not, is it also not permissible for a man to be supported by a relative, close or remote? If a nation compensates a man for the time he spends at sports, time which he might have spent at his regular job, does he still remain an amateur? Apparently so, for this is what Australia does for the men it sends to the Olympic Games.

It is said that the Russians subsidize those who make sport into a significant career. If so, the Russians seem to be more clearheaded on this issue than the rest of the world. Might not an employer, rather than a nation, see to it that there is no financial loss suffered by those who train or who qualify for participation in games? Why is a subsidy by a nation more noble than one by some other organization? Suppose that there is a nation which is unable to pay for sending athletes to the Olympic Games or to some other competition: why should it not be permissible for individuals in that nation or elsewhere, or for other nations to make it possible for those athletes to participate? Since the Olympic Games are supposed to offer competitions for individuals and not for representatives of nations—despite the fact that they are selected by nations, and paraded and decorated under their national flags—is it right that some men, unsupported by their nations, be precluded from participating, while others, living in countries that are richer or more willing to support their athletes, are given the opportunity to compete?

These unanswered questions show that there is not much clear understanding as to just what the term "amateur" connotes. And if this term is unclear, its normal correlate, "professional," also can have no steady, unambiguous meaning. The American Cyclist Union, a while back, tried to solve the problem by the acknowledgment of a third group of players, the "proamateurs." These were men who drew salaries but did not race for money. It was not long, though, before this category was abandoned, for most of the cyclists who drew salaries wanted to race for money. The situation was soon as confused as it had been before.

There are professional contests in which the winner takes all and the loser gets nothing. Only one is paid. Are they both professionals? No one seems ever to have denied that they were. Is a professional, then, only one who would like to be paid? But many so-called amateurs also would like to be paid. That is why they convert their trophies into cash. Is a professional one who works, with or without a contract, in the hope that he will be paid should he be victorious? But team players are never victorious as individuals, and many an amateur has a well-understood contract with his college or club, which demands that he practice and be successful if he is to continue to be freed from the need to pay for his tuition or equipment. Does a man still remain an amateur if he thinks of his participation in sport as a sound investment for a successful financial future? If not, how innocent must a man be to qualify as an amateur? Is a man a professional if he earns money from work related to his participation in games? If so, Bannister, in writing a book about his preparation for breaking the four-minute mile barrier, must have been a professional. Would he have been more of a professional if he had endorsed some product on television, or if he had been interviewed or had conducted interviews for pay? Is a man a professional if he is supported and trained and educated just so that he can participate in a sport? If so, we have many professionals in our colleges.

It is not unknown for a college to provide room and board, free tuition, and some cash to outstanding or conscientious athletes. Should a man prove unable to meet the standards of the varsity team, or should he not be sufficiently assiduous in training, he is then not only removed from the team, but has his "scholarship" taken away as well. If anyone is a professional, he surely is, though his pay is often far below what he earns in fact on behalf of his school. Is a professional, then, one who is receiving adequate compensation, or at least compensation above the niggardly sums which colleges pay to outstanding athletes? Does one become a professional if one is given his uniform and equipment? If so, what poor boy athlete is not a professional? And what "little leaguer" could avoid being termed a professional, since his uniform is paid for, and other subsidies are provided by supposedly well-intentioned adults. "Professional" like "amateur" is a term riddled with ambiguities.

An amateur, strictly speaking, is one who plays a game for no other reason than to play it. He cannot but benefit from his participation; he will undoubtedly be tested there; he will want to win; he will, more likely than not, enjoy himself even while under pressure or at the edge of exhaustion. But it will be the game with which he is concerned. A professional, strictly speaking, is one who takes some end other than the playing of the game to be his primary objective. His aim may be to win, no matter how, to entertain the spectators, to give encouragement to his government, to get publicity, or to make money. It makes no difference which of these it is. He is a professional if his play is governed by considerations which do not follow from the nature of a contest or a game.

If these characterizations of the amateur and professional have any merit, many a player will have to be called an amateur even though he is well compensated, and many another will have to be called a professional even though he receives no pay. It will require us to reclassify as amateurs those who had been called professionals merely because they had played in games with those who earned a living playing in some sport. Almost all of the public which devotes some time to participating in sports, since it does this as an occasion for the joyous utilization of whatever skills it has attained, will, on this view, be taken to be amateurs. All, in fact, will be amateurs just so far as it is the game with which they are primarily concerned. The question as to whether they are also financially rewarded will be simply irrelevant.

Money is not necessarily a power for turning men away from the bounded world of sport; it can serve to free them sufficiently so that they can concentrate on being athletes. To promote amateur athletics, money should be so used as to make it possible for athletes' minds and bodies to be freely expressed in sport. This will mean that many an amateur will need financial aid. Today some compensation is provided when genuine need can be demonstrated, but the demand that need be shown can be embarrassing, and the sums now offered are hardly worth the requesting. Why should demonstrated need be a criterion for determining whether or not an amateur is to receive compensation?

So far as a nation, its schools, and its corporations are interested in furthering the cause of amateur sports, it is incumbent upon them to make it possible for qualified men to participate. If the men are not to be bothered by monetary matters, they should be compensated for whatever loss of income or opportunity they suffer through their devotion to an athletic career. This, most emphatically, does not mean that the men are to be paid in scholarships and academic privileges, but only that athletes are not to be hindered because they are unable to earn enough to have free time to spend in athletic preparation and participation.

Social Security benefits, today, are given to men who are seventy-two years of age or older, without regard for what they might be earning. In a similar spirit, one could treat amateur athletes as being entitled to financial aid up to a given sum, regardless of the state of their personal finances. The fifty-dollar limit, which the Olympic Committee has put on the value of prizes that can be properly received without question, stands as a tacit acknowledgment by that stern body of the fact that financial rewards are not entirely denied to the amateur.

It is not easy to determine what kind of work is to be judged as improper to men who engage in amateur sport. We verge on petulance when we deny an athlete the right to earn a living by teaching, coaching, and promoting sports in educational institutions. Perhaps a case could be made for excluding from the ranks of amateurs all those who coach varsity players, but what argument could one offer for excluding those who teach athletics to the rest of the student body or in secondary schools, or who have permanent posts in the primary schools? Yet these teachers may have capitalized on their athletic prowess, and some of them do help students to prepare for eventual organized competition. The International Olympic Committee would presumably exempt a teacher of civics or history from the charge of being a professional; the distinction between him and his colleague teaching physical fitness or gymnastics is invidious. And some men, as part of their job, may have to teach in both areas. The current official attitude on amateurism would require us either to change our educational programs, or to condemn the men even though they were subject to conditions in no way within their control.

An adequate subsidy given to all players, without regard for their financial status, will minimize the need to pry into their personal affairs, and yet make it possible for everyone to enter wholeheartedly into the noncommercial games for which they are qualified. The U.S. government does not ask those it sends on trips whether or not they could afford to pay the passage themselves; it gives everyone a per diem or per mile allowance, and lets it go at that. It sets an example athletic associations could well follow.

Today, amateurs are allowed to carry the insignia of some organizations, even though the athlete is paid in some fashion for doing so. With equal warrant the athletes could be asked to carry the insignia of any organization—club, business, college, or nation—that makes their participation in a sport possible. And they might as well be paid openly by the supporting organization. Were they properly helped, the athletes would not, though, be paid to win, penalized if they did not, or rewarded if they did. The organizations would support them as long as they met universal, preassigned conditions of fitness, training, and participation; the decisions and administration of those organizations would, ideally, be subject to review by neutral judges.

One might reply to some such suggestion as this, that amateur athletes do not deserve support from anyone. It

could be argued, as it was in more austere times, that
athletics takes one away from more important work and
should in fact be discouraged. Or, what is a more congenial line today, it could be argued that the benefits which the
athlete derives from sport more than compensate for the
sacrifice of time and money that he is compelled to make.
But there is no incompatibility between being paid and
benefitting in other ways as well.

A subsidy for an amateur would normally be well
below the compensation a professional deserves for the
work and entertainment he is paid to deliver. As a rule, the
professional is a more consistent and better player than
the amateur, and makes a profit for his employer. The
amateur is almost always one who has not yet developed
sufficiently, who is not yet as good as he might be. And he
often represents a nonprofit-making institution.

Though amateurs sometimes win in contests with professionals, more often they lose. Their experience is limited
and they do not have as much at stake as the professional.
Occasionally they may give themselves to the game more
fully than the professional does, uninterested in counting
the cost to themselves. But then, though exceptional in a
performance or so, they fail to do well over the long haul.
The professional normally gets more money because he
produces more.

More likely than not, a professional player was a first-
rate amateur to begin with, and started in the professional
ranks because he thought he could mature into a first-rate
professional player. Had he not been a distinguished amateur he would most likely be working at low wages under
poor conditions at tedious, unsatisfying work; if he did not
develop into a full-fledged professional player he would
soon find that a professional career was not so attractive as
some other. Because he usually has had a career as a
strong amateur, the professional has had the benefit of
needed teaching and experience on which he can continue
to build. With few exceptions, he has met severe competition persistently and successfully. The assumption that he
is a superior athlete is rarely unjustified.

A typical professional is a seasoned player. He has had

an opportunity to improve his judgment and his timing, to subletize his skills, and to learn where he is strongest and where he is weakest. Consequently, he is at once more adroit and more wary than an amateur can show himself to be. By and large, the professional knows what to expect, what he can count on himself to produce, what kind of situations are likely to arise, what he may be called upon to do, what he can expect of his teammates, and something of the strengths and weaknesses of his opponents, whose performances and records are sometimes made available to him.

On an absolute scale, the professional is a comparatively young man. Rarely does he continue to play into the forties, particularly in sports requiring endurance, strength, and speed rather than accuracy or steadiness. In the world of sport, though, he is a comparatively older man. Despite the fact that he may be only in his early twenties, he is normally already well trained, with a good deal of experience to make him more at home in himself and in the game than an amateur is or can be. He has had time to increase his strength and improve his judgment. He is more persistently and intensely occupied with sport, and faces more severe, crucial challenges than amateurs usually can. He, therefore, has had more of an opportunity to improve his playing. The very length and character of his experience allows him to develop and express a skill that the possibly superior vitality and recklessness of the younger amateur rarely can counterbalance. Though every crisis is new, to be solved then and there, it is a fact that the professional has had to face more crises than an amateur usually does, and therefore, despite his stability in habit and style, is better equipped to make radical but sound decisions again and again.

Like every other craftsman, the professional works on a means for the production of an end having a nature and a career outside his contrivance or control. The carpenter makes a chair for people to sit upon; whether or not they sit on it, and how, is not his concern. In a similar spirit, the professional athlete must somehow produce pleasure in the spectators and profit for his employers—consequences which are supposed to follow from his masterly pursuit of his sport. His sport is a means to an enjoyment and profit for others; what that pleasure and profit are like or how they are used is not his affair except so far as they determine whether or not he may be permitted to continue in the ranks of competing professionals. The amateur, in contrast, is more like an artist, occupied with making something excellent then and there. Pleasing spectators or enriching an organization is not an intended, desired, or necessary consequence of his participation in athletics. For the amateur the game is an end in itself.

The motivation of the professional is strong and steady. He has, for the time being, made sport his career. It is his work. As a good craftsman he wants to do his work well. He wants to perform superbly and to satisfy those on whom his livelihood depends. At his best he will be graceful, a delight to observe. But whatever excellence he exhibits is qualified by his need to meet the demands of employers and spectators. Unlike the amateur who ideally has other interests which occupy him, having no relation to what he does in sport, the professional, even while he makes sport central to his life, uses it as a means for producing goods for others and eventually for himself.

The typical professional has played more often, and under more trying conditions than the amateur. Because of his more frequent playing he has more deeply entrenched habits. His expectations are better grounded, his movements are surer, and his style is better established. Not only does he make fewer errors, but his actions are not so frequently nor so conspicuously ineffective as are those of the amateur.

Because the professional often has a family, and has financial and other obligations that he feels compelled to meet, it is desirable for him to avoid distractions and to reduce his involvement in other enterprises. In contrast, the amateur is more subject to the temptations and confusions which plague those who are comparatively without responsibility. He denies himself because he desires to, where the other denies himself because he must. Necessity is always stronger than desire.

If the amateur is a student he has to devote some time and attention to his studies. It is not easy to cut him off—though some schools try—from all contact with students who are bent on learning. He is at least dimly aware that there are books and libraries, scholars and classrooms, and an occasional teacher of art, science, or one of the humanities. This is true even for those who have "academic" scholarships which permit them to take pseudo courses in the history of football, the mechanics of weight lifting, and the "philosophy of sport," leaving them free to spend most of their time and energy in the gymnasium or on the field. The professionals are more disadvantaged. Though some of them were once true students, few of them any longer have an opportunity to use, inside or outside the game, what might have been learned in the course of an academic schooling. Their work is too demanding to make it possible for any but a few to have energy and time left over; they are not in the mood to engage in the resolute pursuit of any good not relevant to their sport.

The professional is a specialist who usually works together with, as well as under, other specialists. This fact helps to explain his greater skill and signal success. It also helps explain why it is that he may be in poor physical overall condition and yet function admirably in a game. Professional football players who are not required to run tend to put on weight. Some of them are so badly bruised in the course of a game that it takes a number of days before they, bandaged and rested, are able to carry out their specialty another time.

Though better machines than amateurs, though more experienced, more mature, and more responsible, professionals are not usually better human beings. They have had longer time and more opportunities to achieve this result, but they also have been prevented from giving much attention to anything other than the problem of becoming better in their sport. Strictly speaking, they are, therefore, not really better athletes. They are only better players. Where they once competed as amateurs, keyed to the effort to be and perform excellently, they now seek only to function well as paid craftsmen. There is nothing disgraceful in this, any more than there is in the efforts of seamen or salesmen. The work they do is desirable, wanted, and reputable, but it is work at a means. The amateur is occupied with an end.

The professional is a workman, an employee, a man who plays for hire under the supervision of a foreman who doubles as guide and control. Money has been invested in him. He is property, whose primary role is to repay that investment by using his ability to play in a way that will satisfy his owners because it satisfies the spectators, usually by a victory. The amateur, too, wants to win; his coaches also want him to win. But the winning belongs inside the game, where it offers a measure of what has been done. The professional wins in order to satisfy others. If he catches the interest or sympathy of the crowd, he may satisfy the spectators and owners, even though the performance is well below standard. He will then have produced the result he is paid to produce.

Though the professional, as a rule, can outplay an amateur, he will play at his very best only when the circumstances of the game demand it. His owners and coaches want him to do a first-rate job, but only so far as this is consistent with his continuing to hold the interest or the favor of those who pay to watch.

Aware that his livelihood depends on his ability to perform over a period of time, the professional tends to minimize risks. He would like to do a fine job day after day; he takes pride in his work, but not to such a degree that he will do a superb job at some one time if this means he will be unable to do much on a subsequent occasion. He has signed himself up for a period, during which he expects and is expected to continue to do good work. He will not be inclined to, and his employers do not expect him to, force himself to move to the point of exhaustion and possible injury. Because his future is predicated on his persistent ability to perform as he should, he, his owners, and his coaches want him to conserve his strength and to be judicious, so far as he is thereby helped to produce the desired result. But the amateur is sometimes ready to push himself to the limit even if this means that he jeopardizes the possibility of doing well again. The coaches of amateurs normally want them to be more judicious. But the amateur does not always heed. Not infrequently he is indifferent to the possibility of accident, injury, or the failure that follows on an attempt to do what is beyond his capacity.

The vitality and spontaneity which the professional had when he was younger inexorably slips from him. Because he is older than the amateur, he usually has slower reflexes. Though he may have superior judgment and skill, and perhaps even courage (where this is understood, after Plato, as knowing what to fear), he is not engaged in the task of building his character. Not only were the foundations and the struts of his character laid while he was an amateur, or when he was rehearsing for the time when he could perform as a professional, but his efforts were soon qualified by the pressure he himself and others exerted to make him function like a professional, occupied with winning, or whatever else assures him his wages, because it satisfies those who employ him.

"Good losers are losers" was an observation made by a professional. It testifies to his conviction that the primary task of the professional player is to win—a conviction which is regrettably shared by many a high school coach, particularly of basketball, and by some college coaches, particularly of football. We seem here to have an analytically true proposition, like "a white cat is a cat," or "an honest man is honest." But it is neither analytic nor true, even when taken to refer only to professionals. What it intends to convey is that a player is not to take a loss in good spirit, that he is to protest against it, even to take it as an affront. This may be proper behavior for a professional if it pleases the spectators and the owners. It is not proper for an amateur, who presumably has no one to please but himself, and then only by performing as well as he can. His urge to win is to be expressed in the guise of a concern to perform excellently in a game, and not, as a professional sometimes must, in the guise of a concern to win because and so far as this is what is wanted by those who pay to have him play.

A professional may be modest and cooperative. Many of the professionals are sound workmen who together do a fine job. They may enjoy participating in the sport and may grow in stature in the course of playing. But neither of these is asked of them. All that the professional is required to do is to enable others to disport, to be relaxed, amused, diverted, thrilled, inspired. At root, he is an entertainer.

Entertainment is a business, engaged in to make a profit. Though an amateur game is not designed to entertain, any more than a theatrical performance is, but to exhibit the excellence that can be obtained in this way, it, too, can be made to serve the ends of business. To be used for entertainment, an activity need not be engaged in for that reason. But if entertainment is to be made into a business, it must be so conducted that a profit is made.

Sometimes alumni force a college to make sport a business by giving it money and exerting pressure to have sports emphasized and promising players admitted. The intent is often noble. The alumni are generous with their time and money, and genuinely concerned with their school and the men. They would like to glorify their institution and to provide some young men, who otherwise would be denied, an opportunity to go to college. In effect, though, a college often prevents the men from being educated, since it requires them to spend their time doing what will not necessarily promote their intellectual or spiritual maturation. Those students who have proven themselves to be promising athletes are too often treated primarily not as students, but as apprentice professionals. The alumni would do more justice to their own institution if they saw to it that it did what it ought to do, both for the teachers and the students. Teachers need to be given a maximum freedom to learn and to teach, while students should be enabled to concentrate on the vital work of growing up through the development and use of a strengthened mind and body. No student, even one of great athletic promise, should be required to devote most of his time and attention to athletics. The theses: athletics is desirable; promising athletes should be encouraged; education is more than book learning, need not be rejected in order to support the claim that a college is not primarily an institution for promoting the athletic abilities of a gifted few.

Alumni pressure is partly the reason why coaches in some colleges try to assume an attitude toward their students similar to that adopted by the coaches of professionals. As is often true of imitations, the copy is at some remove from the original, and inevitably lacks its clarity and pertinence. A successful coach of a professional team may assume only a managerial or supervisory role in relation to his men, but the coach of amateurs fails if he is not a guide and friend, a teacher and man, devoted to the welfare of his charges. He betrays his calling if he attends mainly to the pleasing of those who watch the game or of those who were graduated from the school at an earlier date. The betrayal is provoked by those who define his success as coach by the comparative number of victories which his team provides in relation to the number of its defeats, or the number of victories that are achieved over traditional rivals. The victories do tell us something, particularly when one compares schools having somewhat the same student composition, but they do not tell us enough to make them criteria for determining who is and who is not a good coach of college athletics.

Most institutions need alumni support. This is sustained and increased by making the alumni feel proud of the school—a matter promoted by the athletic achievements of the current students. But this is not the only way in which the loyalty and money of the alumni can be elicited. In any case, it offers no justification for making some students play in public as though they were professionals.

A university supplements a college with graduate schools of various kinds. So far as those schools are designed to prepare men for careers in business, architecture, engineering, medicine, or law, they are vocational schools, even if they are conducted on a high level. It is dubious policy which allows such schools to be joined with colleges as part of an institution of higher learning. The values and bent of those schools are so different from those of the colleges that they can neither help them nor be helped by them. The two may, in fact, because of their competing needs for funds, space, administration, and the time of teachers, frustrate one another.

It is the obligation of graduate schools to prepare those who are to be leaders of basic disciplines, by helping them master the principles which are illustrated in the material that the colleges communicate to the young. There is no warrant, therefore, for a graduate school to engage in the training of men in vocations. There is even less warrant for a college doing so. Neither is a place where men are to be made into craftsmen.

A college has no more right to find a place for the training of professional athletes than it has for the training of professional plumbers or deep sea divers. The young men there are to be given the opportunity to be perfected by mastering more than can be achieved by a disciplined young body, keyed by the mind to bring about a successful display of physical skill. They are to be helped to carry out the ideals isolated in the graduate schools, and are to enrich the principles studied there, so as to be launched on a lifelong adventure of becoming full men. In both the graduate schools and in the colleges, and particularly in the second, the pursuit of bodily excellence is to be encouraged, but only so far as it does not hobble or obscure the desirability and actual pursuit of longer-ranged endeavors contributing to the making of a civilized man.

Professionals and amateurs are different in need, prospect, task, and objective. The one works for money, the other plays as part of an adventure at self-discovery and growth. The one wants to do a workmanlike job that has value for his employers, whereas the other seeks to help bring about a game well-played. The task of the professional is to please, usually by means of a victory; the task of the amateur is to function excellently in the game. The objective of the one is economic security and advancement, but the objective of the other is to become more of a man. The differences do not preclude the possibility of amateurs playing against professionals, or even of their forming teams with them. Professionalism is not a taint or a stain which on contact forever darkens the virgin soul.

Nor does there seem to be any good reason why one

might not be an amateur in one sport and a professional in another. "Amateur" does not denote a state of being but an attitude. There is no need to suppose that the attitude, if assumed in one place, will necessarily be assumed in another. This fact is not jeopardized if amateurs and professionals compete againt one another, as they do in open tournaments.

Much could be gained by allowing men to switch back and forth in their status as amateurs and professionals. Indeed, if we are interested in knowing just how far a man can put the shot, how fast he can run a mile, how accurately he can shoot, the question as to just what status he has seems to be irrelevant. It clarifies nothing in these areas to keep two sets of records, one for the individual who apparently is not being financially recompensed, and another for one who is rewarded with money or other financially viable awards. Amateurs need to be segregated from professionals when their distinctive abilities, tasks, and objectives would be perverted, but not otherwise.

The issue appears to be more complicated when we attend to team play. Should one allow professionals and amateurs to be on the same team? I am inclined to think not. On some teams certain positions are pivotal. If occupied by professionals, an undue advantage will be given to their side by virtue of their superior experience and maturity. Many incalculable factors would then be introduced into team play. We would leave open such questions as whether it would have been better had more professionals or fewer been on the team, and whether it would have been better to have allowed the professionals to do more or less than they had. Fairness would require that, at the very least, they be matched by other presumably equal professionals in similar positions. But these perhaps are not weighty considerations.

A team made up only of amateurs or professionals, because of its homogeneity, allows us to accept its achievements without further question. We can, of course, ask what might have happened had such and such a man played in place of another, or what might have happened had such a contingency not arisen. In the end we must content ourselves with taking the performance in the game to be a finality, expressing what this or that team can do. Allowing professionals to be on the same team with amateurs presumably makes for no more ambiguity than that provided by a match of mixed, i.e., male and female, doubles in tennis.

No apparent harm is done in having professionals and amateurs compete with one another, so long as no one is made to compete on uneven and unevaluable terms. Such competition is invited, however, when college students are asked to play against teams which include men who are older and have had much longer training, wider experience, a career not possible to the rest, and no scholastic interests.

The objection against having professionals on the same team with college students will not down because their diverse backgrounds and attitudes make their similar actions have such different meanings. The activities of amateurs and professionals should initially be evaluated on different standards. But only if we can find a way of relating these different standards will it make much sense to match the men in fact or in theory. A similar problem confronts us when we try to compare the performances of men and women.

AMATEURS and professionals differ in prospect and objective, and usually in experience and skill. They are to be sharply distinguished, without being prevented from playing together or against one another under controlled conditions. Women are not always so readily distinguishable from men, particularly when they are clothed, or when sex differences are not determined by an examination of their sexual organs, but by a microscopic study of the composition of their cells. Normally, though, we have less difficulty in distinguishing them from men than we have in distinguishing professionals from amateurs. What is far more difficult is the settlement of the question: are women athletes to be viewed as radically and incomparably different from men or as comparable with them, both as amateurs and as professionals?

Whatever difficulty we may have in identifying an individual as a man or a woman, athletic bodies have shown no hesitation in laying down conditions and rules which apply to one and not the other.

At the Olympic level, women are not permitted to lift heavy weights or to throw the hammer. They are, however, permitted to put the shot, hurl the discus, and throw the javelin. Similarly, they are barred from the pole vault, the high jump, the high hurdles, and the longer foot races, but they are permitted to compete in the long jump, the low hurdles, and the shorter races. They are also barred from the more strenuous team games, but in 1964 they were permitted to compete in the milder game of volleyball—the only team game in which there is no possibility of direct body contact between opponents.[1]

There is no serious competition in which women are matched against men. Rather, in those sports in which men and women participate together, they play as partners, with women generally accepting the supporting rather than the dominant role.[2]

At the international level, some forms of competition appear to be categorically unacceptable, as indicated by the fact that women are excluded from Olympic Competition in . . . wrestling, judo, boxing, weight lifting, hammer throw, pole vault, the longer foot races, high hurdles, and all forms of team games, with the recent exception of volleyball. These forms appear to be characterized by one or more of the following principles: an attempt to physically subdue the opponent by bodily contact; direct application of bodily force to some heavy object; attempt to project the body into or through space over long distances; cooperative face-to-face opposition in situations in which body contact may occur.[3]

Some forms of individual competition are generally acceptable to the college women of the United States . . . swimming, diving, skiing, and figure skating . . . golf, archery, and bowling . . . characterized by one or more of the following principles: attempts to project the body into or through space in aesthetically pleasing patterns; utilization of a manufactured device to facilitate bodily movement; application of force through a light implement; overcoming the resistance of a light object. . . . Some forms of face-to-face competition are also generally acceptable . . . fencing, . . . squash, badminton, tennis.[4]

There is considerable justification for these decisions in the results of tests and studies which have been made on women by themselves and in comparison with men. Women have comparatively less muscular strength and lighter arms, do not use their muscles as rapidly, have a longer reaction time, faster heart rates, and achieve a smaller arm strength in relation to their weight than men do. Their bones ossify sooner, they have a narrower and

1 Eleanor Metheny, *Connotations of Movement in Sport and Dance* (Dubuque, Iowa, 1965), p. 53.   2 *Ibid.*, p. 55.
3 *Ibid.*, p. 49.   4 *Ibid.*, p. 50.

more flexible shoulder girdle, smaller chest girth, and smaller bones and thighs. They also have wider and more stable knee joints, a heavier and more tilted pelvis, longer index fingers, and a greater finger dexterity. They have shorter thumbs, legs, feet, and arm length, a smaller thoracic cavity, smaller lungs, smaller hearts, lower stroke volumes, a smaller average height, lower blood pressure, fatigue more readily, and are more prone to injury. Their bodies are less dense and contain more fat; they have less bone mass, and throw differently.

Some women are outstanding athletes and have better records than most of the men involved in the sport. Some women have made better records in the Olympic Games than were previously made by men. But it is also true that when women compete in the same years with men, the women's records are not better than the men's. Marjorie Jackson won the 100 meter race in 1952 at eleven and one-half seconds, but the best time made in 1896 by a man was twelve seconds. In 1896 the best time for the men's 100 meter free style swimming race was one minute and twenty-two seconds, but in 1932 Helene Madison made the distance in one minute and six-tenths second. More spectacular advances are reported of Russian women in the shot-put and discus. That these and other women can more than match the records made by men in other years is understandable when we take account of the fact that women begin their athletic careers at an earlier age than they once did, that they are willing to practice for considerable periods, that they are benefiting from improved training methods, that they are using better equipment than they had previously, and that more of them are participating in contests and sports.

Women are unable to compete successfully with the best of men, except in sports which emphasize accuracy, skill, or grace—shooting, fancy skating, diving, and the like. Their bones, contours, musculature, growth rate, size, proportion, and reaction times do not allow them to do as well as men in sports which put a premium on speed or strength.

It is part of our cultural heritage to make an effort to

avoid having women maimed, disfigured, or hurt. That is one reason why they do not usually engage in and are not officially allowed to compete in such contact sports as boxing, wrestling, football, and rugby, with inexplicable exceptions being made for karate and lacrosse. In the United States women gymnasts do not compete on the long horse, and since 1957 they do not perform on the flying rings, apparently because they there overstrain and injure themselves. A woman's shoulder girdle is different from a man's.

One way of dealing with these disparities between the athletic promise and achievements of men and women is to view women as truncated males. As such they could be permitted to engage in the same sports that men do (except where these still invite unusual dangers for them), but in foreshortened versions. That approach may have dictated the different rules which men and women follow in basketball, fencing, and field hockey. Where men have five players on a basketball team, women have six, and are not permitted to run up and down the court. Men fence with foils, the target of which is the torso ending with the groin lines, with épées, the target of which is the entire body, and with the sabre the target of which is the region above the waist, including the head and arms, but women fence only with foils and then at a target of which the lower limit is at the hip bones. Women's field hockey, a most popular team sport, is played in two thirty-minute halves whereas the men play in two thirty-five minute halves.[5] The illustrations can be multiplied. But enough have been given to make the point that in a number of cases the performances of males can be treated as a norm, with the women given handicaps in the shape of smaller and sometimes less dangerous or difficult tasks.

Men and women can be significantly contrasted on the average and on the championship level as stronger and weaker, faster and slower. So far as the excellence of a performance depends mainly on the kind of muscles,

5 On these see Frank G. Menke, *Encyclopedia of Sports* (New York, 1963), and Parke Cummings, ed. *The Dictionary of Sports* (New York, 1949).

bones, size, strength, that one has, women can be dealt with as fractional men. This approach has considerable appeal. It not only allows us to compare men and women, but to acknowledge that some women will be outstanding, and, given their handicaps, surpass the men. But we will then fail to do justice to the fact that there are men who are more like most women in relevant factors than they are like most men, and that there are women who are more like most men in these respects than they are like most women.

Simply scaling women in relation to men in terms only of their physical features and capacities, can lull us into passing over a number of important questions. Are women and men motivated in the same way? Do they have the same objectives? Is the team play of women comparable to that of men's? Negative answers to these questions need not blur the truth that men and women are of the same species, and that what is of the essence of human kind is therefore present in both. If it is of the nature of man to seek to become self-complete, both male and female will express this fact, but not necessarily in the same way. They may still face different problems and go along different routes. The very same prospects may be realized by both of them, but in diverse ways. Their characteristic desires give different expressions to a common drive; similar activities do not have the same import for both of them.

Comparatively few women make athletics a career, even for a short time, and fewer still devote themselves to it to a degree that men do. Many reasons for this fact have been offered. Social custom, until very recently, has not encouraged them to be athletes. Fear of losing their femininity plays some role. Also, the appeal of a social life quickly crowds out a desire to practice and train, particularly where this forces them to be alone and without much hope of being signally successful. Swimmers, champions at thirteen and fourteen, seem bored with competitive swimming as they move toward the twenties. But more important than any of these reasons seems to be the fact that a young woman's body does not challenge her in the way in which a young man's body challenges him. She does not have to face it as something to be conquered, since she has already conquered it in the course of her coming of age. Where a young man spends his time redirecting his mind and disciplining his body, she has only the problem of making it function more gracefully and harmoniously than it natively can and does.

Men are able to live in their bodies only if they are taught and trained to turn their minds into bodily vectors. And they can become excellent in and through their bodies, only if they learn to identify themselves with their bodies and what these do. Normal women do not have this problem, at least not in the acute form that it presents to the men. A woman's biological growth is part of a larger process in which, without training or deliberation, she progressively becomes one with her body. What a man might accomplish through will and practice after he has entered on his last period of biological growth, she achieves through a process of bodily maturation. By the time she passes adolescence she is able to live her body somewhat the way in which a male athlete lives his.

A woman starts with an advantage over the man in that she masters her body more effortlessly and surely than he does his. If he is to be one with his body, he must prevent his mind from continuing to venture according to its bent, and must make it into a director of the body. He, but not she, has to deal with the body as though it were somewhat resistant to a drive toward its own perfection, and needs to be restructured, redirected, and controlled so that it becomes as excellent as it can be. With less effort she becomes better coordinated and more unified than he; she does not have to turn her mind away from its own concerns to make it function on behalf of the body. It never, despite her genuine interest in intellectual matters and her flights of fancy, is long occupied with the impersonal and nonbodily.

A woman is less abstract than a man because her mind is persistently ordered toward bodily problems. Emotions, which are the mind and body interwoven intimately, are easily aroused in her as a consequence. There are times when she will give herself wholeheartedly to intellectual pursuits, and may then distinguish herself in competition with men. But easily, and not too reluctantly, she slips quite soon into a period when her mind functions on behalf of her body in somewhat the way in which a trained athlete's mind functions on behalf of his. A woman, therefore, will typically interest herself in sport only when she sees that it will enable her to polish what she had previously acquired without thought or effort.

The athlete becomes one with his body through practice. Competition in games continues his practice, and in addition offers him a means for measuring his achievements in comparison with those obtained by others, and by himself at a previous time. No less than he, a woman wants and deserves to be measured too. By competing in games, she can learn where she stands. There she will discover just what she can bodily do and therefore what she is as a unified being. Usually, though, it is easier for her to judge herself by her attractiveness, and measure this in terms of its social effects. Where a man might be proud of his body, she is proud in her body; where he uses it, she lives it as a lure.

This account raises some hard questions. Why do not more women become athletes? Is it because they find that the advantage that they have in their comparatively easy and satisfying union with their bodies, makes athletic exertion and competition of not much interest? Is that why women athletes are often so young and stop their careers so soon? Why are not men, who have become one with their bodies, content with the result? Why do they go on to use that body, to identify themselves with equipment, to test themselves in contests, and to make themselves into representatives in games? Do they think of their attractiveness as too adventitious and episodic to be able to give them the kind of satisfaction they need? Why is not a good physique enough for all men or even for a good number of those who embark on an athletic career?

An almost opposite set of questions arises when we assume that biologic urge and social pressure tend to make men use an impersonal and women a personal measure of the success they achieve as embodied humans. Why do some men avoid all athletics? Why is it that some women follow an athletic career? It is too easy an answer, and one not apparently supported by the facts, to say that neither is normal. Many a man appears well adjusted, healthy, happy, and admired, despite the fact that he participates in no sport. Many women athletes are attractive; some are married; some have children. We beg our question when we assume that women athletes are men *manqué*, females without femininity, a fact supposedly evidenced by their devotion to an athletic career; we beg it, too, when we assume that nonathletic men are emasculated males, a fact supposedly evidenced by their unconcern with athletic matters.

If perfection can be achieved through the use of a perfected body, one should expect that women would want to compete with their peers. The fact that most do not, cannot be altogether ascribed to the social demands that are made on their bodies and their time. They are not biologic and social puppets. If they were, must we not also say that men are puppets as well, and that they do not devote themselves, as women do, to the task of making themselves attractive, because this is not a socially respectable goal for them? And what should we say then of those who withstand the pressures? Do they alone have a free will enabling them to counter what the others are driven to do? But a free will is not an adventitious feature, like hair, or bow legs, or a snub nose, resident in only some humans; if some women and men have will enough to withstand natural forces, surely all the others have it too, and might be expected to exercise it.

It is sometimes said that women feel challenged by men and yet know that they are not strong enough to overcome them through force. Their best recourse is to try a different route. This is an old story, told again and again in song, play, and novel, and for that reason alone should give us pause. From this perspective, the woman athlete is seen to be at a disadvantage in comparison with men, and must try to become equal or to prove herself superior to them by deception or flattery, or by disorienting them or taking advantage of their weaknesses. But she can also be taken to suppose that she is suffering from an unfair disadvantage, and must strive first to put herself in the position where her biological and social status is on a footing with his. The first of these alternatives sees women as inescapably inferior beings who compensate through wiles for what they cannot obtain through open competition; the second takes her to be disadvantaged and the disadvantages are to be overcome by discipline and determination. Neither alternative is satisfactory; neither takes adequate account of the joy, the devotion, the dedication, and the independence of spirit exhibited by many women athletes, their concentration on their own game, and their indifference to what the men are doing.

Training and practice can be friendless and boring. A sport such as skiing leaves one much alone. Nevertheless, there are women who train and practice; others ski in competitions with great intensity. While making enormous efforts and sacrifices to become highly skilled, they refuse to obscure the fact that they are women. They emphasize their femininity. It would be obviously wrong to say that they reject their sex or that they are less feminine than non-athletic women. It is no less incorrect to say that they train, practice, and perform only in order to ensnare or to show themselves to be the equal of men.

A woman must train and practice if she is to become an athlete. This demands that she make an effort to stand away from her body. The result she obtained through biological maturation she must for a while defy.

Most women do not make the effort to train or to participate because they are not subject to the tensions that young men suffer—tensions resulting from the discrepancy in the ways in which their minds and bodies tend to be disposed; the women have already achieved a satisfying integration of mind and body. Nevertheless, women can improve the functioning of their bodies. This is best done through exercise. And it can be helped through a vital participation in games.

A woman who wants to be an athlete must, for the time being, stand away from her body in preparation for the achievement of a different kind of union than that which she naturally acquired, and then must work at reaching the stage at which a man normally is. He starts with a separated mind and body; she must produce this before she can enter on an athletic career. She has to make a sacrifice of a natural union before she begins her athletic career, while he must for a while sacrifice only the pursuit of merely intellectual matters.

A man, of course, has achieved some union of mind and body, but it is not as thorough as a woman's normally is; she, of course, has had her intellectual moments and has found them desirable, but they do not last as long nor come as frequently as his do. Embarked on their athletic careers, both must make similar sacrifices of time and interest in other tempting activities. But some of them—security, a family, and a home—appeal to the woman more strongly and at an earlier age than they appeal to the man, and as a consequence she is prone to end her athletic career sooner than he.

Comparatively few women interest themselves in sport, and when they do they rarely exhibit the absorption and concern that is characteristic of large numbers of men. They do not have as strong a need as men to see just what it is that bodies can do, in part because they are more firmly established in their roles as social beings, wives, and mothers, than the men are in their roles as workers, business men, husbands and fathers, or even as thinkers, leaders, and public figures.

The number of people who give themselves whole-heartedly to an athletic career is not large. More men do so than women, but not enough to make the women who do have the shape of aberrational beings who are to be accounted for by means of a distinct set of principles. Both women and men seek to be perfected. But a woman finds that her acceptance of her matured body, promoted by her carrying out biological and social functions, offers a readily available and promising route by which the perfection can be reached.

Team play does not have much of an appeal to most women. The contests women enter are usually those in which they function as individuals alongside one another. Women are evidently more individualistic in temper, more self-contained than men. They live their own bodies while men spend their time and energy on projects, some of which demand team work.

Like men, women inevitably represent something other than themselves, and in the last resort, like men, represent man as such and at his best, given such and such a nature and such and such rules determining how he is to perform. But despite their status as a member of some team, and as a representative of all of us, women do not normally assume a role which is carried out in the light of the way in which others carry out their roles. They do not readily function as teammates.

There are, of course, exceptions. Women make good partners in tennis, and good members of teams in field hockey, basketball, and lacrosse. These exceptions do not belie a general tendency of women to perform as individuals. That tendency is supported by the fact that team sports invite undesirable injuries, and the fact that a woman's acceptance of her body, gradually intensified as she develops, encourages an individualistic outlook. This persists even when she makes a strong effort to abstract from her natural bodily condition and tries to identify herself with her body in the way male athletes identify with theirs.

Considerations such as these make desirable a distinctive approach the problem of how to interest women in athletics. Apparently, they must be made to see that it is good to separate oneself from one's body for a while in order better to unite with it later. One must make evident to them that the later union is a better unon but of the same kind as that which they natively acquired. Some young women have been able to see that this is a truth which gymnastics, swimming, diving, skating, and skiing sustain; other sports could be smilarly supported.

Once women have decided to engage in athletic activities they must, like men, train and practice; otherwise they cannot hope to do well. Their training follows the same general procedures followed by men, with account, of course, being taken of their difference in musculature, strength, and attitudes toward exhaustion, injury, and public display. Since they do differ from men in these regards, there should be sports designed just for them, enabling them to make maximal use of their distinctive bodies. Thought should be given to the woman's lower center of gravity, her greater flexibility in the shoulders, girdle, and fingers, to her greater stability in the knee joints, and to her greater heat resistance, if we are to give her opportunities for attaining a degree of excellence comparable to that attained by men, and this without taking her to be a fractional male. Though basketball was not designed to take advantage of neglected muscles or organs, but merely to provide an opportunity for men to play in summer and winter, with a minimum amount of easily available equipment, etc., it testifies to the truth that a sport can be a fresh creation, made to satisfy definite purposes. Other new sports could be created; some of these should be built around the use of a woman's body. The rules that govern women's games, particularly those involving teams, today often pay attention to what women can do and what they wish to avoid. Still further rules could be introduced which promote the perfecting of women, by making it possible for them to use their distinctive bodies in distinctive ways.

The sports we have today are heterogeneous. They do not explore every side of the human body; they are not grounded in an understanding of the main bodily types. More often than not, they are accidental products of history, slowly modified to take advantage of various innovations and to avoid discovered limitations. It is not likely that they are now in the best possible form for men; foreshortened versions cannot be expected to be altogether appropriate to women.

Apart from softball and what is called women's lacrosse, thinking about women's athletics has tended to emphasize gracefulness, accuracy, and coordination, particularly in those sports where some attempt is made to avoid imitating the men. There is an inclination to treat their sports as developments and extensions of the dance. Part of the reason for this, undoubtedly, is our socially inherited view of women's capacity and function; another part is traceable to the fact that women have come into

educational institutions and public activities in only comparatively recent times; a third reason is the firm conviction that women should be graceful rather than strong or
swift. It is also true that thinking about women's athletics
has been characterized by a singular lack of imagination,
inventiveness, and concern.

Little choice has been given to women to do more than
dance or to adapt the sports which men pursue. Rarely has
there been an attempt made to observe and objectively
measure what they do. Even in those educational institutions reserved for them, the needs of women are not given
the attention they deserve. Women's high schools and
colleges often yield to the temptation to become vocational
schools preparing women for an eventual career as home-
makers and mothers, as though it were the task of an
educational institution to prepare students for the kind of
lives previous generations led, or which most of the students will most likely lead. The institutions seem to have
forgotten that it is their task to promote the self-discovery,
the awakening of interests, the extending of the imagination, the civilizing of students, to set them on the way
toward becoming enriched, matured beings.

Calisthenics and gymnastic programs, long ago
pushed aside in men's schools, still find a large and sometimes a primary place in the physical education of women.
Calisthenics is exercise without equipment; gymnastics is
exercise making use of equipment; both have as their
objective the promotion of all-round development, and perhaps gracefulness. They are thought to be ideal means for
making the body healthy and well coordinated. Their prac-
titioners sometimes compete with one another in exhibitions. In contests and games, calisthenics and gymnastics
have at best only a minor, incidental role. They may, of
course, be mastered as part of an athletic training course,
aimed at the production of a different type of result. But
then they are used only to make the body fit to engage in a
contest or game which is not covered by a calisthenic or
gymnastic program.

The gymnastic programs in vogue today are largely
combinations of the German, French, and Swedish. The
Germanic strain emphasizes strength, the French graceful-

ness, and the Swedish mechanical precision. Once, each of these was pursued independently, under rigid codes, with set exercises and well-defined steps and stages. Around the turn of the century all were forced to give way to a "natural" gymnastics which concentrated on the development of the entire body. The large place such a program continues to have in women's schools confirms the view that women are thought to have a matured and accepted body, and that they need only to polish it.

"Gymnastics" comes from the Greek. Its literal meaning is "engaging in exercise nakedly." The Romans disapproved of the nakedness. We have continued to follow the Romans, but with some appreciation of the French gracefulness and the Swedish precision.

In the end, the very devotion to the cause of making fine bodies defeated the gymnastic programs from remaining in a dominant position in the men's colleges. Once given the chance to train for games, students revolted against doing set exercises as ends in themselves. They found them to be tedious, repetitious, meaningless.

Today, fitness programs are being reintroduced for men. This may lead to a welcome reintroduction of strong gymnastic programs for them, parallel to those now supported in women's colleges. Men will perhaps return to them again, once they see gymnastics as not only making possible a better participation in games, but as enabling them to become splendid incarnated beings.

A game is a sequence of turning points, each of which must be dealt with appropriately if the activity is to terminate successfully. At each moment the player shows what he has mastered and what still remains to be done. Having dedicated himself to the task of doing all he can, he then finds that he must bring to bear all his power and emotional capital to achieve the best results. The participation forces him to make and live through the crucial decisions, and possibly add to his skills. The benefits are not predicated on his sex. Women, too, should be prompted to train, to prepare, to practice, so as to be ready to test themselves in relation to others, and thereby discover how excellent they have made themselves become.

A decent and civilized man controls his body along the

lines required by society, a well-mannered man controls his body along the lines of convention, and an intellectual controls his body to enable himself to concentrate on other matters, while an athlete controls his body so as to be able to identify himself with his equipment, and to master the obstacles that confront him. This last opportunity is denied to women when they are not provided with sports that are regulated and programmed to their structures and rhythms.

One of the aims of a good athletic program is the development and intensification of good character. With the growth of professionalism in the schools, it has been cynically remarked that character building is the most that coaches of losing teams can produce. Were that true it would be enough. Character building justifies an emphasis on athletics in the high schools and colleges. And it is no less needed by women than it is by men. They, too, can profitably learn how to meet crises, how to withstand fear, and where to draw the line between self-indulgence and excessive restraint. And they can learn these things effectively, as men now do, in the gymnasium and on the field. Because the building of character is one of the tasks of education, both women and men should be given the opportunity to prepare themselves for vigorous participation in relevant sports.

Character is built by engaging in limited, well-controlled acts. By imitating what had been splendidly done in the large, the young are helped to grow. We then teach them how to make a proper estimate of who they are and what they can do, by promoting their correct assessment of when and where they are to advance and retreat. Like other virtues, assessment is a habit; like all habits, it is strengthened through repetition. A game allows for its manifestation and provides additional opportunities to entrench it further.

The adoration of the crowds, of the young, and of girls, can make a male athlete misconstrue just what he has achieved, what he is yet to achieve, who he is, and what he might become. The virtues which he painfully acquired in practice are then muted and sometimes distorted; he begins to lose focus and to misunderstand the nature of sport. Women are fortunate in that few of their games come to the attention of the public; they are thereby enabled to avoid most of the misconstructions which beset male athletes. But it is also true that men have in their games a unique opportunity to show what they can do under well-specified, controlled, yet trying circumstances. Men are normally put to tests much more difficult than women face, and as a consequence are able to attain heights denied to them.

The comparative neglect of team sports by women entails that they have fewer opportunities to see themselves as needing to work on behalf of the rest, to make sacrifices for others with whom they share a common objective, and to function in coordinated roles. Because they have fewer occasions when they can carry out difficult tasks together with other players, they do not have the opportunity to master specialized skills, or to know the kind of bodily mastery which others have achieved and of which they make effective use.

Women need to be disciplined and self-disciplined, trained and self-trained, both as individuals and as members of groups. They should have the right and the privilege of contributing in judgment, skill, and imagination to the making of a distinguished game. They, too, have need for and deserve to be suffused with the pleasure that comes from a game well played. They, too, can gain by belonging to something bigger than themselves, such as a tradition-bound sport.

Even when women have little aptitude or interest, they can profit from athletic activity. Physical fitness and bodily tone are thereby usually improved. The women most likely will become healthier, perhaps more graceful, and gain some sense of the fair play that proper playing demands. They might thereby become better adjusted to themselves and to others.

Maladjustment is a form of illness. He who is inharmonious is not well. The movement from the state of being ill to that of being well is therapy or cure. Athletics, because it enables one to move from a poor to a better state of being, can be viewed as a branch of medicine, but one which fortunately finds room for the expression of spontaneity, ingenuity, and judgment. Sport is, of course, not to be treated as primarily an agency for promoting health —or anything else for that matter—regardless of how important this is. Sport is an end in itself. One can become perfected by engaging in it, but it does not have even that perfection as its aim. Perfection is an inevitable consequence of sport only when this is properly pursued in an enclosed arena where men and women find out what man can bodily be. If health is also achieved, so much the better.

Athletes run the risk of overexerting themselves. They expose themselves to strain and the possibility of injury, with a consequent lessened tolerance to disease. Appetites are developed in training which continue to be insistent later, making an accumulation of fat more likely, and, therefore, shorter breath and conceivably a shorter life expectancy. There is a proneness to accidents, particularly when challenging and unpredictable situations have to be faced with quick decisions and appropriate action. An error can scar a life, psychologically and emotionally as well as physically. No one likes to see women subjected to these risks. Still, a risk is not yet a failure. Women need to risk more; only if they do, can they hope to gain all that is possible for them.

A well-trained athlete can rightly expect to engage in sport throughout his life, providing that he so alters his interests, intentions, and efforts that he can keep abreast of changes in his age and physical condition. There is no reason why a woman should not be able to continue in a similar way, and maintain a trim, firm body, suffused with a desirable tone, for an indefinite period. If her athletic potentialities are taken with as much seriousness as a man's, it will become more evident than it now is that sport concerns not only males but mankind, and deserves to be viewed as a basic enterprise, devoted to the production of the excellent in and through the body.

General discourse of this sort deals with idealized types of men and women, and is rooted in speculations for which there is little empirical warrant. Its primary justification is that it opens up possibilities for investigation and may help one focus on issues otherwise slurred over. To some degree it rests on the observation that young men's energies overflow to an extent that the energies of women of the same age do not. Young men are restless and exuberant; vigorous action seems natural to them, while women are content to move smoothly, using their energies to improve the union of body and mind that is natural to them.

Sport is a young person's most promising opening into excellence. Unfortunately, no one has a clear and well-substantiated knowledge as to what a career devoted to sport exactly imports for either men or women. Most of what is claimed for it today is the product of rapid empirical summaries, not a little prejudice and hope, and some limited experiments. We would be on surer ground if we knew how to compare what was done in one sport with what was done in another, and how the various sports were related to one another, for we would then be able to place them all before us and see what they, severally and together, might mean for all, professionals as well as amateurs, women as well as men.

14.   the standardization of sport

MEN are men everywhere. We can stop with this observation and justifiably allow all men to compete in all sports, without restriction or qualification. But it is also true that men differ in strength, experience, background, ability, and commitment. We, therefore, make it a practice to have children compete only with children, freshmen only with freshmen, young men only with young men, and, usually, the old only with the old.

Rarely do we pit women against men, either in individual or in team sport. In its 1965 statement, the National Joint Committee on Extramural Sports for College Women stated the accepted view on competition between the sexes. "Men should not play on women's teams and women should not play on men's teams. . . . Men and women playing together may compete against other men and women . . . provided the activities do not involve body contact." [1] Accepted practice would seem to make this official statement almost unnecessary; the separations are maintained by the force of custom. There is value, though, in stating explicitly and officially what is both desired and done. One is then better able to deal with hard cases and with violations; lines drawn in advance show where lines are to be drawn in fact.

In some sports, contestants are classed according to weight. Wrestlers and boxers compete only with those in

---

[1] Quoted in "The Role of Sports in the Culture of Girls," by Laura T. Huelster, *Proceedings*, Second National Institute on Girls' Sports, National Education Association (Washington, D. C., 1966), p. 122.

their own weight classes. In other sports, such as judo and karate, there is a hierarchy of excellence, and contests are held only between those on the same rung. We take such distinctions to be irrelevant in shooting, fishing, bowling, and dressage competitions; excellent results in these sports are obtained by heavier and older as well as by slimmer and younger men.

Evidently, so far as competition is concerned, there are at least two types of sport. In the one, we seek to determine just what the best attainable result will be; competition here is sufficiently wide open to permit anyone who has a reasonable hope of success to show what he can do. But in the more common types of sport, age, size, weight, training, skill, and sex are recognized to make such a difference to the hope of success that competition is restricted to the members of a class, all of whom are somewhat similar in one or more of these presumably relevant features. Sometimes it is desirable to limit the competition further; the disparity between players in the same age, weight, sex, etc., class may be too great to make a contest between them worthwhile.

One way of improving a match is by seeding, the practice by which strong players are freed from the necessity of playing early rounds in an elimination contest so that they will be sure to meet one another. The idea implicitly supposes that some unknown players, qualified to enter the competition, may defeat proven, strong ones. Seeding does not preclude such a defeat; an unknown player may survive all the elimination rounds, and end victorious. Seeding merely prevents one strong player from meeting another too soon, or a known weaker player from defeating a known stronger one early in the contest. The idea has been extended to trial heats where, in order to make different trials more interesting, good performers are distributed among the different heats. All of the contestants may be required to compete in some preliminary heat, but only a few good athletes, at most, are made to compete with one another. The same device could be employed in contests between professionals and amateurs, or men and women, young and old, etc.

We can think of seeding as a way of distinguishing known stronger players from players whose records are not known to be as good, and then allowing the latter, after having met certain conditions, to compete against the former. We can also view all other limited competitions as being the outcome of a process of seeding in which different grades of players are not permitted to come into competition with one another. In the one case we have a moveable, in the other a fixed, barrier between types of competitors.

Handicaps, in which some advantage is given to the disadvantaged in the effort to make the competition one between equals (though they may still in fact differ in weight, or sex, or experience), work on a principle different from that which governs seeding. A handicap compensates for the advantages which some enjoy, by subjecting the advantaged to limiting conditions designed to bring them to the level of the others; or conversely, it takes account of the disadvantages of some by granting these better conditions or more points, so that they will have as much of an opportunity to be victorious as those who are acknowledged to be superior players. Evidently it allows a wide variety of individuals to compete with a reasonable expectation that they will be successful.

Seeding and handicaps apply to competitors in the same contest. Records, in contrast, particularly in field events, report the achievements of men in different places, at different times, and under varying circumstances. The records abstract from supposedly minor differences in terrain, temperature, wind, and humidity. As a rule they take account of some of the larger differences. Indoor and outdoor records are, therefore, distinguished. They are so sharply distinguished, in fact, that no world's track or field record can be made indoors. Intercollegiate records in racing are invalidated if the following wind exceeds three miles an hour. Automobile time trials must be made in both directions, and are then averaged in an attempt to allow for any difference that might have been produced by sun, wind, or track. These, however, are only half-hearted measures. If one who runs with a strong wind at his back is unjustly favored, he who runs with a slight wind at his back is also unjustly favored over another who has a slight wind against him, or who runs in a dead calm. He who runs with a following wind of two and a half miles an hour has a five mile an hour advantage over one who runs against a wind of that velocity. But today the records take no account of such facts.

There is nothing wrong in having a man run with a strong wind at his back or in his face. What is wrong is the refusal to attend to and to weigh the advantage and disadvantage which the wind produces in a given contest. We cannot provide uniform conditions everywhere, but we can take note of the prevailing advantages and disadvantages, and give them a weight, negative or positive, in the final report. Similar adjustments can be made for those who are favored or hindered by temperature, humidity, terrain, and the like.

We need a statement of ideal conditions, and a formula for assigning handicap values for divergencies from them. Professionals can then be calibrated with amateurs, the young with the old, and men with women. By giving different values, in addition, to differences in experience, age, skill, and strength, competition can be equalized even though the competitors are evidently quite disparate. If this is done, all, and not merely certain conspicuous differences under which competition is conducted, would be given a value in the final result. For the first time in the history of sport we would have a fair, objective, universally applicable scale in terms of which the outcomes at different places and times, under diverse conditions, produced by individuals and teams in different stages of development could be compared.

Records in the modern sense date from around 1880. Before then the reporting was not reliable and the timing not very precise. The tenth-second interval is a rather recent innovation; it was not recognized by the IAFF or the AAU until 1926.[2] Measurements could be more exact. Progress in that direction is fortunately now being made through the improvement of timepieces, photography, re-

2 George P. Meade, *Athletic Records, The Whys and Where-fores* (New York, 1966), pp. 17, 30 ff., 61.

cording, and reporting. But we have still a good distance to go. Diving and ice skating exhibitions are judged with the unaided eye; gains and downs in football are measured crudely, with inadequate controls. Too much in many sports is left to quick, unchecked decisions.

So far as we are content merely to ask all competitors to try to be as excellent as possible, it makes little difference where they stand in some elimination contest, in situations for which they are not as prepared as others are, or under circumstances which help or hinder them. Exact measurements will not be needed. But if we are concerned with knowing just what men can accomplish, or in having a uniform set of records, the actual deviations in conditions from an acknowledged norm for all should be carefully calculated in the result.

An alternative method for providing for the standardization of sport would consist in ignoring all differences among the competitors. Olympic Games are sometimes played in hot countries and sometimes in cold, and at considerable heights above and at heights close to sea level, without any consideration being given to the differences these might make to the result. No attention is paid to the fact that athletes from hot or high countries are competing in hot or in high places against those who have been accustomed to cold or to sea level. With the same warrant we could ignore differences in other circumstances, or in ability, sex, age, and professional status. An excuse for such ignoring can be found in the fact that men who were thought to be in a disadvantageous position, have sometimes outdistanced all others.

Although hot climate evidently represents a physiological handicap, it does not necessarily render the attainment of athletic success, even at Olympic Games impossible. Some of the world's best runners came from Jamaica and the winners of the field hockey tournament were Indians [in the British Empire Games of 1954].[3]

3 Ernst Jokl, M.D., *Medical Sociology and Cultural Anthropology of Sport and Physical Education* (Springfield, Ill., 1963), p. 107.

This alternative proposal is not better than the other. In effect it treats advantages and disadvantages as so many lucky or unlucky occurrences, on a footing with the contingencies which crop up in the course of an ordinary contest or game. If we were to deal with the performances of professional and women athletes from this perspective, refusing to take account of how they differ from amateurs and men, respectively, athletic success will be almost entirely the prerogative of male professionals. Women amateurs, to be sure, can sometimes outdistance men in rifle, figure skating, and dressage, with their emphasis on control and accuracy rather than strength. Perhaps they can more than hold their own in some endurance contests, though we cannot be sure just what they can do in endurance competitions, in good part because they have not entered them in appreciable numbers. William W. Heusner observes,

Theoretically, the capacity of women to conserve sodium and chloride to increase extra-cellular fluid and plasma volume, and to decrease urinary volume should enable them to perform well in endurance events and to withstand heat better than men.[4]

They will, though, be at a distinct disadvantage in relation to men in any competition where strength is a large factor. And strength plays some role in every athletic activity.

It would be good to have an ideal set of standards, and to compensate mathematically for advantages, or to provide handicaps answering to differences in endowment, length of experience, and the prevailing conditions. Whatever makes a difference to the result should be noted and its value calculated in the final report. Undoubtedly there will be some factors that we will have to ignore. Some teams have had the benefit of better coaching, or have had the support of a sympathetic group of spectators. But we have no reliable way of measuring the effect these have. Could we, though, measure these advantages it would be

4 William W. Heusner, "Basic Physiological Concepts as They Relate to Girls Sports," *Proceedings*, Second National Institute on Girls' Sports, National Education Association (Washington, D. C., 1966), p. 140.

tempting to say that they nevertheless should not be calculated in any result, since they represent a desirable norm
which all should exhibit. But does one not then have a good
reason for also ignoring the advantages that superior ability, strength, and weight provide? It seems so. Consequently, one would have to abandon the practice of handicapping when the abler and more experienced play against
comparative novices. We are forced to conclude, therefore,
that we must ignore certain advantages, not because they
should not be considered in making matches or in keeping
records, but because we have no way of handling them.
We must be content to compensate by points or by handicapping and seeding only those who, perhaps as a result of
these advantages, are demonstrably superior. And this will
require that we apply common measures to all.

Racing stewards think certain drugs give horses an
unfair advantage. If so, we do not know just how to
calculate the exact effect of the drugs. What is needed are
exact determinations of what can be accomplished with
and without them. Our knowledge of the effects of other
drugs is also not clear enough. Nor do we seem to know
what is to be permitted to men, and why. Today it is
customary to allow the use of mild stimulants and some
familiar drugs, despite the fact that they are used to make
one more alert or to dull pain and thereby make it possible
for one to continue to compete. The use of some other
drugs is forbidden because they are thought to give an
undue advantage to their users. Yet no one seems to know
whether or not this advantage is great or small, or just how
long it lasts.

A strong case could be made out for the proscription of
drugs known to have a permanent deleterious effect, but a
large part of the issue is untouched by such considerations.
Why permit the use of coffee, tea, aspirin, or even sugar
and fruits to be taken at half time or during a marathon
swim, and forbid the use of alcohol, particularly where this
would help a player to overcome shyness or some other
inhibition? Why not permit all contestants the use of the
same drugs, at least the well-proven harmless ones? Those
for whom the drugs are most effective will of course gain
an advantage. But a similar result follows on the introduc-

tion of flexible vaulting poles, runners' starting blocks,
springy golf balls, thinner bats, and so on.

Usually, it will be fairly easy to provide a sound estimate of the contribution to the final result that is made by
large environmental factors. It would be hard, but certainly not impossible, to give different values to different
ages, weights, and years of experience, thereby making it
possible to compare competitors and records now separated
into supposedly incomparable categories. An objective set
of records could then be obtained, despite the fact that they
are made by different types of men, in different places and
times.

Weight seems to have little or no bearing on the results achieved in shooting with the rifle or the revolver.
Sometimes age does not seem to be significant. The age
range in the 1952 Olympic Games was fifty-three years.
One fencer was twenty and another was forty-nine; one
gymnast was fifteen and another forty-five. A seventeen
year old won the 200 clay pigeon contest; in fifth place was
a man of sixty. Once men pass beyond childhood (and
until they become quite old) age seems to make little
difference to what they can achieve in fly casting or archery. Nor does experience always appear to provide an
advantage. Youngsters sometimes beat more seasoned
swimmers. Ilsa Konrads at fourteen broke the world's
record for 440 yards in 1960.

Differences in sex offer a more difficult problem of
adjudication. Sometimes it has no bearing. Women have
made records in shooting, and have won competitions
against men. But women, as was already remarked, do
have abilities and anatomies which differ in signal respects
from men's, putting them at a disadvantage in certain
types of competition. Even in diving and gymnastics,
where they perform so well, they lack the strength to make
the high jumps necessary for the performance of certain
complicated turns and rolls. Nothing in principle, though,
prevents us from placing a numerical value on the difference which distinguishes the musculature, girdle, and
strength of men and women, thereby making it possible to
produce a single set of records for them all.

If we are willing to go this far—and why should we

not?—we will have to look into the question as to whether
or not there is a sufficient difference in the metabolism,
resiliency, musculature, anatomy, and perhaps even opportunity, to warrant the introduction of handicaps, in fact or
in calculation, for the members of different races. American Negroes do superbly in the sprints. Is this because
they enjoy a physical advantage over whites? They are not
conspicuous among marathoners. Is that because they lack
some factor which white marathoners have, to their advantage? No one seems to know.

If there is a real difference in the bodily capacities of
Negroes and whites, we ought to handicap one or the
other. There are men who would withdraw at this suggestion in the fear that it would solidify prejudice and weaken
the cause of civil rights. But these political considerations
have no place in sport. Granted that the question of civil
rights, prejudice, etc., are to be considered, it still may be
the case that a handicapping on the basis of race may have
no undesirable effects. The recognition of the physical
advantages enjoyed by men over women has not entailed a
denial of women's political rights, nor has it apparently
intensified male prejudices against them. The contrary
appears to have happened.

Problems like these could be avoided, it has already
been suggested, by taking all competitors as they are. Any
advantage, native or acquired, that anyone might have,
would be disregarded. We would attend only to the question of who was victorious and by what amount, and how
this compared with what had been achieved at other times.
Whatever favored the winner would not be remarked;
records would merely show the results. In this way we
would learn what the best athletes could do under the most
propitious conditions. If we follow this line, it will be
difficult to deny to any feature the status of a given, and we
would have no reason to object to any circumstance, no
matter how extraordinary. We would also have to abandon
the attempt to standardize sport.

Seeding and handicap practices, and the refusal to
allow baseball to be played in the rain, men to run with a
strong wind at their backs, and the like, make evident that

we are not willing to abstract from every circumstance. Our unwillingness would be willful were games part of the daily world or of nature, for these are affected by contingencies of the most diverse kinds with which we have to make do. But because games are encapsulated occurrences, governed by rules which men invent and enforce, it is within our province to deal with circumstances as we like, ignoring some and attending to others. We ought to note those that make a signal difference in the results. This is what we now do in many cases. The question that remains over is whether weight should be given to many more factors than is now done, or whether we should be content to decide the matter as we traditionally have, by allowing it to come up every once in a while in the course of the discussions by official bodies. But it is hard to justify a haphazard process, particularly when its operation results in arbitrary selections and evidently unfair evaluations. A vigorous and persistent standardization is desirable, to make possible a comparison of results achieved in a sport at different times, in different circumstances, and by different types of contestants.

All contests and games of a particular type seem to be within the province of one type of athlete. It seems reasonable to suppose we can make intelligent comparisons between races at different distances; some runners, after all, hold records for a number of them. There is, to be sure, a great deal of difference between a sprint and a marathon, but we could conceivably move from one to the other through the mediation of the distances run in between. It makes sense to equate a forty-five second 440 yard race with a four-minute mile, or to compare running, hurdling, and jumping, since they are closely related skills. It has been determined that the record rate falls off differently in a shorter race from what it does in a longer.[5] But how compare the shot-put and a sprint? How compare baseball and lacrosse, or tennis, golf, and diving? That they are not altogether incomparable is evident from the fact that we do

5 David B. Dill, "Fatigue and Physical Fitness," *Science and Medicine of Exercise and Sports*, ed. Warren Russell Johnson (New York, 1960), p. 389.

sometimes scale them on the basis of spectator interest, money spent on them, and (where we have professionals) money earned. We could conceivably use more pertinent measures, such as the amount of strength exhibited, the grade of difficulty involved, or the degree of gracefulness demanded or achieved. Today different values are assigned to different dives, to figures skated, and to the events in the decathlon, primarily on the basis of supposed difficulty. A similar procedure could be followed in judging the achievements of men in all other sports.

If we are to have a single set of records we must know how to relate the achievements in one contest or game to that of any other. We could equate all champions, and take the records that they have made in the different sports to provide standards in terms of which other competitors are to be measured. Or better, we could assign weights to different sports; by giving those weights a quantitative value we would make possible the comparison of the results in one with those of any other. If now we specify what would be ideal outcomes in each sport, we could then scale actual performances on the basis of their approximation to the ideal. The hurdles might be said to be more difficult than sprints by such and such a fraction; the record in the shot-put could be treated as a fraction of that made in the hammer throw because of the presumed lesser demands made on the performer. Team sports could be related to one another and to individual sports by some similar device. In all these cases we would, unfortunately, often be called upon to make arbitrary decisions, and in many a case those decisions would be unfair. But more justice would be done than is possible today.

Standardization presupposes some method by which one can compare player with player, contest with contest, circumstance with circumstance, and sport with sport. It could be so vigorously pursued that each of these could be given a value with reference to the others, so that, for example, a player of such and such known excellence will be assigned a value which can be compared with that given to such and such a circumstance. The advantage which a champion natively enjoys might then be compared with a favoring wind or a lucky move. But once again our decisions would be somewhat arbitrary and often unfair.

The more comprehensive the assignment of weights to different sports, games, participants, and circumstances, the more do we make athletics into a world where men compete as equals. We also make it possible for them, despite a difference in age, sex, and experience, to be in the same contests with one another, each with his appropriate handicap or weighted value. We need have no more fear that the contests will all end in draws. They do not today, despite great efforts made to have evenly matched competitors.

If there is a scoreless tie, or a dead heat, whether or not the competitors are well matched, something will have been decided. Instead of one, a number of men will have brought about a single result. It will still be true that superiority will have been allowed to manifest itself in the course of rule-abiding efforts. The great danger in an equalization of competitors through handicaps, modification of scores, and the like, lies in the other direction; wide differences amongst competitors might made a contest take on the semblance of a mob scene. This possibility could be minimized by having different groups compete separately. Standardization would then be restricted solely to the evaluation of the results produced.

He who wins a contest reveals himself to have some advantage over the loser, and that advantage is in part produced in the course of the contest. Though we want individuals and teams to play against individuals and teams in similar circumstances, our desire to have superiority demonstrated means that we want men to be evenly matched only in those features that can be discovered in advance of the contest. Though we want them to compete under conditions which allow for a fair comparison with what is done elsewhere, our desire to have fair comparisons means that we want the contests conducted under uniform conditions, leaving it to the actual struggle to bring out what in fact distinguishes one athlete from another.

A victory offers testimony to a comparative excellence when contestants are evenly matched. When they are not, the victory as a rule shows the advantages which a man may have because of his experience, sex, youth, etc. When the disadvantaged wins, because of his handicap, his result is significant; the handicap makes good the loss that the disadvantage entails, thereby treating the outcome as though it were made by man at his best. Once again we make it possible to show, not what this or that individual can do, but what can be done by man.

15.   a metaphysical excursus

MOST men live without vision or wisdom. The few who act
as large-sized men, do so only part of the time. Rarely do
any of us push ourselves to the sticking point. Even more
rarely do we raise our heads above the multitude of tasks
and details that besiege us daily. The athlete avoids this
sad prospect by temporarily accepting a life which makes
it desirable for him to learn to control his body and the
agencies by means of which that body will meet the challenges of other bodies and the world about. As a consequence, though he does not thereby acquire vision, he
escapes for a time from some of the confusions characteristic of daily life; and though he does not thereby become
wise, he does benefit from the wisdom inherent in a well-
toned, skilled, effective body.

Like all other men, the athlete is obligated to do the
best he can in every case. Unlike most other men, he
dedicates himself. As a consequence he accepts an obligation and makes a strong effort to fulfill it. He therefore
prevents his body from acting on impulse, to make it the
servant for achieving excellence. For a short period he uses
his native freedom with maximum effect, to place himself
for a moment alongside artists, religious men, and inquir-
ers of every stripe.

The athlete's world is set over against the everyday
world. Economic demands and the satisfaction of appetites
are for the moment put aside. This is also what is done by
ethical men in their endeavors to realize ideal goals. Artists
and historians similarly bracket off their distinctive, dynamic spatiotemporal worlds. They are matched by reli-

gious men who make both private and public efforts to achieve a closer contact with and to conform to the demands of their God. All turn from the world of common sense and its practical demands to try to come to grips with distinct finalities.

Nature, the ideal Good, and God are ultimate and everlasting. Each has its own characteristic particulars which depend on it for their being, just as it depends on them for articulation and effectiveness. The scholar and the athlete, the one through study and knowledge, the other through action, are directly related to limited versions of these ultimate finalities, and directly related to the unlimited form of another finality, which I have elsewhere termed "Actuality."

The more a man cuts himself off from the world around him, in order to identify himself with what is ultimately real, the more he opens himself up to the presence of Actuality, and is able to make use of it as the common referent for the particular items that environ him. Whenever he says "it is true that . . ." or "it is the case that . . ." he refers to Actuality as that which sustains forever what it is that is true or is the case. By becoming one with his body, the athlete in an analogous way makes what he does be more clearly that which is in fact and forever the case.

All particulars are contingent; none remains in existence forever. They now are, because they *have* being, because they for the present share, in a limited and distinctive way, the being of a finality. In his acceptance of himself as a body, the athlete faces Actuality, the being which that body and related particulars equally participate in. He, therefore, can become aware of himself as one who, despite his prowess, successes, and awards, is on the same footing of reality with all other men, and eventually with all other space-time particulars.

As the Bhagavad-Gita long ago affirmed, the man of action, once he has detached himself from the pragmatic import of his efforts, achieves what the contemplative does, once he has turned his mind away from contingencies to dwell on that which is forever. By a distinct route the athlete, too, can arrive at the result the yogi seeks. The distinction that existentialists like to draw between men and all the other entities in this space-time world, he completely abrogates in a dynamic acknowledgment of an eternal reality which sustains all.

The athlete is a man of action who responsibly tries to bring about a public result. Because he separates his activity from its fruits he becomes a part of a distinct, bounded situation. The dynamism of that world he has pushed aside, enabling him to create another domain with its own beginning, ending, process, and laws. What he is and what he does is for the moment thereby severed from the rest of the world.

Like an artist, the athlete is occupied with producing something with which he can live for a while, and which, so far, enables him to be self-sufficient. He does not make and is not interested in making something that is beautiful, or in grasping the very being of space, time, or energy; instead he holds himself away from everything else to give himself wholly to a game. Since he is no longer subject to the daily conventionalities and practices which overlay and obscure what is taking place, he is in a fine position to heal the breach that daily separates him and the world beyond. To be sure, he lives inside other conventions, but these are not supposed by him to be the very structure of reality, and he is, therefore, more able than most to return to his daily tasks with some sense of what is stable and fundamental there, and what is not.

Occupied with the present, directed toward the future, the man of action as a rule spends little time in mastering what links him to the past. That is why history rarely reveals him to be doing much more than continuing the processes which had been begun earlier by predecessors. Had he undergone anything like the degree of training to which the athlete submits himself, he would be more judicious, and would be readier to act with greater freedom and a sense of what is the case. Because he not only plays in a game but participates in it, the athlete engages in acts which preserve the past of his sport. His acceptance of rules, which bind his opponents as well, helps make the game a new occurrence within a distinctive history.

Like every other man, an athlete is a distinct individual. He, too, lives out his life in ineluctable privacy. But because of his dedication and his willingness to subject himself to tests which probe to the depths of his preparation, character, and creativity, he is sharply outlined.

Like a religious man who turns from the world to open himself up to his God, the athlete places himself before whatever eternal and impersonal judge there is. He accepts as basic the position that he will be judged objectively, and irrevocably. The religious man is, to be sure, more actively occupied with his presumed judge than the athlete is. Through his faith he tries to come closer to his God, whose evaluations are of vital importance to him. The athlete, instead, is content to allow himself to be judged by men, and makes no effort to come in closer contact with whatever eternal judge there is. In compensation, he can often watch his judges in action, and is able to learn, as the religious man cannot, just how he compares with others.

Both in religion and in athletics men are welded together intimately. Neither result has much lasting power. If the religious man is right, he also makes it possible for his God to be at once immanent in that whole and a better focused object outside it. The athlete must instead be content with nothing more than the totality that he and his fellow players together constitute. He makes less of a claim than the religious man does, but for that reason he does not take account of realities that may have much to do with his present and eventual welfare.

By participating in a public game with others, the athlete makes an intimately related whole with them. The more the players act together, despite competition, to produce a common game, the closer is the bond uniting them all. Athletes make more vital that harmonization of men which religious men suppose God's presence in the world entails.

Like every other body, the athlete's decays and eventually passes away. But there is also a sense in which he nevertheless continues to be. Since he has abdicated from all other positions to make himself a man who is an effective, excellent body, he has defined himself to be an incarnation of those persistent laws which cover the operation of that body. He is one with those laws, their very embodi-

ment, and is so far forever. As an individual he passes
away, of course, but his individuality is irrelevant to the
more basic fact that he has made himself into a place
where those laws for the moment are. The bodies of other
men also embody those very same laws. But those men
have not altogether identified themselves with their bodies
and so far, though instantiating the laws, are not eternal-
ized as these.

All men illustrate cosmic truths. All are localizations
and carriers of structures which last forever. So far as
anyone embodies these he, in a way, forever abides. But
only he who identifies himself with a reality which those
laws govern can be said to be able to benefit from the
eternality of those laws. Something similar to what the
mathematician attains when he thinks, the athlete attains
when he acts.

Today we are so aware of the press of time and the fact
of mortality that any reference to immortality arouses dis-
trust. And there is so much crassness exhibited by athletes
as to make suspect any account that has them appear to be
more than men who are able to use their bodies a little
better than others can. But it is not to individuals in their
individual distinctive private nature that these observations
apply; it is to those individuals as caught up and almost
swallowed in the role of ideal athlete.

All of us are acquainted with the eternal in many
ways. The numbers we write down are but marks to
enable us to understand better the eternal possibilities
which mathematicians know. They are the chemicals
that allow us to read the invisible writings of eternity.
The ideals of truth, beauty, and goodness, which obligate
us all, though realized in partial and distorted forms, are
possibilities that remain forever, unaffected by their lack of
realization or by any realization we can manage. More
evident, perhaps, is the fact that the truths of logic are
necessities forever outside the corrosive grip of time. But
any truth is a truth forever. It is always true that I am
sitting here before my typewriter on January 29, 1968,
revising once again what I had written on January 22d,
1966.

Each one of us represents all of mankind. When we

assert something to be the case we assert it not merely for ourselves, or as expressive of ourselves, but as something which any other could assert. When I say "This is a book" I am not saying "This is a book for me," "This looks like a book to me," "I think it is a book," but that it is a book in fact. Ignorance, errors of judgment, differences in vocabulary, and an incapacity to see what in fact I confront will prevent another from knowing whether what I say is true or no; but if it is true, it is true. It will remain true even if no one knows it or no matter who it is that knows it.

Our judgments and our evaluations purport to be formulations of what is objective, permanent, and true, not subject to the vicissitudes of our individual biases, likes, or careers. To know what is, is to escape the remorseless flux of time.

When we attend to any truth we remove ourselves from the transient world, becoming one with eternity. The athlete, in his commitment, vivifies this fact. He not only represents all mankind—as we all do—when he judges and knows; he represents it in his effort to achieve a maximal result in his sport. The world of sport intensifies the meanings which any man in the course of his life inevitably expresses in his judgments and decisions. The athlete is sport incarnated, sport instantiated, sport located for the moment, and by that fact is man himself, incarnated, instantiated, and located.

Each of us is a unity of "local matter" with the meaning of man. The unity has only a short life. But the matter and the meaning continue to be. The athlete unites his local matter with the meaning of mankind, enriched and mediated by the meaning of excellence which he seeks to embody. When he understands himself to encompass these two abiding components and to provide a unique mode of union for them, he is in principle one who is the copresence of two eternities. His recognition of other athletes, as men who uniquely unite matter and meaning, is a recognition of them as also exhibiting the copresence of those eternities. Serving as distinctive carriers of what he also carries, they become his copresent counterparts. This fact is shown in team play and the respect accorded them.

Where others structure situations according to their affections and whims, the athlete submits himself to stringent rules, and dedicates himself to a superb performance, to make himself one who loves too coldly, perhaps, but persistently and well. In his play he exhibits in a steady, impersonal form that love which some men on occasion extend toward a few.

a selected bibliography

index

a selected bibliography

Anthology of Contemporary Readings, An Introduction to Physical Education, ed. W. Aileene S. Lockhart and Howard S. Slusher. Dubuque, Iowa: William C. Brown Co., 1966.

Armbruster, David A., Sr., Leslie W. Irwin, and Frank F. Masker, *Basic Skills in Sports for Men and Women*. St. Louis: C. V. Mosby Co., 1963.

The Art of Officiating Sports, ed. John W. Bunn, et al, 2nd ed. Englewood Cliffs, N. J.: Prentice-Hall, 1957.

Balke, Bruno, "Work Capacity at Altitude," *Science and Medicine of Exercise and Sports*, ed. Warren Russell Johnson. New York: Harper and Row, 1960.

Beissen, Arnold R., *The Madness in Sport*. New York: Appleton-Century-Crofts, 1967.

Boyle, Robert H., *Sport—Mirror of American Life*. Boston: Little, Brown and Co., 1963.

Brouha, Lucian, "Training," *Science and Medicine of Exercise and Sports*, ed. Warren Russell Johnson. New York: Harper and Row, 1960.

Callois, Roger, *Man, Play, and Games*, trans. by Meyer Barash. Glencoe, Ill.: The Free Press of Glencoe, Inc., 1961.

Cerutty, Percy Wells, *Athletics: How to Become a Champion*. London: Stanley Paul, 1960.

Conditio Humana, ed. Walter von Baeyer and Richard M. Griffith. New York: Springer-Verlag, 1966.

Cummings, Parke, ed. *The Dictionary of Sports*. New York: Roland Press Co., 1949.

Cureton, Thomas Kirk, Jr., *Physical Fitness of Champion Athletes*. Urbana, Ill.: University of Illinois Press, 1951.

Dill, David B., "Fatigue and Physical Fitness," *Science and Medicine of Exercise and Sports*, ed. Warren Russell Johnson. New York: Harper and Row, 1960.

Doherty, J. Kenneth, *Modern Training for Running*. Englewood Cliffs, N. J.: Prentice-Hall, 1964.

Drummond, J. C. and Anne Wilbraham, *The Englishman's Food: A History of Five Centuries of English Diet*, rev. ed. London: Johathan Cape, 1957.

Dyson, Geoffrey H. G., *The Mechanics of Athletics*. London: University of London Press, 1964.

Espenschade, Anna, "Motor Development," *Science and Medicine of Exercise and Sports*, ed. Warren Russell Johnson. New York: Harper and Row, 1960.

Esquire's Great Men and Moments in Sports. New York: Harper and Bros., 1961.

Fredrickson, P. S., "Sports and the Cultures of Man," *Science and Medicine of Exercise and Sports*, ed. Warren Russell Johnson. New York: Harper and Row, 1960.

Henderson, Robert W., *Ball, Bat and Bishop*. New York: Rockport Press, 1947.

Hooks, Gene, *Application of Weight Training to Athletics*. Englewood Cliffs, N. J.: Prentice-Hall, 1962.

Huisinga, Johan, *Homo Ludens, A Study of the Play-Element in Culture*. Boston: Beacon Press, 1955.

Isocrates, Vol. III, trans. by LaRue Van Hook, Loeb Classical Library. Cambridge, Mass.: Modern Library ed., 1961.

Johnson, Warren Russell, ed. *Science and Medicine of Exercise and Sports*. New York: Harper and Row, 1960.

Jokl, Ernst, "The Athletic Status of Women." *British Journal of Physical Medicine* (November 1957), 4.

————. *The Clinical Physiology of Physical Fitness and Rehabilitation*. Springfield, Ill.: Charles C. Thomas, 1958.

————. *Doping*, Proceedings of the International Seminar, International Council of Sport and Physical Education, UNESCO. New York: Pergamon Press, 1965.

————. *Heart and Sport*. Springfield, Ill.: Charles C. Thomas, 1964.

————. *Medical Sociology and Cultural Anthropology of Sport and Physical Education*. Springfield, Ill.: Charles C. Thomas, 1964.

————. *Nutrition, Exercise and Body Composition*. Springfield, Ill.: Charles C. Thomas, 1964.

————. *Physiology of Exercise*. Springfield, Ill.: Charles C. Thomas, 1964.

————. *The Scope of Exercise in Rehabilitation*. Springfield, Ill.: Charles C. Thomas, 1964.

————. *What is Sports Medicine?* Springfield, Ill.: Charles C. Thomas, 1964.

Koppett, Leonard, *A Thinking Man's Guide to Baseball*. New
York: C. P. Dutton, 1967.

Kreuzer, Ferdinand J., *International Research in Sport and
Physical Education*, ed. Ernst Jokl, M.D. Springfield,
Ill.: Charles C. Thomas, 1960.

Krout, John Allen, *Annals of American Sport*. U. S. Publishers
Association. New Haven: Yale University Press, 1929.

Lampros, S. P., and N. G. Politis, *The Olympic Games*. pt.
i, *The Olympic Games in Ancient Times*. Athens,
Greece: C. Beck, 1896.

Le Cava, G., "A Statistical Review of Boxing Injuries," *International Research in Sport and Physical Education*,
ed. E. Jokl and E. Simon. Springfield, Ill.: Charles
C. Thomas, 1964.

Lentz, Arthur G., ed. *United States 1960 Olympic Book:
Quadrennial Review*, New York: U. S. Olympic Association, Inc., 1961.

McIntosh, P. C., *Sport in Society*. London: C. H. Watts, 1963.

Mead, George H., *Mind, Self, and Society: From the Standpoint of a Social Behaviorist*, ed. Charles W. Morris.
Chicago: University of Chicago, 1934.

Meade, George P., *Athletic Records, The Whys and Where-
fores*. New York: Vantage Press, 1966.

Menke, Frank G., *The Encyclopedia of Sports*, 3rd rev. ed.
New York: A. S. Barnes, 1963.

Metheny, Eleanor, *Connotations of Movement in Sport and
Dance*. Dubuque, Iowa: William C. Brown Co., 1965.

The Olympic Games: Rules and Regulations, Eligibility Code,
General Information, Information for Cities which
desire to stage the Olympic Games, Bibliography.
International Olympic Committee. Lausanne, Switz.:
Louis Couchoud, S.A.

Pratt, John L. and J. Benagh, eds. *The Official Encyclopedia
of Sports*. New York: Franklin Watts, Inc., 1964.

Proceedings, Second National Institute on Girls' Sports. Washington, D. C.: National Education Association, 1966.

Quadrennial Review, Period of 1961–65, U. S. Olympic Committee, Olympic House. Washington, D. C., 1966.

Royal, Darrell and Blackie Sherrod, *Darrell Royal Talks
Football*. Englewood Cliffs, N. J.: Prentice-Hall, 1963.

Rudeen, Kenneth, *The Swiftest*. New York: W. W. Norton,
1966.

Salak, John S., ed. *Dictionary of American Sports*. New York:
Philosophical Library, 1961.

Sapora, Allen Victor, and Elmer D. Mitchell, *The Theory*

of Play and Recreation, 3rd ed. New York: Ronald Press, 1961.

Schapp, Richard, *An Illustrated History of the Olympics*, 2nd ed. New York: Alfred A. Knopf, 1967.

Schöbel, Heinz, *The Ancient Olympic Games*, trans. by Joan Becker. Princeton, N. J.: D. Van Nostrand Co., 1966.

Segal, Erich, "It is Not Strength, But Art, Obtains the Prize," *The Yale Review*, LVI, No. 4 (June 1967), 606, 607, 608.

Sheldon, William H., et al. *The Varieties of Human Physique*. New York: Hafner Publishing Co., 1963.

Slusher, Howard S., *Man, Sport, and Existence: A Critical Analysis*. Philadelphia: Lea and Febiger, 1967.

Smith, George Alan, *Introduction to Mountaineering*. New York: A. S. Barnes and Co., 1967.

Sports Illustrated Book of Football. Philadelphia: J. P. Lippincott, 1960.

Veblen, Thorstein B., *The Theory of the Leisure Class*. New York: Modern Library, 1931.

The Wonderful World of Sport. New York: Time-Life Books, 1967.

Ziegler, Earle F., *Problems in the History and Philosophy of Physical Education and Sport*. Englewood Cliffs, N. J.: Prentice-Hall, 1968.

index

Abilities: of runner, 103
Absorption: in play, 70
Acceptance: of the body, 36, 75, 80–81
Accidents: and athletics, 228
Accomplishments: of athletes, 84
Accuracy: definition of, 127; promotion of, 128–29; skill and grace, 128; attempts to achieve, 129; contrasted with correctness, 129; gross result and, 129; in the large, 129; perfect, 129; test for, 129; absolute, 130; as perfection within limits, 130; endurance and, 130; of women, 214
Achievement(s): and contextualism, 83; of athletes, 84; physical, limits of, 141
Act(s): changing character of, 42; complex, 42, 47; coaches and complex, 42; unit, 42; aptitude and, 43; training and, 46; as present, temporal occurrence, 47; beginning of, 47, 71; encompassed, 47; end of, 47; progression in, 47; subdivision of, 47; coaches stressing, 48; present, 58; desire eliciting, 59, 60; wanted, 60; interrelated relevant, 61; intention eliciting, 62; of attention, 65; impersonally justified, 71; program and, 72; improper, of athlete, 86; vital, and watches and clocks, 118; in a game, 158
Action: controlled, and strength, 126; violent, 126; and participation, 166
Actors: youthful, 11

Actuality: athlete facing, 244; scholars and athletes, 244
Admiration: aroused by professionals, 192; of amateurs, 192
Adroitness: strategy and tactics, 87
Advantages: in games, 181; in war, 181; weighing of, 233; and drugs, 236; affecting results, 239
Adventure: young men encouraged to, 45
Advice, bad, 49
Age: and Olympic Games, 237
Aggression: Freudian views of, 32; in professional sports, 32; sex and, 32; sport as outlet for, 32–33; as a drive, 33; sport and success, 33; self-completion and, 35; man's, 176; games and, 177–78, 184–85; rules and, 178
Agility: and flexibility, 96
"Agon": a game incorporating, 175
Agriculture: role in economy, 9
Alertness: without attention, 59; flexibility and, 96
Alumni: forcing college to make sport a business, 207; institutions needing support of, 208
Amateur(s): admiration of, 192; contrasted with professionals, 192–211; rich men as, 192; definition of, 193–94; young men as, 193; as one not receiving money for success in athletics, 194; definition by Olympic International Committee, 194; as one who does not play with those